Education and Federalism in History of Ambazonian Resistance: The Gymnastics and Folly of Assimilation

Peter Ateh-Afac Fossungu

Mwanaka Media and Publishing Pvt Ltd,
Chitungwiza Zimbabwe
*
Creativity, Wisdom and Beauty

Publisher: *Mmap*
Mwanaka Media and Publishing Pvt Ltd
24 Svosve Road, Zengeza 1
Chitungwiza Zimbabwe
mwanaka@yahoo.com
mwanaka13@gmail.com
www.africanbookscollective.com/publishers/mwanaka-media-and-publishing
https://facebook.com/MwanakaMediaAndPublishing/

Distributed in and outside N. America by African Books Collective
orders@africanbookscollective.com
www.africanbookscollective.com

ISBN: 978-1-77928-533-1
EAN: 9781779285331

DISCLAIMER
All views expressed in this publication are those of the author and do
not necessarily reflect the views of *Mmap*.

Table of Contents

Introduction

Chapter 1: The Politics Of 'Minority' in Multiculturalism: Democracy and Self-Determination in the Perfect Nation
Surveying Democracy and Defining Federalism
Collective Participation Abusing and Claiming Self-Determination in 'National versus Federal' Human Rights Game
Intimacy of the 1972 and 1984 Name Changes and the Theory of New-Old Name Revival Equals Sublimation
The Mathematics of Secession and Special Majority for Amendment: Two Simple Majorities Equal a Special Majority?
The Solid Federal Edifice Theory Teaching a Pig to Sing
Who Defines National Policy in Systems Based on Constitutionalism?
Monosity as Prerequisite for 'Pluralistic Democracy': Illusive National Unity and the Monopolization of Citizens' Destiny

Chapter 2: Pointless Multiculturalism and Multipartism: Testing the Deepness of Assimilation Waters with the 1985/83 Education Cases and Cultural Minority Exchange
Exchanging Authentic Minority for Settlers and Indigenes: The Students' 1985 Letter Vehemently Opposed Manipulation and Assimilation
The Secrecy of Population Politics in Cameroon
The 1990 Multipartism Law Reinforcing the Single-Party State?
Deconstructing the Law's Threats to West-Central African Political Geography: Federating for Security?
Ignorant Democrats Prop Up Dictatorship

Chapter 3: The Constitution and the Education Domain: The Assimilationist Philosophy of the Education Law under the Equality Microscope
Inventing Federalism from Nowhere: Power Sharing in Foumban?
The Sex of Patriotism and Equality: Gender Politics in Cameroon via the 1997 Legislative and Presidential Elections
Grasping the Designs of the Education Law

The National Education Board and/or the PROBAC Board: The Ministerial Duplication Story Evidencing Education as Top Priority? Cementing Assimilation with PROBAC/G.C.E. Differentiation: Obliteration of the G.C.E. Board?

Chapter 4: Deciphering the Subtle Prevention of Biculturalism: Epsitologizing the Purpose and Objectives of Education in Cameroon and Ambazonia
On the Purpose of Education in Cameroun: Addressing the Dog-Breeders
The Roots of Developing through Confusing and Incomplete Rules and Laws
Epsi and the Objectives of Education: Parlement and the Golden Lesson of Unity of Purpose
The Anglo-War-Cry of Inverted Minority
Penalizing Students for the Creation of Universities

Conclusion
Bibliography
Mmap Nonfiction and Academic Series

Introduction

This book focuses on educational dualism and federalism, showing the sphere of education to be the stronghold of the Ambazonian resistance to outright assimilation. I argue in regard of education (and language & legal systems[1]) that Cameroon's over-sung cultural or educational dualism was a charade – a sham epitomized by its assimilationist 1998 Education Law (known as *Law N° 98/004 of 14 April 1998 to Lay Down Guidelines for Education in Cameroon*). I demonstrate how this piece of legislation, rather than reaffirming Cameroon's biculturalism as it avowed, was hell bent on effacing any semblance of cultural or educational dualism still resisting assimilation. Also, that the continuous and persistent employment of terms such as cultural dualism, bilingualism, and so forth, in legal texts in Cameroon was only to confuse the international community especially from seeing exactly the kind of 'ethnic cleansing' which was and still is taking place in the neo-colony. Certain definitional precisions I made in the Introduction of my earlier book (Fossungu, 2025) would facilitate a better grasp of this one. Better peruse and read in that Introduction here. I can, with fair accuracy, evaluate the two "sub-systems of education" in Cameroon not just because of what I have read in books and other writings. Most importantly, my knowledge on these matters also comes from my experience as a teacher who taught for a long time in both sub-systems at both pre-university and university levels.

Differences and diversity, if properly managed, are supposed to be Africa's strength. The channel for properly managing them is federalism. But rather than give the differences and diversity their proper channel that is called "federalism as a form of *decentralized* government" (Stevenson, 1989: 3, original emphasis), the Cameroon administration, for instance, did only impose the unitary hyper centralized state and then continually promoted what Bringer (1981: 4) describes as the official fanning of the "internal friction within the... bench and tensions between East Cameroon and West Cameroon judges due to different patterns and levels of education and

---

[1] Largely covered by Fossungu (2021 & 2018, respectively) but inextricably tied to education.

5

qualifications." The government's confusing policy was that of fanning the differences (for divide and rule purposes) but at the same time refusing that the two educational "sub-systems" responsible for these differences were different. This was simply being brainless since the differences are so deep-rooted and could not just go away simply because someone was trying to behave as if nothing was different. To better demonstrate this, the two systems are briefly compared as I extensively examine the effect on national unity of one wanting to assimilate the other, rather than co-existing with it as the Education Law confuses people in Section 15(2): "The above-mentioned educational systems shall co-exist, each preserving its specific method of evaluation and award of certificates."

Many writers are often bewildered by the actual formation and continuous existence of the Federal Republic of Cameroon (FRC) or Cameroon. This "njumba-no-be-married" union is said to have been sanctioned by *Loi N° 61-24 du 1er septembre 1961 portant révision constitutionnelle et tendant à adapter la constitution actuelle aux nécessités du Cameroun réunifié* (hereinafter Federal Constitution, which was not the Union Treaty at all, according to Mola Njoh Litumbe). The singularity of the FRC is indeed noted in several respects. For instance, unlike Franck (1968a: 8) whose discussion "touches not upon the failure of what was, but of what might have been," I am here examining what was, although not being in fact what should have been. (Hence, Litumbe's fine reminder that Njumba No Bi Married which has become the signature to countless Ambazonian freedom songs such as "Don't Vote – You Are Not Cameroonian".) Yet, the FRC being studied here had, surprisingly (until 2017 with President Biya's declaration of his genocidal war on Ambazonians), never disintegrated like the West Indian Federation which (some experts say) created at worst hostility and at best apathy, being seldom able to produce the kind of concrete advantages which could have engendered support for the Federation (Flanz, 1968: 113). Neither had the FRC even broken down, in the words of Franck (1968a: 8), into "resembling more those peculiar ex-lovers who, having broken up, still continue to meet and engage in love-hateful domestic bickering that end sometimes in sex but never again in marriage."

That is not all that gives the FRC its unusualness. Writing ten years after its formation, Le Vine (1971: 1) stated that Cameroon's experiment in federalism is not without its unusual aspects. It was then the only federal union of French-speaking and English-speaking territories on the continent (not excepting the Ghana-Guinea-Mali union, which never went beyond the rhetorical stage) and the first attempt to blend the political offspring of French, English and United Nations tutelary experiences. The only other African bilingual territorial merger has been that of the Somalis that resulted in a unitary state long before the FRC that is said to have done same in 1972. Did the FRC indeed end in 1972?

Chief Obafemi Awolowo has reviewed most of the political unions around the world [see Obafemi Awolowo, *Thoughts on Nigerian Constitution* (Ibadan: Oxford University Press, 1966) at 28-48]. But the FRC could be distinguished from most other broken political marriages such as Britain/Ireland, Northern/Southern Rhodesia, India/Pakistan, all of them, according to Franck (1968a: 8), being profoundly poisoned relations among former partners; as well as from the Scandinavians whose *sang*-Freudian correctness disguises their mutual alienation. To leave most of Cameroon's other distinctive conflict-ridden (but not even clashing then) characteristics aside, the *successful* Cameroonian English/French marriage is bound to knock a lot of people off balance. Especially viewing, for example, the experts' findings that federalism could not even materialize in East Africa (between three English-speaking countries: Kenya, Uganda and Tanzania) despite all the mystique of unity that remains a reality vividly perceptible to the political sense there (see Franck, 1968a: 7-8; Southall, 1974: 138; & Okondo, 1964). But that surprise must substantially dwindle when some hard facts (that are wrapped in confusioncracy) about Cameroon are grasped. For an appetizer, it is undeniable that the conditions at the time of the UPC rebellion in French Cameroun no longer prevailed during the 'Anglophone Problem' and the rules had to have changed accordingly. The fact that the risk of the disintegration of Cameroon had long gone is seen clearly in the statements of the current President of the Republic (POR) that would be praising the dynamism of

7

Cameroonians to cooperate despite their marked differences. In Biya's (1986: 31-32) words, "These [ethnic, cultural and regional peculiarities], in some respects, are national socio-cultural resources, given their unquestionable contribution to the dynamism and co-operation for which our country is well known." I, therefore, think it is about time for African states to rethink their way of doing the business of governing their diverse populations. Time and dialogue are certainly on our side. We needed genuine 'Dialogue for Lasting Peace' (Ikeda, 1987: 248-269) in Cameroon. Like several experts,[2] Maneli (1994: 3 & 9, 104-105, 11 & passim) tells us that Perelman, for instance, considers dialogue not only as a simple exchange of ideas but also as a social category that promotes an endless competition of arguments to establish the best possible solution in each situation and at a given time. Dialogue is not something known to the LRC gangster regime.

Other than confusion and manipulation, what could account for the uniqueness of the FRC just noted? Was the FRC a federation and why was it formed? Was the FRC motivated by a desire to both protect human rights and avert some imminent problems common to the federating entities? Was the FRC really the result of "historyless" political science or simply that of an "ulterior something"? This issue must be examined because political science without history has been largely condemned for its fruitlessness. Classical authors on federalism such as Wheare, Dicey, Geoffrey Sawer, Durand, Livingston, Friedrich, Tarleton, Elazar, and Riker certainly formulated their theory without taking "*compte du cas camerounais, trop récent et trop mal connu*" (Benjamin, 1972: 147). That is, without taking 'into consideration the case of Cameroon that is very recent and thus not very appropriately known or studied'. Can it also be said with conviction that the Cameroonian "Fathers of Federation" did not know of the existence of the theories of those experts when they formulated their "Verbal Federation" in Foumban?

---

[2] See Annette T. Rottenberg, *Elements of Argument* (New York: St. Martin's Press, 1985); and Earl Rubington and Martin S. Weinberg, "Social Problems and Sociology", in Earl Rubington and Martin S. Weinberg (eds.), *The Study of Social Problems: Five Perspectives* 3rd edition (New York: Oxford University Press, 1981), 3 at 7.

The correct answers to these questions are found in the principal and general question(s): What is federalism and what gives impetus to its adoption? As it is usual with almost all institutions, the meaning and purpose of federalism are intertwined. Both its meaning and purpose can be seen in (1) *what* it is adopted to do, and (2) *how/why* it is able (or unable) to do it. While the first point has to do with the sickness to be cured by federalism, the second touches on the kinds of principles upon which the federation is based. Both these factors are principally shaped by (3) the forces pushing for and/or against a federal union; that is, *why* federalism is adopted. All these points are important and are discussed in this study, but the third point (the Invisible Hand of Federalism) is the most important since it is the key to the others and therefore that which directly involves how the institutions and/or history and/or culture of the federating components are/is to be treated in the union.

The first Chapter handles the politics of minority in multicultural democracies, seeking to know if the perfect nation is compatible with multiculturalism. That is, it studies the inconsistency of the perfect nation with multiculturalism and collective participation. The second focuses on the first bold moves from the Biya regime to assimilate the Ambazonian educational system within the desire to ignore or sidestep the notion that there was an 'Anglophone Problem'. The third interrogates the appropriate constitutional domain of education to properly grasp the philosophy of the Education Law. The fourth then deciphers the use of *epsi* (or monthly stipend to students) to prevent biculturalism. There is a conclusion.

Chapter 1

The Politics of 'Minority' in Multiculturalism: Democracy and Self-Determination in the Perfect Nation

You cannot take your certificate of victimhood to the negotiating table. You cannot take your certificate of all the wrongs that have been done to you to the negotiating table. It is about power. You don't have it, you don't matter. You don't have it; you don't have a voice. The failure to build power before they moved to Ambazonia to establish a Parliament was the beginning of the Ambazonian Problem. Leaving the Eastern House [in Enugu, Nigeria], moving to Buea to set up self-governance without the ability to protect and secure it? Moving on to 1961 before the discussions of the plebiscite or federation there was nothing to defend the interest and protect the power of the Ambazonian people. [Spokesperson Asu Lucas, "Dr Cho Ayaba and Norway: Cameroun's Strategy of Containment" 6 March 2025 on ACN TV]

On 6 November 1982 Paul Biya (who, since 1975, was President Amadou Ahidjo's Prime Minister) became the President of Cameroon by virtue of a one-manish hurriedly made constitutional amendment of 29 May 1979. According to Biya (1986: 10-11), "Despite our country's immense economic potentials, material comfort is still the prerogative of a privileged minority, while poverty is the lot of the majority of Cameroonians.... Such injustice existed and is still widespread in our society, leading to a great deal of frustration and eventual resignation." President Biya could not have been seriously regretting the existence of these forms of injustice in then Cameroonian society when he was tenaciously clinging to the root cause of the same – the perfect nation which is inconsistent with multiculturalism, ushering in Kontchoumeterized participation (instead of the usual), and a new kind of 'pluralistic democracy' that completely banishes federalism and multipartism.

Federalism is such an important human rights protecting instrument in governance that it was a principal topic of discussion at one of the triennial congresses of the International Political Science Association, held in 1964 in Geneva. Majeed (2008: 5) sees federalism as an important method of good governance in which political accommodation and understanding become sound practices amid conflicting ideologies, disparate groups, and seemingly irreconcilable positions. Given that a decline of the legitimate political order results in a decline of the moral authority of the nation-state, he concludes, the link between the need for good governance and federal power-sharing is obvious. Federalism, according to Frank Trager, has thus been prescribed and applied as a remedy to a great variety of political, economic, social, cultural, and other ailments at all levels of state organization. Federalism is not a fixed point on the map but a tendency that is neither unitary nor separatist. In Aristotelian terms, federalism is the median between those two polar positions, and thus the true opposite of the two (Trager, 1968: ix & x). Federalism has thus been prescribed and applied around the world with varying degree of success. Why it has not succeeded (or will not succeed) in Africa is simply because of confusion and manipulation from the intellectuals and other political elites; thus, calling for the keen scrutiny of the role of the intellectual in politics as well as the accurate meaning of "intellectuals in politics".

According to Fohtung (1995) and Ahidjo (1996), Paul Biya had spent so many 'patriotic' years of his shadowy life in some of the highest offices of Cameroon, pretending to be something else so as to get to the almighty POR position in which, with the mere stroke of his pen, he could secure the hanging of his predecessor as well as decree his beloved Perfect Nation. The perfect nation is then a fait accompli in 1984 and nothing, absolutely nothing, on earth could therefore take this darling outmoded 'perfect nation' away from the POR. That can only happen over his dead body, or to be precise, the death of 'bilingual and bijural Cameroon'. (And he did the killing through the war he forced on Ambazonia, didn't he?) That thesis from the critics can well explain why, despite all the bitter challenges directed at the 1984 name-change

11

and the grave dangers it posed to national unity, it was again reaffirmed and confirmed by the opening article of the 1996 Constitution (known as *Loi N° 96-06 du 18 janvier 1996 portant révision de la Constitution du 02 juin 1972*): "The United Republic of Cameroon shall, with effect from the entry into force of this law, be known as Republic of Cameroon (Law N° 84-1 of 4 February 1984)." This 1996 reaffirmation logically leads to the questioning of what had happened to the 'only one Cameroon people' attained in 1984 (as justifying the name-change – see Fossungu, 2025: 99-100). Elusive national unity, always appearing and disappearing! Does that not *happen* simply to justify perpetuity in power? Answer the question with the 'monosity' prerequisite for 'pluralistic democracy' (below) that is also guilty of sexing patriotism and equality.

Surveying Democracy and Defining Federalism

Democracy and collective participation are intertwined concepts but for convenience I will first briefly survey democracy before seeing if there was collective participation (or self-determination) in Cameroon, as claimed. Both de Jorge (1993: 304, 301-302, & 306) and Biya (1986: 36) have found democracy to have universal characteristics. Based on the realization of this universality, the various forms of democracy have been briefly surveyed by the *Encyclopedia Britannica* (2002: 5) and other writers like Archer and Reay (1966: 163-64) who have advanced and described these four variants: direct democracy, representative democracy, economic democracy, and liberal or constitutional democracy. How is Ambazonia to be looking at it?

We understand the world is now global. We cherish some western norms and values. We cherish eastern norms and values. Some of the cultures are similar, their experiences are similar because of migratory patterns. But there are some things that are intrinsically African, and the black people are an endangered species who should be protected wherever. And we must develop economic policies that take into consideration the fact that for hundreds of years we have not had opportunities. The events within the continent in the past years and months and in the past weeks should get Ambazonians to begin to prepare themselves. I spoke to the General this

12

morning and I gave firm instructions on the level of preparation that they must have should there be a military takeover in Yaoundé. And I want all of us, Ambazonians, wherever you may be, to prepare yourself for such an eventuality. It would be a huge opportunity for our country and for our struggle. We are taking this seriously (Ayaba, Ngoketunjia: September 2023).

It is liberal or constitutional democracy that is currently in vogue and fits into the question at hand. Liberal or constitutional democracy is a form of government, usually a representative democracy, in which the majority exercise their powers within a framework of constitutional restraints designed to guarantee all citizens individual and collective rights (such as equality, freedom of speech and of religion). As Riemer (1983: 121) further explains, while some ideals of liberal democracy may change in both theory and practice, certain fundamentals will remain the same (the universal features). Its persistent democratic ingredients include (i) popular rule, (ii) freedom, and (iii) equality; while the persistent liberal ones include (a) constitutionalism, (b) protection of basic rights, and (c) political and economic competition and free choice both at the ballot box and in the marketplace. Riemer (1983: 121) adds that factor (c) here has changed from a laissez-faire position to one that favours government intervention in the interest of the public welfare, social justice, and fair play. These requirements could partly explain why most genuine democracies of today do have some form of Bill of Rights (like the USA's) and Charter of Rights and Freedoms like Canada's *The 1982 Canadian Charter of Rights and Freedoms*, Part I of the *Constitution Act, 1982*, being Schedule B to the *Canada Act 1982* (U.K.), 1982, C.11; and *The Charter of Paris for a New Europe*.

How is Africa faring in the matter? Ambazonians and the Sahelians think,

Africa needs to design an African system commensurate to our own realities. African states need true independence. Political and economic independence that guarantees for the people the right to choose their trading partners and dispose of their resources as they see it fit. That Africa's natural resources cannot be sold out through racketeering systems and keep the people in perpetual debt without any reward from the resources in their Land. We must develop new models of economic development and political theories that suit the continent (Ayaba, Ngoketunjia: September 2023).

Very correct, Dr Cho Ayaba; because what has "evolve[d] in East Asia is a democracy that is quite unlike a liberal democracy, but which produces the good life and wholesome society, economic and social progress and a political and social system that is consonant with the values and traditions of their society" (de Jorge: 1993: 302).

It was to take care of the problems of (cultural and ethnic) minorities, for example, that liberal or constitutional democracy came to prevent the tyranny of the majority by requiring that the powers of the majority be exercised within a framework of constitutional restraints designed to guarantee all citizens individual and collective rights. Politicians and scholars from this type of democracy have hardly spared the minute in reminding themselves of this plain fact. In his 1985 address to scholars at the University of Toronto, Canada, Chicago historian, William McNeil, clearly stated that poly-ethnicity is normal in civilized societies, whereas the ideal of one ethnically unitary state was exceptional in theory and rarely approached in practice. Marginality and pluralism were and are the norms of civilized existence (cited in Driedger, 1989: 3). Canada's Prime Minister Pierre-Elliott Trudeau could not also pass by without warning that a nationalistic government is by nature intolerant, discriminatory, and, when all is said and done, totalitarian. A truly democratic government, to him, cannot be nationalist, because it must pursue the good of all its citizens, without prejudice to ethnic origin (Driedger, 1989: 192). Agreeing with the former Canadian Prime minister is a 1962 Opposition Manifesto which very clearly challenged President Ahidjo's ceaseless drive to create the single party.

National unity such as is defined by certain people is a myth, and this myth borders on utopia. If we were really animated, all of us, by a desire for unity, one would employ a different language than the one we are used to hearing from Radio Yaoundé and the officials. As for ourselves, we believe that unity supposes a minimum of courtesy towards those one wants to unite. But we observe, to our great regret, that this unity will come about only when the holders of power have reduced the other Cameroonians to the rank of slaves.... National Unity with effective competition and activity among all the political and spiritual families of Cameroon. Yes! National Unity in the uniformization of the single party which will lead necessarily to dictatorship. No! (Quoted in Fossungu, 2018: 128-29).

The "perfect nation" seekers must therefore be constantly told in Frank D. Day's strong terms that if the State is held to be an absolute entity, and the repository and first source of all authority, power, right and privilege (as has been in Cameroon), its acts will be deemed to be above judgment; its final purpose will be posited as its own selfish interest – as race was for German Nazism, as Nation was for Italian Fascism, and as Economic Community was for Russian Communism (Day, 1964: 32). In constantly telling them all this is to say that they must adopt a different state-governing strategy that protects human rights and is inclusive, not exclusive. One time Quebec Premier, Lucien Bouchard, also told members of the *Parti Quebecois* how "We must illustrate in policies and in our programs a plan for a country that is inclusive and tolerant [because] We are the government of all Quebecers and we will not turn our backs on a single citizen" (cited in Fossungu, 2021: 5).

Not turning "our backs on a single citizen" means that every citizen counts. Every citizen can only properly matter in a multicultural society if we strictly follow Trudeau's advice that every region and national group should have a wide range of authority and fields to enable it to develop its national characteristics to the fullest. The true solution then is federalism, the best state form through which, like ex-Prime Minister Pierre-Elliott Trudeau, I also think

We must [necessarily] separate once and for all the concepts of State and of Nations and make Ca[meroon/United Africa] a truly pluralistic and polyethnic society. Now in order to do so, the different regions within the country must be assured a wide range of local autonomy, such that each national group... may be able to develop the body of laws and institutions essential to

the fullest expression and development of its national characteristics (cited in Driedger, 1989: 192).

Nigeria must also be listening well here. Federalism proper is thus
the prescribed medication. Like multiparty politics with which it must
marry, federalism is obviously one of the effective modes of separating
powers and dividing competence – both institutionally and territorially
– to save the people and federating entities from autocracy. This is the
state form that African states so badly need to be able to effectively
tackle their ethnic and other conflict-management problems; as well as
to pull together for the betterment of the African peoples' lot on this
planet called Earth. The Sahel is showing the way through the Alliance
of Sahel States (AES). Lack of vision apart, it is evident that this federal
undertaking is something that will not be impossible in Africa: absent
confusion and manipulation. The lack of vision is mostly on the part of
the officials in power who do regard federalism just as negatively as
anything else that preaches the diversification of power centres. But it
does not end there because the absence of vision and integrity would
seem to cut right across the entire African spectrum (Government and
Opposition alike). Truly, as Anyangwe (1987: xiv) has observed, it is
only "lack of vision, integrity and commitment on the part of many
[that] will continue to clog the wheels of that important [federalism]
undertaking [in Cameroon, for example]." A critical and balanced
evaluation of the invisible hand of Cameroon's federalism (also see
Fossungu, 2025) best illustrates this lack of vision, integrity,
commitment, and the accompanying and overriding confusion and
manipulation; all of which would not let authentic history play the role
that is its own in development or nation-building.

Defining Federalism: It has not been an easy task defining federalism
to the general satisfaction of all. Using several definitions (all of which
he set out), Shapiro (1995: 4) thoroughly demonstrated the striking
vagueness of many attempted definitions of federalism, opining that no
easy definitions and pigeonholing will prove adequate. This may largely
explain why Wheare's (1963) celebrated federal principle has come
under fire from Hogg (1996: 99 & 100) for being too rigid in stressing
the separate and distinct spheres of both levels of government. Having
also catalogued several other contrary (to rigid) contributions, Hogg
(1996: 99) found that those too would have so eroded the concept of

16

federalism that it has become too vague to be useful. It is thus not surprising that another expert had made the same discovery six years before Shapiro when, having extensively examined the various attempted definitions at pages 7-9 of his book, Stevenson (1989: 8) also concluded that possibly no single definition of so elusive and controversial a concept could be satisfactory for all purposes. This explicates why several images, according to Majeed (2008: 4), emerged from the eleven studied countries. There is the image of the "divided federalism" of Canada as a contrast to the "integrated and shared federalism" of Germany, with the "quasi-federalism" of India lying in between. The US system, Majeed says, underscores a delegation of powers to the national government rather than a distribution of powers between the national and the state governments – but not without an often strongly coercive centralism. Whereas Canadian fiscal federalism is one of the most decentralized forms of federalism, Majeed has concluded, India's is one of the most centralized.

These complex attempts at circumscribing the concept of federalism cannot however be indicative that definitions should be completely shunned. According to Franck (1968b: 169), what such a definitional problem or diversity simply suggests is not that a single, highly structured definition of federalism is needed. Rather, it is that there be greater understanding of the nearly infinite number of variations that can be played in the federal theme and that the difficulties of engineering a union of nations should only begin when the leaders agree to federate, and their subalterns sit down to work out what is too often called "the details". This thesis is again well seen in *Distribution of Powers and Responsibilities in Federal Countries*. As Majeed (2008: 3) tells us, their study identified similarities and differences among the eleven federal polities studied regarding intergovernmental distribution of powers and responsibilities. In all eleven countries the system is part of the constitutional structure; yet there is wide range of variations among these systems. He goes on to exemplify, stating that whereas the United States and Australia present one type of distribution system, Canada and India present another. Even in Europe, he notes, Belgium presents still another, whereas other European federations such as Germany and Switzerland exhibit a division between the allocation of legislative and executive authority in particular areas.

Majeed's (2008: 3) conclusion is also that in view of differences in forms and scope of various distributions of powers and responsibilities, "it can be surmised that there is no pure model of federalism but, rather, several practical variations within the common framework of federal systems." From the foregoing, the definitional problem, according to Franck (1968b: 169), would also suggest that the content of a federal arrangement need not be governed by any historically fixed pattern; that the concept of federalism is malleable enough to bend with the realities. Indeed, the important conclusion about federation formation which he emphasizes is that it is when the realities are bent to fit into some rigid, historic but unsuitable federal pattern that trouble often begins. This critical and constructive study advances the FRC and the SDF four-state federation project (see Fossungu, 2025) as clear candidates in this stark bending of realities; thus, resulting in the rise of Ambazonia where:

> People who never had an identity suddenly bestowed to themselves an identity which they projected. Anywhere now you hear of Ambazonia you take pride in it. They sing our Anthem; it whispers something into your ears. I ask each and every one of you to believe and have faith in your country. That is the essence of your existence. And I am sure by the time we are done with these discussions your faith in Ambazonia would have increased; and that should translate into commitment to the war of our independence, to the defence of our people, to ensure that we can eradicate, through policing, some of the extortions, the kidnapping for ransoms, that our people have been complaining about. I am very sure it will improve our standing with our people and with the world. Make no mistake, not Canada, not USA, not Norway, not Germany, not Belgium is going to give you any help. They are waiting for you to fail so that they can continue with the old system that they are used to. The international order does not like uncertainty. It wants clarity, it wants certainty. Because it is

very important in terms of investment. They are not coming to rescue Ambazonians. They don't care how many villages are burnt, how many people are killed, until it starts to affect them. We must care for Mamie Appih's death. We must care about Baby Martha. We must care about Sam Sawyer, about General Ivo, General Chacha, and the others who have died in battle. And we must care about the protection of those who are still fighting. Because the only outcome acceptable at this stage is victory for the Ambazonian people. Thanks to everyone. You have a nice Friday. Happy weekend. I will see you tomorrow. Possibly we will be talking about the state of Bui. Good night (Ayaba, Ngoketunjia: September 2023).

That was the proper diagnosis to the problem because a country after all, Pierre Trudeau declared in closing his sane and persuasive stance, is not something you build as the pharaohs built the pyramids and then leave standing there to defy eternity. A country is something which is built every day out of certain basic shared values. And so, it is in the hands of every Afrikan to determine how well and wisely they shall build the country of the future. [Pierre-Elliott Trudeau, *Memoirs* (Toronto: McClelland and Stewart Inc., 1993) at 366]. David Wippman has even argued in agreement that even "the international community supports as the preferred approach to resolving a number of international conflicts the adoption of federal or confederal structures that effectively confer limited independence on subnational groups." [Cited in Fédérick Charette, *Les driots collectifs – de quel droit?* (Thèse de Doctorat, Université de Montréal, 1996) at 204 n.30] That is the straightforward or elementary lesson that Ambazonians too had been preaching in their own fashion under their 'The Force of Argument and not The Argument of Force' (albeit in the wrong context until 2017). But would the Cameroon regime, plagued with *Kontchoumeters,* learn anything from Canada?

Collective Participation: Abusing and Claiming Self-Determination in 'National versus Federal' Human Rights Game

The perfect nation has always been found hiding under the cover of national unity in Africa. For instance, Enonchong (1967: xiv), in his "Preface" directs his "immense" appreciation to Dr John Ngu Foncha (who, with Ahidjo, secretly fabricated the FRC) "for writing the laudable foreword for this first edition of the work. Both for his keen interest in the unity of the nation and preservation of its democratic institutions and his constant plea for justice as the rock-foundation of peace, coupled with his progressive views on what educated citizens should be, cannot be overemphasized." It thus appears not to be by inadvertence that Dr Enonchong's book, which is dedicated "To the Cause of Cameroon Unity and Democratic Federalism" (1967: i), does employ *National Federal Assembly* (NFA) throughout: despite the fact that the Federal Constitution itself talks of the *Federal National Assembly* (FNA), for instance, in Articles 15, 16, 19, 20; and *The Federal Legislature* in its Title IV (Articles 16-22). Is it true that this is self-hatred or what! Tell them, please.

They made you to hate your own. Oh, I am from Douala, you know. I am just coming from Yaoundé. You come and impress people with zero nonsense. It is like all this nonsense we are also talking about in the Diaspora. I come from London, you know. I am from Washington. What the hell is Washington? What the hell is Washington? What the hell is London? Surely, you are hiding in some suburb there with mental torture. You use it to intoxicate Ambazonians. Ah! Hahaha! Hahaha! [some Mankon language] Hahaha! Hahaha! Ambazonians, look, look, look. We are empty. Empty! The only thing we have is Ambazonia. Ambazonia. Me, I have made up my mind. If I die today, my family knows. Whether you cremate my body, tie it inside some bundle. If we are free, take it, you go and bury it in the cemetery of the braves. If we are never free, throw it in the ocean. I live for nothing. Maybe the children would grow up, listen to this video, they would know dad stood for something. They would be proud to say, that is my father (Ayaba, Ndian: 27 August 2023).

Yes, we are nothing without a freed and sovereign Ambazonia. I do believe that genuine federalists will always put the federation (that is, what it is adopted to promote: unity in diversity) before all else, including the uniformization being euphemistically called 'national unity' (diversity in unity, otherwise known as the 'New Ethnic Group'). This explains why such federalists would always refer to an institution as the one in question simply as the Federal Parliament. Or if they must employ the word 'national' they would prefer to talk of Federal National Assembly (FNA) and not National Federal Assembly (NFA). The preferred appellation of FNA is not only because there are other effective non-federal 'parliaments' (legislatures or legislative assemblies) in the Union – ATZ Parliament, MDZ Parliament, & SVZ Parliament for Ambazonia. By FNA, federalists are putting the emphasis on the federation. National unity thus passes through the federation, and not vice versa. NFA stands for just the reverse: 'federation' passing through national unity; thus, in an uncharacteristic fashion, "justifying" the anti-human rights and undemocratic Cameroon Unitary 'democratic federal' arrangements I am interrogating. A democratic federalism punctuated in Article 15 by open-ended emergency powers in the hands of the President of 'Federal' Republic (PFR) of Cameroon, who sees only the assimilation of Ambazonians as national unity. Yet, they would be (1) talking of self-determination while also (2) sexing equality and patriotism.

To the Ahidjo Biya administrations, federalism, designed for self-determination within the state, according to Biya (1986: 30) is "the most effective vector of political destabilisation" used against ethnically diverse states like Cameroon and, therefore, is unacceptable since it is another name for secession – a threat to national unity. Biya further argued that there was even no need for it because of majority rule (see Fossungu, 2025). Do these so-called African leaders even know what they are talking about? Majority rule is not absolute in a liberal or constitutional democracy, which usually takes the federal form for diverse societies. It is not clear (absent confusion of assimilation) why anyone should be talking of the respect of minority rights in the first place when the "majority" *must always* prevail. This is the zenith of the *Political Master Plan of Assimilation* (that has been shown to have been clearly known to 'inner circle' Southern Cameroonians before and in Foumban, part and parcel of which also includes Premier Amadou

21

Ahidjo's (Biya's predecessor's) philosophy of the Francophone majority 'dealing' with the Anglophone minority on a "footing of equality". Talking about the suspected conspiracy for the annexation of the Southern Cameroons at the 4th Committee of the 13th Session of the United Nations General Assembly in February 1959 (this February again!), Amadou Ahidjo of *La République du Cameroun* is quoted by the 1999 Independence Proclamation[3] as having declared that "we do not wish to bring the weight of our population on the Anglophones. We are not annexationists, in other words, if our brothers of the British zone wish to unite with an independent Cameroon, we are ready to discuss the matter with them, but we will discuss on a footing of equality."

Brotherhood also has always been the magic word with the Foumban actors only and until they have attained their ulterior goals. Isn't this speech very purposefully philosophical? And isn't it just as vague as the phrase *an intellectual in politics*? I pose all these questions because it can be, and has been, strenuously argued below that '*bringing the weight of our population on the Anglophones*' is exactly what the Francophone leaders did in order to opt out of the federation (if a true federation it was indeed) and into the unitary assimilationist state: by having East Cameroonian participation in the 1972 questionable referendum on the basis of one-person-one-vote and thereby 'drowning the voices of West Cameroonians' who were against the change. This would not be the case in a true federation as I have already stressed and would do so again in the Intimacy Game.

Intimacy of the 1972 and 1984 Name Changes: The Theory of New-Old Name Revival Equals Sublimation

The 1984 name-change that revives the contested name (Republic of Cameroon) cannot be divorced from the even more controversial and anti-multiculturalism one in 1972. The first important question is that of why Camerounese (East Cameroonians) even had to participate

---

[3] See The Proclamation of the Restoration of the Sovereignty and Independence of the Southern Cameroons, Buea, Southern Cameroons, December 30, 1999, available at <http://www.southerncameroons.org/index3.htm>.

in the 1972 referendum, if indeed this was a veritable federation. To bring out the significance of this query, I can only liken the 1972 referendum (its secrecy and deception apart) to 'the Rest of Canada' participating in a referendum on Quebec's sovereignty, with the Quebec Premier being the campaign manager for Ottawa. Is this what will happen in a federation proper or in Canada? But that is exactly what happened in Cameroon. Then Ambazonia (West Cameroon) prime minister was the campaign manager for the 'glorious revolution.' N.N. Mbile of the ruling Cameroon People's Democratic Movement (CPDM) party is quoted as saying that during that "courtesy-fool" referendum it was even the then West Cameroon prime minister (and federal vice-president – what a federation!), Solomon T. Muna, who "served as campaign manager... and brought that 99.9 per cent 'yes' for the unitary system." [Philip Njaru, "Mbile Warns SCNC: Secession is Act of War – No Body Will Let Go Rich Anglophone Territory" *The Herald* (25-26 September 1996), 1. Also see Konings and Nyamnjoh (1997: 210)] Why do the "intellectuals in politics" see white but keep telling us that it is black? Who was/is oppressing 'the English-speaking minority' in Cameroon? It duly explains why

LRC has messed it up completely, deliberately. They never knew this day would come because they believed so much in their own arrogance. They have so much contempt for us. Why? Because they measured us based on how the Fonchas and the Munas acted. If those guys banged the table and left, if those guys threatened to set up an army to defend our Land, they would know that these are men who would give birth to lions. Rather, those guys were fighting themselves to see who would become the better slave. And LRC then considered that the offsprings of the Fonchas and the Munas could only be slaves. We would think like them, act like them; and that is why they became so brutal each time we rose up. They became so arrogant each time we spoke out. Because they asked themselves, how dare you? If your forebears succumbed without protest, who the hell do you think you are? And then they recruited, and this is the worst part, this is the worst part about the occupation of our Land. They recruited thousands of

23

enablers. Tens of thousands of them and imposed them as our speakers, our window to the world. Solomon Tandeng Muna, when I was in primary school in Ngembu, will land with a helicopter and all of us will go there and we are clapping for him. He is taken in a limousine into his luxurious home, and they slammed the gate lock. He never cared about the road that passed in front of his own house. He never cared about the lives of the people who lived in Ngembu, living in misery. Water in Ngembu was put through community services. He left nothing. He brought nothing. They fought for themselves. Cameroun concluded that the offsprings of these men can never be lions (Ayaba, Ngoketunjia: September 2023).

The "Anglos War-Cry' thesis (see Fossungu, 2018: 137-38) also elucidates why most French-speaking majority do not seem to see that federalism would benefit everyone, not only the English-speaking minority. I also think that, but for the human rights 'war cry', most French-speaking Cameroonians would have opted for the stance that only the English-speaking had to vote in the 1972 referendum since they alone had voted in the United Nations plebiscites to join French Cameroun. (Their funny attitude also in the face of the Ambazonia/Cameroun war has been very telling too to the theory.) Of course, it is difficult to see how the 1972 referendum result would have been any different, with West Cameroonians alone participating. "The eclipse of Foncha and the rise of Solomon T. Muna, who eventually became prime minister and vice-president," Bjornson (1991: 24) also indicates, "illustrate how Ahidjo marginalized people who cultivated their own constituencies at the same time that he rewarded those who offered him their unqualified support.... He [Muna] was the one who transformed West Cameroonian administrative structures in accordance with Ahidjo's desire for a unified system."

Yet, other sources have suggested that Ambazonians did not put up a great fight in 1972 largely because of the manner of effecting that year's change and of its implicit assumption of the continuous existence of two identities in "United" Republic of Cameroon (URC). Unlike his successor, it has been argued, President Amadou Ahidjo had the *courtesy* (in effecting his 1972 change of the federal to unitary appellation) to go through the controversial referendum that Mensah-Gbadago has castigated as the embodiment of the most significant of manipulations by which Cameroonians were made to opt for a unitary state and this has gone down in history as the most significant date in the political history of Cameroon (cited in Fossungu, 2019: 62). Taking roots from the secretive Federal Constitution, it is then not surprising that Anyangwe (1987: 133 n.18.) also states that the "1972 Cameroonian constitution [as well] was never publicly debated and discussed. Even its actual drafting was shrouded in secrecy, and the people were called upon in a referendum to vote for a constitution whose contents they knew nothing about." A University of Yaoundé (UNIYAO) law professor also indicates that the 1996 Constitution is no exception to the secretive trend (Ondoa, 1996: 11 & 14).

Not everyone sees the 1972 change as a gross deception practised on the Cameroonian people though. There are other experts like Enonchong (1967: xii) who would instead describe its initiation in 1961 as "the Great Reunification Day", and Lantum (1991: 20) sees the 1972 event proper as a "great event [which] signalled the successful harmonisation of the political institutions during the ten years of the preceding period during which we all belonged to the '*Federal Republic of Cameroon*'" (emphasis as in original). The controversy over, or manipulation on, the issue is nowhere more accentuated as in the politics of minority protection and annexation by coup d'état, etc. Ambazonians had, since the 1984 name-change, been arguing that changing the country's name from FRC to URC in 1972, at least, still indicated that there were two or more entities that had come together. Their history (or story), they maintained, was thus still alive in the 'United' that replaced 'Federal'. What is *indeed* in those names anyway?

Also talking about the great expectations from the formation of the FRC, Konings and Nyamnjoh (1997: 207) have lamented that "Contrary to expectations, this did not provide for the equal partnership of both parties, let alone for the preservation of the cultural heritage and identity of each, but turned out to be merely a transitory phase to the total integration of the anglophone region into a strongly centralised, unitary state." The bulk of Southern Cameroonsians thus preferred to see the controversial 1972 transformation not in terms of what it was but in terms of its standing with the one in 1984. Thus, while this change in "1972 marked the overt beginning of [the] systematic subjugation, marginalization, assimilation and annexation of the Southern Cameroons", the argument of SCFAQ (Question 5) proceeded, "There was however some recognition of the bi-cultural nature of the state in the structures of the United Republic of Cameroon." Was that enough for not standing up then? Ayaba, do crisebacologists not get your point so well? Yes, even Benjamin Franklin would say that they clearly deserve neither liberty nor safety (see Fossungu, 2024: 47).

The 1972 transformation picture, SCFAQ (Question 5) pointed out, was very different from Biya's 1984 change that consummated the assimilation and annexation "with Decree N° 84-001 of February 4th, 1984 [which had the effect of] reverting the country to La République du Cameroun, in an attempt to completely obliterate and annex the Southern Cameroons. [That is why] Many Southern Cameroon[s]ians intensified their vocal opposition to the [1984] annexation of their territory." Aaccording to Gorji-Dinka (1991: 5), the 1984 change from URC to the Republic of Cameroon was a forceful annexation and assimilation since 'Republic of Cameroon' is the name of French-speaking Cameroon before the 1961 reunification. For this charge, they easily invoke the Federal Constitution, by whose first paragraph of Article 1, the FRC "is formed, as from 1st October 1961, of the territory of the Republic of Cameroon, henceforth called East Cameroon, and the territory of Southern Cameroons formerly under United Kingdom administration, henceforth called West Cameroon."

They also invoke two interestingly confusing ('The New-Old Name Revival Equals Sublimation') theses. First, that *La République du Cameroun* (East Cameroon) consequently seceded from the 1961 Union so that, second, they in Southern Cameroons – their own pre-federation name that they had since 1984 also revived – were no longer bound by *any* agreement to stay together (Gorji-Dinka, 1991: 5). Pomerance similarly argued that the Eritrean secessionist movement erupted because of Ethiopia's violation, in 1962, of the 1952 federation agreement that had established Eritrea as an autonomous unit. [M. Pomerance, *Self-Determination in Law and Practice* (The Hague: Martinus Nijhoff, 1982) at 115 n.382a] Moosnitec also held, for example, that the uniformists within the Hindu majority in India, in their drive to assimilate the Muslim minority, were breaching the two fundamental principles (of democracy and of secularity) of the Indian Constitution of 1950. [Th. Moosnitec, "La montée de l'intégrisme hindou" *Jeune Afrique* (18-24 mars 1993), 60.] Is the Southern Cameroonsian argument as forceful as that of the others, notably Eritrea's? The Southern Cameroonsian argument could have been as forceful *only* in 1972, if there was indeed a federation in Cameroon? Was 1972 even the first time that the need for standing up for collective cultural rights and for the Federation presented itself? In short, why was there no massive protest in 1972, the seemingly and palpably right moment for the two-point Southern Cameroonsian argument? Put differently in the words of Stark (1976: 423), "Why was this [1972] change conceded so easily by West Cameroonians? Why was it trumpeted officially as a 'revolution'?"

Other analysts have tried to explain but their explications would only go to buttress the point I am making. Namely, that there was no federation instituted in 1961 in Cameroon. Show me the Union Treaty that was signed and approved by the Parliaments of both LRC and Southern Cameroons, as requested by the architect of Njumba-No-Bi-Married, Mola Njoh Litumbe. None in existence. As the SCFAQ (Question 5) has doggedly argued,

> Many Southern Cameroon[s]ians (then known as West Cameroonians) protested this treasonable annexationist act [of 1972], but had no means of fighting back since the federal institutions had ceased to exist and those replacing them were not in their control. Even though they overwhelmingly rejected the centralized unitary United Republic of Cameroon that was replacing the Federation in the May 1972 referendum, their voices were drowned by those of their numerically superior francophone brothers.

This brotherhood thing always! Can the voices of Quebecers, for instance, be drowned by those of the rest of Canada in analogous manner in the Canadian 'Confederation' or federation? The response is a no; the obvious reason intimately tied to the invisible hand of Canadian federalism that is in no conceivable way comparable to the Cameroonian that was mired by the personification of public debates (see Fossungu, 2025). No *true federation* can indeed be formed in these circumstances (of the a priori personification of public issues); and the proof is in the February Story itself that disunites by uniting. But could the one-person-one-vote application in the 1972 referendum be part of Mr. Ahidjo's 'footing of equality' that he gave to the unwary Southern

Cameroonsians through the UN General Assembly in February 1959? Ahidjo's arguments could then run like this: "You want equality, and you get unqualified equality (or equality in vague terms) which you happily accept and embrace. Then when I start qualifiedly applying unqualified equality, you start to complain: what is really wrong with you Anglo-Fools?" Dr Cho Ayaba, do I not hear you well? The Anglo-Fools could then only feebly retort as follows. Only France's fools (or those who Enoh Meyomesse says "under the French did not really free themselves from France"[4] because of their sheepish belief in the doctrine of "Join me, and you're like me"[5]) would think that self-determination is a possibility in a unitary centralized State with a Supreme-Majority. Most French-speaking "intellectuals in politics" are even fascinated by the argument of Cameroon's one-time external affairs minister that "The dog of the King is the king of dogs." [Ferdinand Oyono, *Houseboy* [translated from French by John Read] (London: Heinemann, 1966) at 24]

Furthermore, one could also argue that the 1972 referendum was what Hogg (1996: 125-27) would see as 'secession by amendment' on the part of both East Cameroun and West Cameroon. Secession is not even the correct terminology to use in the Ambazonia-LRC war, as I have explained earlier; it is one against annexation, not one to secede (see Fossungu, 2025). An argument fortified by the fact that the Foumban 'intellectuals in politics' did not create a "true federation" that would have impeded secession, as theorized by Stevenson (1989: 8-9). Assuming they did, the secession-by-amendment argument would seem to be quite plausible in Cameroon: except that both entities never

---

[4] Larry Eyong, "Enoh Meyomesse: Jailed for Truth or Theft?" [On File with Author, received through email on Wednesday, 28 December 2011]. As SCFAQ (in Question 37) also put it, "A certain infantile attachment between La République du Cameroun and France persists which is completely disgusting to Southern Cameroon[s]ians and which is responsible in part for the rift between Southern Cameroons and La République du Cameroun. Former British colonies are not perfect and many of them such as Nigeria, Ghana, Uganda, etc. have had major goofs since independence but they are still ahead of the French neo colonies because those goofs were their own and they have learned from the experience. As things stand, we do not know when the French neo colonies will crawl, talk let alone walk."

[5] Victor T. Le Vine, "Political-Cultural Schizophrenia in Francophone Africa," in I.J. Mowoe and Richard Bjornson (eds.), *Africa and the West: The Legacies of Empires* (New York: Greenwood Press, 1986), 159 at 163.

28

became de facto two separate countries thereafter (until 2017, thanks to the AGovC led by Dr Lucas Cho Ayaba, who shrewdly and heroically embraced the compelling Argument of Force matching the Argument of Force). Otherwise, why was West Cameroon (Ambazonia) still trying to 'secede' from East Cameroon since 2017 if they said that the latter had seceded 'by unilateral act' from the FRC in 1984? Secession by amendment is thus out of the equation; leaving us with change by means provided by the constitution itself. Did the Federal Constitution's means of change protect the minority as claimed? It did not at all, especially in view of its Article 15 that I have just mentioned above (open-ended emergency powers to the PFR).

The Mathematics of Secession and Special Majority for Amendment: Two Simple Majorities Equal a Special Majority?

The unfamiliar democracy crafted in Foumban has obviously prompted questions from critics such as Canute Tangwa that specifically seek to know what the intellectual must be doing in politics that is infested with political chameleons. "What is the role of an intellectual? Should the intellectual be an active participant or a seer in politics? How can he [or she[6]] avoid brushes with political chameleons?" [Canute C.N. Tangwa, "Siga Asanga's Death and the SDF" *The Post* N° 0067 (8 May 1998), 4.] In response to the queries, de Smith (1964: 280) has held that the scholar must become involved in the events themselves, as an adviser, a commentator, or a partisan; and if he or she ends by being none the wiser he or she will at least be better informed. Again, I ask, is that what they are, or have been, doing in Africa generally? There is no better way to respond than by

---

[6] "I will consider to be an intellectual," Lantum (1991: 20) also very chauvinistically and in a conjuring manner told the questioning youths, "someone with a developed inquisitive and critical mind who applies his [a female can never be an intellectual then?] mind or intellect as rationally and objectively as possible, with full sense of responsibility to illuminate his milieu with the improvement of the common good of humanity as his or her [where is *she* now from?] goal." More of such sexist exclusions are discovered as we go along.

demonstrating the veracity or otherwise of their various theses through the meaning of federalism and associated concepts.

Has Cameroon ever been a federation? That is, as Wheare (1963: 33) would want to know, did the "system of government [in question] embody predominantly a division of powers between general and regional authorities, each of which, in its own sphere, is co-ordinate with the others and independent of them?" Upon the answer to this central question (and those following) lies the heart of the entire confusion and manipulation in Cameroon regarding multiculturalism and human rights. The other associated questions are: Does a federation exist by the mere fact that "federal" is affixed to the name of a centralized unitary country? What are some of the most conspicuous features of the Foumban Constitution that are inimical to the federal spirit and form? Foumban is regarded in Cameroon as Philadelphia is in the USA (or as Charlottetown is in Canada): Is this analogy sensible or simply a subtle part of the historical confusion? Did the President of the Federal Republic stage a coup d'état upon Cameroon in 1972? In other words, did the Foumban Constitution (1961-1972) guarantee fundamental human and institutional rights and especially minority concerns, as most Ambazonian intellectuals do claim? If the answer is yes, then why did the FRC very *peacefully* terminate in 1972 without the existence of two or more countries (such as was the case with Ethiopia and Eritrea)? If the answer to the issue of rights being guaranteed is no, why did the FRC not protect those rights? Did federation (if there was any) in Cameroon *end* in 1972?

I think giving genuine answers to these questions is an important step toward comprehending the groundless theses on human rights guarantees by, and surrounding, the FRC; and, therefore, also civilizing the current federalism and multiculturalism (and, therefore, human rights) debates in Africa generally and Cameroon in particular. Let me use their secession argument and special majority thesis now to fasten it up. It is known from both Njawé and Eyoum'a Ntoh that it is the doing of analytical, incisive and objective reporting (*sans avoir horreur de*

30

la vérité[7]) that principally, if not exclusively, leads to real debates of/on the issues such as those of federalism, democracy, and multiculturalism in Africa. Pathetically, as I indicated earlier, the reverse instead seems to be the rule in Africa. Local government (or federalism) without an independent judiciary and locally elected officials is not worth the name. In the absence of these institutions there is no reason why anyone would then be using the terms federalism and democracy, except for confusion, a mystification that seems to have become the singular characteristic of the "intellectuals in politics". They claim, for instance, that Biya's 1984 change of name to 'Republic of Cameroon' is secession on the part of LRC from the 1961 union (see Konings, 1999: 305-306).

According to a French constitutionalist, "*La démocratie peut être considérée, selon la définition adoptée, comme le pouvoir du plus grand nombre ou le gouvernement du peuple, par le peuple, et pour le peuple ou encore comme le régime qui assure l'identification des gouvernés aux gouvernants.*" [Pierre Pactet, *Institutions politiques Droit constitutionnel* 10e édition (Paris: Masson, 1991) at 85.] The second part of his definition (*comme le régime qui assure l'identification des gouvernés aux gouvernants*) clearly makes the branding of the three Sahel Confederation governments as 'juntas' and 'dictatorships' only the western propaganda against African administrations that serve and protect the interests of their own people rather than being foreign puppets. From Pactet's definition of democracy as government of the people by the people and for the people, it is crystal clear to even any savvy elementary school pupil that secession will not be regarded in the inverted, confusioncratic, and subversive manner (as it was in Cameroon) in a country that is truly democratic. If it is truly a government of the people by the people for the people, secession has already been excluded by self-determination or the absence of repression. Was Ambazonia then repressing

---

[7] See Pius Njawé, "Le vrai débat" *Le Messager* N° 587 (20 février 1997), 1; & Patrick-Thomas Eyoum'a Ntoh, "Qui veut tromper Fru Ndi?" *Le Messager* N° 587 (20 février 1997), 3..

Cameroun (LRC) in the union for the latter to be seceding from it? It is the reverse that would instead hold. Secession is nothing but the legitimate response to the repression of the universal right to self-determination within the state.

This also means that a democratic society, according to Hogg (1996: 124-25), may even have 'the power to secede' embedded in the constitution. As indicated by Konings (1999: 301), the final version of the Foumban Constitution left no room for legal secession from the federation, although some Ambazonian delegates had wanted a provision inserted into the constitution sanctioning the peaceful withdrawal from the federation. Why did they accept what they did not want? And why would there now be such a peaceful withdrawal on the part of Cameroun? My other works (e.g., Fossungu, 2025) might provide an elaborate answer; but to provide for secession in the constitution does not necessarily mean that states or provinces have the right to secede from a federal union *whenever* they just feel like doing so. "If the definition [of federalism] is a valid one," Stevenson (1989: 8-9, emphasis added) has argued, "it follows that in a *true federation* the provinces or states have no right to secede. If such right existed before, they surrendered it when they entered the federal union." This is the elementary lesson; and which is quite normal and logical but does this logic apply to the case of Cameroon? That is, was the FRC a true federation? I answer in the negative since there was no Union Treaty as noted above; and would therefore think that, as there was no true federation in Foumban, the 'true federation impediment' argument from Ambazonians cannot stand. That is to say in particular that the Ambazonian argument that (by the name-change in 1984) *La République du Cameroun* seceded from the Union in 1984 has no firm foundation or any underpinning at all (for more of which, see Fossungu, 2025: chapter 5). What kind of lawyers and constitutionalists (intellectuals) are those Ambazonia sent to Foumban then?

The secession claim from Ambazonians has already been excluded because there was no true federation. As McGill University's Professor Scott's argument goes, "There is no legal basis for any constitutional change – and therefore no right of secession by any province of Canada

– except through the means of change provided by the Constitution itself." [Stephen A. Scott, in David Schneiderman (ed.), <u>After Allaire and Bélanger-Campeau</u> (being a Symposium) as reported in 3:1 *Constitutional Forum Constitutionnel* (Winter 1991), 14 at 15.] What then were the means provided by Cameroon's 1961 Federal Constitution that could justify change in Cameroon such as the one(s) in 1972 (and in 1984)? In other words, was the minority state (Ambazonia) protected in such a way that a nation-wide referendum could not be one of these devices for effecting constitutional change in Cameroon?

The Solid Federal Edifice Theory Teaching a Pig to Sing

There are several theories suggesting the affirmative to the query just posed, especially the Solid Federal Edifice Theory. In this palaver, a lot of people just jump into talking wildly about the 'solid federation' without ever having seen the constitutional or political basis of said solid edifice. This theory claims that the given constitutional means for change under the FRC protected Ambazonians from any change that they did not favour. In the proper words of Ntenga's (1997) Solid Federal Edifice thesis, the Foumban Federation, "made up of the State of West Cameroon and that of East Cameroon", undoubtedly "was built on a solid foundation known as 'the Federal Constitution.' While laying the foundation stone in Foumban in 1961, the architects and builders of the Edifice agreed that no part of the building shall be modified without the knowledge and express consent of both parties and the sovereign people of Cameroon." Other similar theses such as the SCFAQ's do claim in its Question 5 that,

> The July 1961 constitutional conference in Foumban defined the structure of the union between La République du Cameroun and the Southern Cameroons as a Federation. This agreement led to the Federal Republic of Cameroon that came into being on October 1ˢᵗ of 1961. The two parties co-existed happily till 1972 when the President of the Federation Mr.

33

Amadou Ahidjo unilaterally *and in violation of Article 47 of the Federal Constitution (which prohibited any action that would threaten the existence of the federation)* abrogated the Federal arrangement with Proclamation DF 72-270 of February 6th, 1972, abolishing all federal legislative, judicial and administrative institutions and removing *all guarantees that protected the rights of the minority Southern Cameroons* in the Federation (emphasis added).

According to the Chairman of a political party too, "Unification was based on Federalism and Equality of status, on Unity in Diversity, on equality of all Cameroonians.... that is why the United Nations gave Southern Cameroons independence on the basis of Federalism. We unified on the understanding that we would operate a Federal System, in which we will live in a mighty, united, economically, strong Cameroon Nation, guaranteeing all citizens of every race and religion, inalienable fundamental and civic rights, equal opportunities and respect for the bicultural character of our people" (Ngwana, 2009). This book strongly disagrees with these theories and, to buttress its contrary view, I am going to take a keen look at the constitutional amending formula of only the Solid Federal Edifice, not to go so much into those of other federal constitutions (as to which, see Fossungu, 2019: 127-48).

As the experts have made it clear to us, essential elements of constitutionalism and respect for the rule of law are constitutional stability and the certainty and predictability that go with this. In fact, as they have concluded, a constitution will lose its value as the supreme law if it is frequently and arbitrarily changed to suit the political convenience of the ruling elites (Fombad, 2014: 425). Yes, this is particularly the case with Cameroon and the "Central African region [which] is seriously lagging behind the rest of the continent in progress towards constitutionalism and respect for the rule of law" (Fombad, 2014: 448). No doubt then that Cheikh-Tidiane Gaye has said that conflicts in Central Africa were so serious that they were a menace to security and peace in Africa as a whole (Fossungu, 2023: 234). Let the amendment tale in then to certify. According to the amendment

34

formula in Article 47 of the Foumban 'Federal' Constitution (its equivalent being Part XI (Articles 63-64) of the 1996 Constitution),

> Any proposal for the revision of the present Constitution which impairs the unity and integrity of the Federation shall be inadmissible. The power to initiate the revision of the Constitution shall belong equally to the President of the Federal Republic, after consultation with the Prime Ministers of the Federated States, and the Deputies of the Federal Assembly. Any proposal for revision submitted by the Deputies must be signed by at least one third of the Members of the Federal Assembly. Proposals for revision shall be adopted by simple majority vote of the members of the Federal Assembly, provided that such majority includes a majority of the representatives in the Federal Assembly of each of the Federated States. The President of the Federal Republic may request, under the same conditions as for a federal law that a second reading be given to a law revising the Constitution.

Every sentence of this amending formula is topic enough for a whole book of its own. I am not going to write those books within this one though. I will just stay on the issues of *coup d'état/annexation in 1972* and of Ambazonians being guaranteed protection under the Federal Constitution, especially against change that they did not want. This will entail finding out (1) whether two simple majorities equal a special majority and (2) whether there was any place for judicial review in the FRC. Citing Albert W. Mukong (ed.), *The Case for the Southern Cameroons* (Yaoundé: Cameroon Federalist Committee, 1990), p. 18, Konings and Nyamnjoh (1997: 210) have indicated that on 6 May 1972, Ahidjo announced in the National Assembly that he intended to transform the Federal Republic into a unitary state, provided the electorate supported the idea in a referendum to be held on 20 May, thereby abrogating clause 1 of Article 47 of the Foumban document which read as outlined above. Even if the constitution were to be amended, they further pointed out that it should not be done by referendum, because clause 3

35

of Article 47 stipulated 'that proposals for revision shall be adopted by simple majority vote of the members of the Federal Assembly, provided that such majority includes a majority of the representatives... of each of the Federated States.'

It has thus been largely alleged that Ahidjo staged a coup d'état in 1972 by not respecting Article 47's special majority, which some scholars like Enonchong (1967: 21, citing Federal Article 18) regard as "the entrenchment of special clauses as a necessary safeguard against the imposition of wanton legislation on any unwilling state." Konings (1999: 300), commenting on the praised article, has lengthily observed that,

> Curiously, Ahidjo eventually allowed a Southern Cameroons recommendation to be incorporated into the constitution which created a potential safeguard against the adoption of federal legislation harmful to one of the federated states. Article 18 created a procedure whereby the president might require a bill to be read a second time, either of his own accord or at the request of the prime minister of either federated state. At the second reading, the bill had to receive the approval of a majority of the national assembly members from each federated state. This element of a 'second reading' was one of the few respects in which the constitution envisaged curtailment of the powers of the federal authority through the actions of state representatives. Although this provision could have made a significant contribution to the safeguarding of West Cameroon interests, it was never actually applied.

My view is that it never could have been any safeguard even if applied. It is already stated but I think I should take it over again. Federal Article 18 that Enonchong cites in buttressing his "special clauses" thesis, provides that "Before a law is promulgated, the President of the Federal Republic may request a second reading thereof, either of his own motion or at the request of either of the Prime Ministers of the Federated States. On second reading, the law shall be adopted only if the majority specified in the preceding article comprises a majority of the votes of the deputies of each of the Federated States." On its part, the preceding Article 17 simply stipulates that "Federal Laws shall be adopted by simple majority of deputies." The question to pose here is: do two simple majorities equal a special majority? A reading of Cameroon's amendment formula (Federal Article 47) and the other articles cited would hardly show any special majority. Lantum (1991: 21) tells us that the "intellectuals in politics" in Foumban in 1961 possessed "An intelligence quotient towering high above the average, to learn and understand the world with unusual perspicacity." This, it must be emphasized, is describing the architects of the FRC, especially the ones from Ambazonia.

Foumban was plainly an All-Male affaire (see *Record of the Conference on the Constitutional Future of the Southern Cameroons, Held at Foumban 17th to 21st July 1961*: Buea, 1961) despite attempts from certain writers to emasculate the facts. For example, Enonchong talks of the 'Foumban Constitution Assembly' "delegates to which included chiefs, representatives of all political parties, of religious and trade union movements and *members of the Cameroon Bar Association*. It was a broad-based conference with the object of encompassing views from *all sections of Cameroon national life*" (1967: 83-84, emphasis added). All this, I must indicate, is untrue and can only go to further the confusion and manipulation in regard of the Foumban Enterprise. To even leave the hot female issue out for now (see Chapter 3), you can simply want to know from them what 'the Cameroon Bar Association' here consisted of. Was it that of East Cameroon or that of a "federal" Cameroon that they were still about to create? Dr Ayaba should once more tell these worthless lawyers to 'shut the hell up. They should shut the hell up... [and] Depart from the system and join the fighters on the ground' (Fossungu, 2023: 227).

Whatever the case, I think any ordinary educated person must appreciate what I am saying about the Foumban "special majority" without necessarily having to be the intellectuals with towering IQs. But I am sure these ones (if they are really what we are being told they were), would, perforce, even more easily realize that the requirement of a vote by simple majority: provided this includes a *majority* (not *necessarily* a special one, it must be noted) of the representatives – *in the federal assembly* – of each of the two constituent states, does not in any way transform the first simple majority into a 'special majority'. Perhaps the point being made here can become very lucid (if not already obvious) if it is expounded upon mathematically, and there is certainly much more difficult mathematics called *Noddometrics* awaiting these 'intellectual' in "*An entirely democratized single party*" (Biya, 1986: 45, emphasis is original). Surprised? "Many of you [who] must be hearing about this subject for the very first time" are counselled that, "As you prepare for NODDometrics, keep in mind that you can never be an expert at democracy to qualify for admission. You will always find yourself becoming a novice at everything. Because…the School's authorities would not even hesitate in announcing to all such experts on non-NODD democracy that they still have a lot of learning to do (preferably in Cameroon's own Advanced Democracy School) to deserve the 'expert' title. And if, for curiosity, you were 'humble' enough to denounce your well-considered views and are admitted, this is what would follow." [Peter Ateh-Afac Fossungu, "Doing *Noddometrics* in the Advanced School of Democracy" *The Herald* N° 608 (15-17 May), 10]

The FNA had fifty members with one-fifth of them being from Ambazonia. I am drawing from *Law N° 64-LF-1 of 24 March 1964*, and Federal Constitution's Article 16 (one deputy to 80,000 inhabitants) and Article 60 (giving population of two federated states: 3,200,000 for La République du Cameroun (LRC) & 800,000 for Ambazonia). A simple majority of 27/50 in the FNA may then be apportioned as follows: 21/40 (LRCans) and 6/10 (Ambazonians). And do not forget too that all members of both camps in the FNA are of the same party. Why do I say so? Because in 1961 the concept of federalism was largely used by some individuals only as a bargaining medium for personal favours from the President of the "Federal" *République du Cameroun* who, on his part, employed the concept solely as a tool, first, for the camouflaged annexation of Ambazonia and, second, for the ruthless crushing of the 'stormy and heady' opposition in Cameroun. For example, to be able to easily achieve their ulterior goals, dealings between the two parties (Ahidjo's *Union Camerounaise* & Foncha's KNDP – Kamerun National Democratic Party) that 'created the federation' were shrouded in top secrecy, contrary to what some 'intellectuals in politics' such as Enonchong (1967: 83-84) do present. The parties to the secret pre-Foumban and post-Foumban dealings (not without the Ambazonian translator) did sufficiently reap their fruits of the secrecy. For instance, 'the secretive Foumban Constitution' required in Article 53 that, until 1964, deputies to the FNA be nominated by the respective legislative assemblies of the two federated states.

This questionable requirement, according to Benjamin (1972: 21), especially enabled President Ahidjo (whose *Union Camerounaise* party then controlled the LRC Assembly) to muzzle the Opposition in LRC and keep them out of the national or 'federal' level (and, what other level was there?). This equally applies to the Ambazonia Legislative Assembly which was dominated by Prime Minister/Vice President John Ngu Foncha's KNDP, thus also excluding EML Endeley's KNC (Kamerun National Congress) opposition party from the 'federal' level. All this could simply not have been the case if those federal deputies were elected directly. That is, if the provision that specified the principle of representation (80,000 inhabitants per deputy) took effect from 1961. Deputies from the southern part of LRC should then not have necessarily been persons favouring Ahidjo's measures and policies; an apt example buttressing the point here being Deputy Daniel Kemajou who, in his valiant opposition to the acquisition of *pleins pouvoirs* by Premier Ahidjo in 1959, affirmed: "No and again No! Better to die in dignity than live in slavery and dishonour" (see *Journal Officiel des Débats, Année Legislative* 1959-1960, First annual ordinary session, plenary meeting of 23 October 1959 at 29).

Any genuine 'intellectual in politics' (excepting the Intellectual in Process Manipulation) must then hardly need to be another Lord Denning of England to truly fail to see how a simple majority becomes a special majority simply because there is another simple majority from both sides of the Mungo River right there in the FNA. To further regard the formula for this kind of majority as something which is "even more significant" (Enonchong, 1967: 90), simply beats the imagination. Enonchong (1967: 90) then proceeds to praise the "special procedure clauses under article 47 of the Federal Constitution for its amendment" before concluding that "Constitutional amendments are the exclusive jurisdiction of the National Federal Assembly." Like all the others before and following, the thesis on fundamental rights guarantees "is like trying to teach a pig to sing: it usually succeeds only in annoying the pig." [Don Macpherson, "Bouchard Not the Life of His Party" *Montreal Gazette* (15 December 1998), B3.] This unnecessary annoyance is plainly evident through a casual look at legislative functions at the federal level as well as the federal-state domains (see Chapter 3). The more so as there was no independent judge to confirm or disallow it, or even to say whose interpretation (Enonchong's or mine) is the correct. All that is preposterous except the learned doctor is talking about a different enactment than the Article 47 that I have laid out above.

Who Defines National Policy in Systems Based on Constitutionalism?

The theory positing human rights protection under the Foumban document quickly provokes a series of associated questions that are stiffly posed by the very first sentence of the Article-47 amendment formula that everyone seems to be clinging on. Some of these questions have to do with the person or organ that decides on the inadmissibility of the proposal for amendment. Who similarly defines what "impairs" the unity and integrity of the State? Blackletter academics and lawyers fail a lot in their responses all the time. Aimed at securing a deeper understanding of the law as a social phenomenon in Africa, therefore, this book, though looking at the issues of confusion in governance and human rights there through the eyes of a lawyer, goes a step or two further by viewing the whole system intact. It does not scrutinize just the legal or concerned constitutional enactment in isolation. I think it is through research *on* (and not just *in*) Cameroon law (risky and over-ambitious as it obviously is) that the Cameroonian confusion can be largely understood, if not entirely grasped.

Dunlop (1991: 68 & 67) understandably warns that research *about* law is a much larger and riskier enterprise, with all the inherent dangers involved in over-ambitious interdisciplinary research. All this is because law in this instance can be discussed as an historical phenomenon, as a cultural, philosophical, or political idea, or as an institution having social, political, or economic consequences that can be examined empirically. Here, Dunlop pursues, law can be read as a story without necessarily making assumptions about rationality or value that the research *in* law tends to involve, seeming always to involve disciplines other than law. One is driven, the Alberta professor concludes, to examine history, the social sciences, cultural studies, philosophy, and literature to carry out the project. This global or zoomedeyed approach (my signature too) has an unrivalled advantage. Above all else, it enormously aids anyone capable of managing it to grasp and master a lot of the confusion within/about Cameroon's constitutional and political set-up. My zoomed-eyed view of the 1998 Education Law in the chapters below is also a clean case to the point.

The Federal Constitution in Article 8 made "The President of the Federal Republic of Cameroon, Head of the Federal State and Head of the Federal Government, [who] shall uphold the Federal Constitution and shall ensure the unity of the Federation and the conduct of the affairs of the Federal Republic." Was Ahidjo then not merely 'ensuring *the unity* of the Federation' in his 'conducting of the affairs of the Federal Republic' when *he* thought 'Federal' was not unity enough as 'United' is, in 1972? Cameroon's Unitary Constitutions (being the modified but much more potent equivalence of the Federal Article 8) do not only also make '*Le Président de la République, Chef de l'État,*' the Courts, judge and umpire over the "*respect de la Constitution*" but also make him the only person who "*définit la politique de la nation.*"[8] Was Biya also not just defining that policy in 1984 when, to him, there was then only 'one Cameroon people', and nothing left to be united as implied in the URC? No one will then be wrong to say that any "constitutional tradition" in Cameroon (if there was anything like it at all) "varies with the foot of the POR." That being the case, as I have questioned in regard of multipartism (in Chapter 2), who can then ever try to engage the POR in debates over these matters without being considered by him (the only and final judge on the matter) as threatening the [head of] State's "unity" that he alone "shall ensure"?

Some legal minds have therefore properly pointed out that this type of drafting embedded in Cameroon legislation, done "by the cronies of the executive called *Administrateurs civils*" and "investing powers... [in] one man can only be seen in a dictatorial regime where the legislature is the puppet of the executive" (Etinge, 1991: 6). The barrister, therefore, submitted that it is not the POR who ought to define the policy of the nation, concluding that it is the Constitution, the supreme document of the land, the sentinel of all freedoms and liberties which is drawn and agreed upon by the people. This legal expert is obviously right because, by Section 14 of the Nigerian Constitution, "sovereignty belongs to the people of Nigeria from whom government through the Constitution derives its powers and authority." As Etinge (1991: 6) then crowned his brilliant argument, "If the president is invested with that power" (as he was and is in Cameroon), "then fifty Presidents will define fifty policies for a nation." This is axiomatic. Had the Canadian or American Constitutions, for example, been drafted in that manner, then John A Macdonald (for the former) and George Washington (for the latter) would have "defined" their respective country's policies: with their numerous successors having the same opportunities of defining and redefining, which, in effect, simply means amending and re-amending

---

[8] *Loi N° 91/001 du 23 avril portant modification des articles 5, 7, 8, 9, 26, 27, et 34 de la Constitution* [1991 Constitution], Article 5 (*nouveau*). The 1996 Constitution's Articles 5 & 11 reinforce the same stance.

the documents.[9] This would obviously mean (especially in the United States where there is a "fixed term of office" – there is none for Canada) that the country would not be what it is today – after no less than forty-seven presidents. For, would some "mad" presidents not have defined the policy to be the demise of the Union as Mikhail Gorbachev did to the defunct Soviet Union? *Son Excellence* El Hadj Amadou Ahidjo did just that in Cameroon in 1972, with his successor, Paul Biya, eventually driving the final nail to Cameroon's coffin in 2017 by openly declaring war (which was covert until then) on "a part" of their 'one and indivisible nation'. Do these people even think at all?

Coup d'etat, you call all that? In other words, as Enonchong (1967: 227-28) himself wants to know, "How then must the [various] legislatures and the executives be kept strictly within their constitutional domains? Who will tell each of them that it has overtly or covertly allowed its function to flow out of the pale of its constitutional authority? On the answers to these questions [must] depend the determination of the body in the Cameroon federal system which can and will define the limits of the various powers distributed by the constitutional instrument." Who decides what "impairs" unity, etc. when there is no independent judiciary as well as no independent territorial units/institutions? Is the absence of an independent judiciary and of locally elected officials in Cameroon not the main reason (according to their very own secession theses) why LRC was able to so easily "secede" (renege, is the correct term) from the FRC 'by unilateral act' (Hogg, 1996: 127-29), be it in 1972 or in 1984 (and yet still being part and parcel of the FRC that now wants to reconstruct Ambazonia)?

> LRC is on a campaign of reconstruction. They want to reconstruct what they did not construct. Every day in their own country, people are dying on highways, narrow highways. They

---

[9] Is President Donald Trump not guilty here with his recent Executive Orders that override the Constitution, especially regarding birthright citizenship? It is amazing that Americans do not see their dictators and thieves but are quick to brand African patriots like Colonel Gaddafi of Libya and Captain Traoré of Faso as dictators and thieves! Who are the real thieves? Good thing is that Africans are wiser now to know the game being played.

cannot expand those highways, but they want to reconstruct Ambazonia. We don't know if they are reconstructing what they have destroyed, or they are reconstructing what they built. Absence of any possibility in terms of access to hospitals, to good schools, schools that are tailored towards helping the children of Ngoketunjia know the potentials within their state, and how to educate themselves to tap into those opportunities and potentials (Ayaba, Ngoketunjia: September 2023).

I think the claim of the minority's protection under the Foumban Constitution in the context of Federalism, Separation of Powers, and Constitutionalism in Africa is frivolous. Nevertheless, the people in power in Africa, especially Cameroon's must study treatises such as H.S Commager's *Majority Rule and Minority Rights* (Gloucester, Mass.: Peter Smith, 1958), as well as de Smith's (1964). By the way, if the Biya administration is so interested in the *respect for majority decisions*, why is Mr. Biya still the POR of Cameroon when the overwhelming majority of Cameroonians have on several occasions voted him out, as shown by Konings and Nyamnjoh (1997: 214-216), Howard French and many others? [See Howard W. French, "President Re-Elected in Cameroon: Biya Returned in Lacklustre Vote that Augurs Poorly for the Country's Future" *The Edmonton Journal* (14 October 1997), F12.] Not to harp on the ongoing Tchiroma Stolen Election Victory Affaire that has plunged LRC into destruction, hear it also live from a confused citizen to the SDF opposition leader, Chairperson Ni John Fru Ndi:

They have disenfranchised us by not registering us. They have manipulated the electoral register, refused to issue cards to the few they registered, and finally refused proclaiming the results as they were. Mr. Chairman, you said during the last rally in Bamenda that you will set the pace for new democracy in Africa and Mr. Biya too is setting the pace for his own sterile democracy. What was the need for this election when they cannot accept the verdict of the ballot box? [Cosmas K. Keba, "Fru Ndi, What Next?" *The Herald* N° 471 (13-15 June 1997), 4]

Monosity as Prerequisite for 'Pluralistic Democracy': Illusive National Unity and the Monopolization of Citizens' Destiny

See them disqualifying Professor Maurice Kamto, a potential winner of their 12 October 2025 presidential elections; and then also trying to arrest Minister Issa Tchiroma Bakary who left their government to challenge Paul Biya for the presidency on 12 October 2025 and having the best chances of a landslide victory. Yet they would be talking of democracy? There is just no point in bragging about majority rule *only* in situations where it would mean oppression. But that is precisely what "advanced democracy" is all about – advancing before democracy to preclude the latter's birth and growth (Fossungu, 2018: 24-25). That is the persistent stance from the Unity Palace that looks at federalism not as a means of channeling, but as the actual cause of, the country's multifarious diversity – cultural, ethnic, linguistic, and religious. According to the authorities, this diversity has been standing in the way of democracy and must be eliminated for the purposes of national unity: only after the doing of which can pluralistic democracy (if that is not tautological) come. It is tautological to talk of "pluralistic democracy" because democracy must necessarily be pluralistic to be democracy. The specialists have defined it in the simplest terms as "An open, *pluralistic* governmental system, allowing for the free expression and flow of ideas and for rival political groupings" (Pearson and Rochester, 1984: 593, emphasis added). The oneness of the Cameroonian People (perfect nation) of 1984 was the prelude to this "pluralistic" democracy, it was claimed. But why was this tautological type of democracy not instituted since 1984 with the existence of only one Cameroon people?

The surprising answer is then that the national unity situation of Cameroon is now different from those of other countries (including even France from where Cameroon dishonestly and largely copies without acknowledgment) since Cameroonians do not yet have the "Perfect Nationhood" which they even had in 1984. What happened? The Perfect Nation of 1984 mysteriously disappeared overnight. That is, just two years later. The higher reappearance of this vanished 'Perfect Nation' in the form of a New Ethnic Group (NEG) was thus

45

imperative. According to Biya (1986: 44, emphasis added), "Having to date ensured the peaceful co-existence of the rich diversity of Cameroonian ethnic groups, it [the Biya administration] can credibly embark on the *higher* phase of its task – that of uniting the ethnic groups into one New Ethnic Group." Some now call it Bululization. Bulu Republic! Until this has been done, the authorities have then claimed, "the realization of this dream [called 'pluralistic' democracy]" simply cannot come to reality principally because it "encounters a major obstacle, that is, the absence of a real [Bulu] nation due to persisting ethnic, religious and linguistic particularisms" (Biya, 1986: 28). Mr. President, these conflicts, and discussions can only be skillfully managed, not eliminated. The management of conflicts is the *art* called politics. Trying to eliminate conflicts forcefully, therefore, the experts have cautioned, is tantamount to being dead and alive at the same time. They have thus written:

> Whether one likes it or not, politics, like sex, cannot be abolished. It can sometimes be repressed by denying people the opportunity to practice it, but it cannot be done away with because it is the nature of… [human beings] to disagree and contend. We are not saying that politics arises solely from the selfish desire of some to have their way, although that is certainly one source of it. The fact is that even in a society of altruists or angels there would be politics, for some would conceive the common good in one way and some in another, and (assuming the uncertainties that prevail in this world) some would think one course of action more prudent, and some would think another (Banfield and Wilson, 1963: 20-21).

It can thus be obvious that being dead and alive at the same time has been the fate of the bulk of Cameroonians, but it was even worse for the Ambazonian minority. The Perfect Nation/NEG exercise then was nothing but part of the generalized confusion in Cameroon, an exercise that assured that the confusionists stay forever in power in their perfect nation; a perfect nation with a perfectly confusing multiculturalism that embodies a type of culture that does not encapsulate history (see Fossungu, 2025). Their further claim which solidifies the denial of history is that:

46

the different quarters of our towns at times show signs of ethnic peculiarities which, in such a particularly explosive spatial concentration, recall the human contradictions of our society…. Our religious divisions themselves are no less sources of social conflict. In this context and in spite of what has been achieved in promoting unity, the demons of tribalism still remain a permanent and serious threat to the stability of our institutions (cited in Fossungu, 2021: 21).

As the Logic of Advanced Democracy then went, the ruling party, "[t]he CPDM, therefore, remains an irreplaceable instrument in the medium term for national unity" (Biya, 1986: 43) because "The CPDM whose responsibility it is *to determine the destiny of Cameroonians* has made a commitment to promote" the NEG (Biya, 1986: 126, emphasis added). It was then, therefore, the irreplaceable mandate of the authorities in place in Cameroon to transform the country's pluralism into one (through the irreversible creation of the NEG) "which is the pre-requisite for the institution of pluralistic democracy" (Biya, 1986: 45). All this being because "The present phase of the history of Cameroon does not permit the institution of a multiparty system. Our Party is, therefore, responsible for the reduction of the existing ethno-cultural divisions in order to promote national integration which is the pre-requisite for the institution of a pluralistic democracy" (Biya, 1986: 127). This is quite amazing or confusing. These authorities that would never want to realize that times have changed were still disputing with the experts who say neither democracy nor federalism can be feasible without some sort of effective separation of powers and multiplicity; stiffly disputing any change to their One-Party System which, according to them, has a "Solid Foundation", spanning over five decades because, as far back as 1966 – just five years after 'federating' – "the political parties were [voluntarily] dissolved and a single new party the *Union National Camerounien* (UNC) was formed, the President believing this necessary to create national unity out of the diversity of the tribes and for reasons of development" (Peaslee, 1974: 83).

The italicized portion of the above quotation (which should normally be *Union Nationale Camerounaise* – CNU in English, see Konings and Nyamnjoh, 1997: 210) is exactly as in the original and can be perfectly understood in the context of the new language or confusion called *Francanglais* (*Francapidgin*, in fact) that is in the offing in

47

Cameroon (see Fossungu, 2021: chapter 3; & Ntemfac Ofege's "Government Should Stop Corrupting the English Language (Culture)" *The Herald* N° 590 (30-31 March 1998), 4). The Etoudi gangsters had long decided, therefore, that "the [unique CPDM] Party will become an important vehicle for spreading the spirit and practice of democracy in our society. The Party must also, above all become a real party of sovereign militants. This objective calls for the fulfilment of certain conditions. For instance, no obstacle, no manoeuvre, whatever its nature…." (Biya, 1986: 45). Of course, Ambazonians demanding fundamental redress to their disheartening situation represented an 'obstacle' that bullets must swiftly eliminate, occasioning the countless massacres. It does explain why since 1982 Biya has been in power whereas during that same period the United States of America has had nine presidents plus, with most of them having been re-elected for a second four-year term; France (itself that is propping them up and forcing all these dictators on Africans) has had about six presidents plus; and Ghana in Africa has seen about nine presidents plus. So, just tell me how Ghanaians are ever going to give even an iota of one ear to Cameroon's talk of African unity when the 'advanced' President Biya talking to them is equal to eight plus of their presidents? And when, moreover, they can easily see the very shabby way Biya had been treating the English-speaking in Miniature Africa?

This book is also critically examining the human factor as it impacted Cameroon's political economy; showing that the country was blessed with everything required for speedy and sustainable development, viewing moreover that it was dotted heavily with intelligent, efficient and patriotic managers from Ambazonia. Real intellectuals in politics or *people weh know road*. I am talking about the natural qualities of Ambazonians, spiced with Ambazonia's unrivalled physical environment and other natural endowments that, with just the right push from the quality governors just described as being present, would undoubtedly have transformed Cameroon into a Paradise on Earth. This situation did not materialize while Ambazonia was under occupation simply because of problems in leadership non-charisma and in non-challenge of historic trivia of the occupier, and not the result of the country's unquestioned diversity, as the colonial apologists called its administrators would claim. A bunch of idiotickerizers are mismanaging Africa and not that it is ungovernable. Its apparent "un-governability" is the result of the deliberately engendered confusion, not of its

48

diversity or any mysterious forces. "To conclude, Your Excellency," Taku (1995: 3) writes, "I have always held the view that what is perceived as a stalemate in the Cameroons is a deliberate choice by the regime of personal powers and not a result of some mysterious forces." The country's impressive diversity per se cannot be such "mysterious forces," as claimed by the Unity Palace occupants.

Barrister Taku is not alone in making the point because other experts, after meticulously going through the 1996 Constitution that is camouflaging biculturalism, have simply concluded that "It is now clear that Biya tends to see power only in absolute categories. Power, to self-professed animal man (Lion man) is real when it is undiluted; when it is a handy tool for liquidating all opposition; when it is the one simple but potent formula for playing God without being encumbered by God's infinite humanness – love and goodness; by simply spelling God the other way round." ["Front Page Comment: Trashcan Stuff' *Cameroon Post* N° 0274 (11-18 December 1995), 1] What Ambazonians are now trying to put in place is a

Land where a mom gets out of bed in Ndop. A bus stops in front of the house, picks up the child, the mom says goodbye, the child is heading to school. The child comes from school with his/her bag full of books, pens, pencils she never paid for. If that child falls sick, with a click on her phone, there is an emergency service there to pick up the child to the hospital. The child is booked in, checked, treated. That mom is going to have faith in the administrators in Ndop. You cannot have faith in a place that offers you nothing but misery. You cannot have faith in a place that if you are sick you die in the corridors of the hospital. You cannot have faith in a place where you drive 200 km there is callé-callé, extortion and brutality by an enemy occupying force. You cannot have faith in a flag that never protects you. You cannot have faith in an Anthem within which you are not represented. My people, we must have faith in our Land. We must have faith in ourselves. We cannot have faith in a country where the people of that country don't even have faith in their own country. That since independence in 1960 there are two men who have ruled LRC. Two men! It is very important for us to know why we are making these sacrifices. And for us to ask what the reward would be. And we are laying them clearly to you at the level of each state, explaining detailly the opportunities that are within those states, how those opportunities would be harnessed and used to uplift the lives of the people within those states and beyond. And what role each of you will play. We are not simply procrastinating. We have the facts about the strength of our country (Ayaba, Ngoketunjia: September 2023).

The best (and most enjoyable) way to learn, according to an expert on comparative government, is to engage in lively, informal discussions with peers. That's just what educated citizens in ancient Greece and colonial America did, with results that left an indelible imprint on world history (Magstadt, 1991: 4). Had the Cameroon leadership engaged (or did they even countenance engaging) in such dialogue with their 'across-the-Atlantic' peers? They did not and would not, most probably because they cannot have anything to talk about in the first place since their governmental variant is not at all listed in the recognized books of democracy. Experts like Georges Védel (in his *Manuel de Droit constitutionnel*, Paris: Sirey, 1949) have seen the emergence of so-called "popular" democracies as raising stiff classification problems not hitherto known to the classical sense of the term, 'democracy'. To that problematic classification must be added the 'advanced' which is peculiar to Cameroon. The Cameroonian additional (or subtractional?) description of democracy must certainly disturb the equability of political and constitutional pundits because they would spend all their lives digging into treatises and books on democracy and never come across anything like advanced democracy (*la démocratie avancée*) – except, of course, they happen to read what Dr Nantang Jua has described as "Communal Liberalism that is the bible of political theology in this country" (Ndi Chia, 1995b). The Yaoundé regime (with its unlisted 'advanced democracy' instead has something else to say in response to Canada's governors; namely, that there was collective and noble participation in the nation-building task on their own side of the wide Atlantic separating the democracies. Was that really it?

This Kontchoumetered regime was obviously out of touch for thinking that the will of the Cameroon people was important in the building of Cameroon's confusing 'serene-and-disciplined' national unity. They do think these citizens did matter, the more reason Cameroon, according to them, was legally and practically a bicultural society (as indicated in the 1996 Constitution, Article 1(3)), being the work of every Cameroonian. According to Biya (1986: 111-12), "Indeed, national unity constitutes the mainstay of this [administration's] action which, to me, ought to be a collective venture because it can be nothing but collective. The concern for concerted and noble action to be conducted with due respect for the originality and dignity of each and every one is one of the aspects of communal liberalism." It is not clear if this is confusion or fossungupalogy (straightforward talk); but experts like Appiagyei-Atua (1999: 97-104) have already offered an elaborate critique of Political Participation among 'Civil Society' in (Neo)Colonial Africa, a conspicuous portion of which Cameroon is.

The Biya administration was still foolishly disputing with the experts by claiming that simply because they had been very vaguely invited "To build a modern Cameroon [which] is a lofty and noble task" (Biya, 1986: 12), Cameroonians, without distinction, were *all* fully participating in the nation-building task. As Biya (1986: 139) thus further claimed, "I do not think and how could I ever think that there are two categories of Cameroonians: ....There is no doubt that the recent past of our country has left the regrettable impression that some Cameroonians were excluded from any real participation in the political life of the country, while a certain class was considered more suitable." Quite apart from the discussion of Gender Politics in Chapter 3 below, this is precisely what Konings and Nyamnjoh (1997:224) were condemning when they stated that "Attempts have often been made to minimalise the Anglophone-francophone divide by emphasising that this did not exist during the German colonial era. At present, Cameroon is officially a bilingual and multi-cultural nation, which many regard as a safe guarantee for the preservation of its differential linguistic and cultural heritage." It is, moreover, hard for me not to doubt how exactly the "regrettable impression" had then changed; and how the Cameroon people were actually having "greater opportunities" of self-determining when (1) patriotism and equality are being officially sexed (Chapter 3) and (2) the biting 'Anglophone Problem' was sidestepped at all costs and some funny concept of 'minority protection' invented for the purpose in Article 57(3) of the 1996 Constitution in the next Chapter.

Chapter 2

Pointless Multiculturalism and Multipartism: Testing the Deepness the Assimilation Waters with the 1985/83 Education Cases and the Cultural Minority Exchange

> When diplomats with the abundance of experience and history on their trail appease tyranny and stoop to blackmail as though Chamberlain's lesson is extinct, when profiteers of genocide and aggression, alien rule, enable and collaborate with the loot and insist on utter brutality with the hope that our defeat would offer them power, lest they forget the cliché. I remind them all that history is a valuable lesson that has stood the test of time (Dr Cho Ayaba, 3 April 2025, from the Dungeon of Norway).

What biculturalism is there in the Education Law's use of educational biculturalism? The drive in Cameroon to assimilate the Ambazonian minority did not augur well with nation-building as the country was visibly heading instead for nation-destruction. "To some observers," Delancey (1989: 1) opens his illuminating book, "Cameroon is a glowing success in recent African history, a site of political stability and economic growth and development." This is exactly the image that the regime wanted to portray through its *politique confusionnelle*, superbly sustained by its useless education curriculum which is:

> Nothing but a curriculum of education that teaches them about fishing in Newfoundland, fishing in Norway, but not fishing in Bambalang. That is the tragedy of occupation. That is the tragedy of a foreign curriculum of education produced by people who don't know your country, people who are interested only in your resources. And nothing about the fish

industry. Remember when we were intoxicated to be singing Vasco da Gamma discovered the sea route to India! Christopher Columbus, he discovered what? America, they say. We were doing or studying fishing in Norway or was it in Newfoundland? Forestry in Norway. These nyamfukas could not teach us fishing in Ndian! The curriculum of education was designed to make you look beyond your own borders. The curriculum of education was designed to make you feel like you have nothing. You must fly into Europe or the USA before you start studying your own history. The amount of knowledge I have gathered yesterday about Lebialem from my COS! I was born in Ambazonia. Yet, I knew nothing about it. I knew nothing. Zero. How much, in terms of intellectual ability, has this struggle offered you? A lot. Just to know thyself. Without this struggle, I would never have known DDC Horace. I would never have known all this knowledge that I am giving to you today. I would never have known that the name 'Lebialem' comes from a twin waterfall. I would never have known that the name 'Fotabong', which sounds like '*Fo te bong*' in Mankon, is a bad chief. Jesus! Just the beauty of knowing my country! The only thing we knew about Batibo was to provoke them on how they speak. The only thing we knew about Pinyin was to talk about them in a derogatory way. The only thing we knew about each other was constructs offered to us by force by the enemy. Now, if you talk about Pinyin, you talk about resistance. If you talk about Batibo, you talk about resistance. The Mankon child from Alabukam didn't want to tell you he comes from Alabukam. *Allah Bukam:* Country of the Crab. Do you want to come from that kind of a place? But now everybody hits their chest, saying I come from Alabukam. Because that is where resistance takes place (Ayaba, Ndian: 27 August 2023).

But, as the Cameroon authorities were still smiling and felicitating themselves for having succeeded in deceiving the North American stranger, to their utter dismay, Delancey (1989: 1) immediately brought out his "American stuff" by carrying on. "To others, Cameroon is a neo-colonial entity, existing under the influence of France, with no benefit of its independence accruing to the bulk of the population, and with revolution and division boiling close to the surface." The 'war of dominance and destruction' between the country's two "sub-systems of education" has always been at the heart of these revolution and division that especially came in only *as a consequence* of the seemingly endless sufferings of the Cameroonian people, particularly since 1984 when assimilation of the English-speaking minority took on an accentuated phase with what Fohtung (1995) describes as "Biya's rise to power [in November 1982 which] was one of those rare political miracles of modern times that almost always winds up in tragedy." It was particularly marked by the 1983 and 1985 moves to assimilate the General Certificate of Education (G.C.E.) system under the guise of harmonization.

The full scale of this tragedy cannot be correctly grasped with just research *in* Cameroon law. Arthurs Report (1983: 66) has provided the distinction of research *in* and *on* law. Equally significant to any sane discussion of Cameroon's nation-building, therefore, must be the relative importance of the non-constitutional factors such as religion, culture, language, distribution of resources, political geography, and, above all, personal and psychological factors like charisma, commitment, friendships, rivalries, and personal ambitions. One can clearly not go beyond the mere words of the constitution (as advised by Benjamin, 1972: 13) without these enumerated elements, most of which also go into making Cameroon political and constitutional history. Experts like Dunlop (1991) of the University of Alberta do prefer to employ research *about* law in opposition to *in* law. Talking about the two predominant influences, he has declared that research *in* law

> is necessarily narrower, though a more coherent, activity than research *about* law. Research *in* law often (perhaps always) consists of doctrinal analysis of legal texts such as cases and statutes. It often (perhaps always) makes assumptions about

some aspects of the legal order, for example, the primacy of the reason and the nature of legal reasoning, as well as political assumptions about the value of a legal system and of the rule of law as a necessary part of the good society. Another characteristic of research *in* law is that it tends not to involve empirical study of the actual working of the legal order or of its economic or social consequences. It becomes the study of a limited set of texts rather than an examination of the actual workings of legal institutions. Finally, legal research *in* law usually does not cross disciplinary boundaries, at least when the operational and political assumptions noted above remain unquestioned (Dunlop, 1991: 67, note omitted).

The Cameroon tragedy is the direct fallout of the absence of safeguards and constitutionalism that Foumban sacrificed at the altar of personal convenience and favours. On "Evaluating Federalism" (Stevenson, 1989: 14-18), it is clear that the FRC is no case from which one can pick certain characteristics to hold out as being the essence of federalism; which is an obvious indication of the fact that there was in reality no federation in Cameroon, notwithstanding Benjamin's (1972: 148) thesis that 'the ideal federal state does not yet exist anywhere' (my translation). Federalism proper, as I see it, cannot exist and function in a society that is wanting in properly enlightened citizens, that is wanting in some basic political and legal institutions, that lacks basic and properly enacted laws, that is marked by the absence of rule of law, and that is defined by the absence of self-control. "At the background of it all," Enonchong (1967: xiii) has explained, "is the age-old idea of the protection of the individual and the right of the national state to carry out its responsibilities in a democratic and progressive society." This signifies that federalism must further constitutionalism and the protection of human rights, all of which, in liberal-constitutional democracies like Canada, "are inseparable from the doctrine of separation of powers, from parliamentary sovereignty, from rule of law, from constitutional supremacy, and from diversification of power centres" (Tremblay, 1993: 66 – my translation).

As I have said, Mr. Biya's tragic rise to power was saluted by some ill-conceived moves on *education* in 1983 and 1985. Konings and Nyamnjoh (1997: 213) have pointed out that in 1983 the Government promulgated an order modifying the Anglophone G.C.E. examination by making it rather like the *Baccalauréat*, and the ensuing demonstrations and boycott of classes were repressed by police brutality at the UNIYAO and in urban centres in anglophone Cameroon. Yes, those two professors are on top of the issue. It was principally the resistance mounted by young Ambazonians to these incessant moves, especially since 1985, which was sooner or later to thrust Cameroon unto the centre stage of "atrocities zones"; what some observers saw as 'another Rwanda-Episode.' [See "Will the International Community Forestall a 'Cameroonian' Rwanda Episode?" *The Herald* N° 319 (13-16 June 1996), 4; "Guerre et paix au Cameroun – L'Etat RDPC nous impose la guerre" *L'Expression* N° 190 (23 octobre 1997), 8-9; Alain Bengono and C. Yaho, "A quelques heures du verdict: le Cameroun au bord de l'implosion" *L'Expression* N° 130 (6 juin 1997), 1 & 4; and Denis Nkwebo, "Temperature élévée: le Cameroun menacé d'explosion" *Le Quotidien* N° 288 (24 octobre 1997), 4] Some journalists even indicated how during a rally of the SDF party "Voices were heard shouting that Kabila's approach [in Zaire] was the only way to oust the Biya regime." [Kum Set Ewi and Peterkins Manyong, "SDF Accuses Biya of Provoking War, Militants Urged to Regroup and Prepare to Defend Themselves" *The Herald* N° 473 (18-19 June 1997), 1 at 3.] Student Lucas Cho Ayaba's able independence voice could be clearly heard even then when many could hardly say the word 'Independence'. The said episode (Ambazonia/LRC war) was inevitably going to happen most probably because, despite the string of academic degrees matching behind their names, poorly educated and unpatriotic administrators could scarcely learn anything at all regarding local government that Kneier (1939: preface) considers to be "the science of the second best." Thus, commenting on the 'settlers' concept in Article 57(3) of the 1996 Constitution that has converted some Cameroonians into 'settlers' in their own country, some critics declared that "My conclusion from his [POR's] haughty and senseless behaviour was that spending long years in formal education systems and earning a string of academic qualifications does not necessarily make one educated, let alone gain wisdom." [Simon J.A. Mope, "So-called Settlers: The New 'Cancer' in Cameroonian Political Discourse" *The Herald* N° 447 (16-17 April 1997), 4]

Exchanging Authentic Minority for Settlers and Indigenes: The Students' 1985 Letter Vehemently Opposed Manipulation and Assimilation

Cameroon's administrators were not listening nor even understanding the role and importance of the 'best political science' that Albert Einstein found to be more difficult than physics. Was it then the question of their not understanding politics because of its difficulty or simply that of deliberate confusion of powers for assimilation purposes? I want to think it is the latter. The numerous misleading theses in Cameroon on the concepts tied to multiculturalism are nothing but part of the generalized confusion in the country; a confusion that is also responsible for hiding itself to many of the people who have attempted to diagnose its engendered problems, as has been deduced especially from the postulation then radiating out from the Ambazonian minority that wanted to secede (or had already seceded but not seceded?) from the oppressive Camerounese majority. What the minority for the purposes of this discussion that was demanding cultural protection is, is a question that would seem to be superfluous. But it is in order in Cameroon because Konings and Nyamnjoh (1997: 208) ably theorized that,

> The Government has not surprisingly devised various strategies to safeguard the unitary [mono-cultural] state, including attempts to minimalise or even deny the existence of an 'anglophone problem', to create divisions among the English-speaking elite, to remunerate some allies with prestigious positions in the state apparatus previously reserved for francophones only, and to repress all actions designed to change the status of the Southern Cameroons.

True to its devilish efforts of minimalisation and denial of the mounting concerns and demands of the real minority (Southern Cameroonsians), the concept of the country's minority had to be largely deformed in Article 57(3) of the 1996 Constitution; creating even more intractable problems by ushering in the notions of *allogènes et autochtones* ('settlers' and 'indigenes') which, to the authoritarian regime, was geared toward protecting the minority. The putting of those concepts into the constitution was only a means of killing two birds (the Ambazonian demands for protection and the hardworking Bamileke) with one potent stone. The Bamileke are very central to the Federalism Question in Cameroon (see Fossungu, 2025: 75), the bulk of them also being 'Anglophones' or the disenfranchised so-called Eleventh-Province People (EPP).[10] I say these people were cleanly disenfranchised or stripped of citizenship because Cameroon then had only ten provinces (which were later called regions by Article 61 of the 1996 Constitution). As they did not belong to any known or existing Cameroonian province, were these EPPs then Cameroonian citizens? All this could have been the price to pay for their love of federalism. The EPP, SCFAQ has explained in Question 3, "are people whose parents and grandparents fled oppression in French Cameroons and settled in Southern Cameroons. The loyalty of these people [as Southern Cameroonsians] should not be called into question but must be nurtured because Southern Cameroons has always practised acceptance of people. It was like that then and it must always be like that in the future. Witch hunts and loyalty tests are not our way."

That could have been acceptable before the open genocidal war, but I do not and cannot see that being the case now at all, especially after 'Defining Being Amba to the Confusionists/Confusioncrats' (Fossungu, 2024: 34-40). That as well must exclude the SCFAQ's (Question 2) definition of a Southern Cameroonsian (Ambazonian) as

---

[10] More instruction on this EPP (whose other recently constitutionalized name is 'Settlers') in Cameroon politics, is also furnished by Peter Ateh-Afac Fossungu, "So-Called 'Eleventh-Province People and/or Settlers'" *The Herald* (29-30 June 1998), 10; Beltus Bejanga, "Position-seekers Should Be Stopped from Calling Other Cameroonians 'Settlers'" *The Herald* N° 446 (16-17 April 1997), 6; Bonny Kfua, "Of 'Minorities' and 'Settlers'" *The Herald* (27-29 May 1996), 4; and "We Are Creating a System of Apartheid in Cameroon – Ambassador Nsahlai [an interview]" *The Herald* (16-17 June 1997), 6.

"Anyone born in the Southern Cameroons or of Southern Cameroons parent(s).... Citizenship of the Southern Cameroons can also be acquired by naturalization. Immigrant residents of the Southern Cameroons who meet civil and other residency requirements can be granted Southern Cameroons citizenship. The conditions for citizenship and duties and immunities that come with it are currently being enshrined in the constitution and laws of the Southern Cameroons. Southern Cameroons citizenship is not based on language (foreign or domestic), ethnic affiliations, ethnic or national origin, race, religion, or any discriminatory factor." We must vigorously contain and banish the childish 'brotherhood' of yester years in Ambazonia because we have already seen enough of these masquerading Camerounese, let alone the French. SCFAQ (Question 30) posits that "Even the French could be conferred Southern Cameroons citizenship if they meet residency and other requirements." What folly! Ambaland is not an immigration country, that fact must be clear enough.

Most French-speaking Cameroonians (especially those traitors in power) were not at all interested in unification and had never been fascinated with federalism mostly because of these hated "citizenship-less" citizens (Bamileke). The "settlers" concept, as shown by Johnson (1970: 56-59), had in earlier years (even before 'independence') been used in an open attempt to boot the Bamileke out of the major cities and especially Douala (Cameroon's economic capital) where they dominated in almost all fields. But the 'Settlers Concept' was never, until 1996, put in the constitution; the putting of which the critics have categorized as lack of self-control. Critics like Eyinga (1996: 7) have then affirmed that, by institutionalizing these things, Mr. Biya indeed awakened the soundly sleeping Ethnic Demon (*"Aujourd'hui, Biya, en mettant ces choses dans la constitution, franchit vraiment le Ribicon"*). The stark lack of self-control in the attitude of Cameroon's administrators has not failed to drag in overly critical comments and doubts about their education.

These critics are not over stretching their conclusions since the worst was still to come. Especially as these concepts of *allogènes* and *autochtones* (like most other constitutional and legal creations in Cameroon, including educational dualism) were yet to be clearly defined in the constitution; since only the POR of Cameroon, of course, would know (as always) the actual content of "th[is] dynamic concept which I yet have to define, and which embodies my image of Cameroon" (Biya,

1986: 112). The POR's real 'image of Cameroon', capped by undefined concepts in laws and unknown laws which they announce as coming later, has been one of creating confusion and thereby abusing human rights without raising the international dust within (sponsoring) international economic/financial circles. When there is revolution and/or division (orchestrated by disagreement over the undefined concepts) or even their semblance, compelling cause under the cover of national unity arises for an all-out wiping of what had until then not been systematically effaced in Cameroon. Clearest case in point is Mr Biya's impulsive declaration of his total genocidal war on Ambazonia from the tarmac of an airport in November 2017. Didn't Africa deserve better than that from Cameroon? Ambazonia, are you listening carefully and taking stock of what to pioneeringly institute?

I also like to believe that that war was inevitable because young Ambazonians were not being fooled by the so-called National Education Board (NEB) that the 1998 Education Law purportedly created in Section 11(2) (more analysis of which is in Chapter 3). The Ambazonian students did not fail in 1985 to see what was really hiding behind the 'harmonization' or NEB. As they stated in their widely publicized Letter,

> The latest unscrupulous attempt we recall with unquenchable bitterness. By issuing confusing announcements on public examinations, MINEDUC [Ministry of Education] was responsible for thwarting the efforts of many Anglophone youths to better their future and that of their families. The students did not sit in for the chemistry "A" and commerce "O" level papers of the just ended G.C.E. examinations. Though there is no doubt that irremediable damage has been done to some of the families concerned, nothing has been done or said to correct the situation. And, instead of calling for justice to fall on those involved in the scandal, the national assembly takes it as an opportunity to press for harmonization of educational systems (we might here ask what became of the G.C.E. Commission?). *Now the simple question we ask is what to expect from someone who condemns a system and is given the opportunity and liberty to select from it? No doubt, total rejection* (Students' Letter, 1985, emphasis added).

Of course, the preference of the NEB was only to be for the French-speaking sub-system. Their entire 6-page Letter, though addressed to their parents, they sent copies to a much wider audience. Copies of it went to "all party chiefs; all mayors; all D.O.s [district officers]; all lawyers and magistrates; all doctors and university lecturers; all Secretaries General and provincial chiefs of services; all directors and ministries; Hon. S.T. Muna; Dr. J.N. Foncha; Dr. E.M.L. Endeley; [and] Mr. E.T. Egbe" (Students' Letter, 1985). These English-speaking students could not have been wrong then because a critic confirmed their views five years later, in March 1990, when he also explained that outright assimilation is what was involved.

> Over the years, a persistent assault has been maintained against the separate and unique cultural (linguistic) identity of this minority: suppression of the federal structure of the country, through which the minority maintained some autonomy in the running of its affairs; the non-appointment of members of this minority to top and sensitive positions in the military, administration, police, Cabinet, and state corporations, as well as in the diplomatic field.[11] It is also being carried out through the economic impoverishment of their area (even though the resources from this area account for about ninety percent of the country's foreign exchange) and by making sure that political leaders of this people (students) lose ability to communicate in nothing but the dominant language by the time they leave the vastly monolingual and mono-cultural university (Fonkeng, 1990: 'Preface & Thanks', 3rd paragraph).

So, the idea really was not that of educational dualism. It was that of the destruction of the 'Anglophone' system and assimilating Ambazonians into the French-speaking system; an educational system

---

[11] The following researchers have also incisively examined the Cameroon civil service and appointment situation: Konings and Nyamnjoh (1997: 213-214 & 225-229), David Tendong, "Civil Service Appointments: Musonge Says Anglophones Have 'Dirty Files', Can't Be Promoted" *The Herald* N°415 (3-4 February 1997), 1 & 3; Peter Ngea Beng, "Anglophones to Be Swept Out in Coming Shake-Up in Parastatals" *The Herald* N° 646 (14-16 Augus 1998t), 1 & 3; and Boniface Forbin, "Parastatals: Why Are Anglophones an Endangered Species?" *The Herald* N° 646 (14-16 August 1998), 4.

that cannot carry international reputation especially when the ministry can "fix" student results just as it likes. According to Johnson-Hanks (2006: 125), in May 1998 (the same year of the Education Law) the MINEDUC "declared an emergency, asserting that education levels were slipping dangerously. It responded by publicly inflating the scores of the *baccalauréat* to ensure that Cameroon's national pass rate would not decline vis-à-vis other Francophone African nations... This well-publicized grade inflation was almost uniformly condemned outside the ministry." As this French-speaking sub-system, with all its perceived shortcomings (more in the chapters below), is the only one that the authorities were bent on promoting and imposing on everyone, Njumba Cameroon's integrity was then in question because, as it was then very evident to anyone with even little brains, the educational system was the one and only area left that had stood out and persisted as the point of Southern Cameroonsian solidarity in the country. [See Francis Beng Nyamnjoh and R.F. Akum, *The Cameroon GCE Crisis: Test of Anglophone Solidarity* (Bamenda: Langaa RPCIP, 2008)]

The idea of protecting the minority from the ultimate dictatorship of the majority is quite laudable. To correctly perform this task, as I have already shown above, constitutional democracy was introduced. But because there in Cameroon this was not the desired goal, the regime could only be pretending to be realizing this noble goal through the sowing of wild seeds that would rather destroy then existing harmony and cooperation among Cameroonians. By and large, Ndi Chia (1995) has posited, the protection of citizens (majority or minority) cannot be worked out by constitutions only because, without lubrication by reason, compromise, sagacity, magnanimity and the greater good, no constitution could even be worth the paper on which it is printed. Fombad (2003) says the same thing in discussing the protection of constitutional values in Africa. The Editor of *L'Effort Camerounais* also could not have put it any better in French in his "Associer toutes les compétences." The Editor of the Catholic weekly threw more light on this:

> *notion d'autochtone (art.57-3) qui, certes, reste à définir, mais dont on peut déjà se demander si elle permettra à l'État de remplir la mission que le préambule lui assigne: 'L'État assure la protection des minorités et préserve les droits des populations autochtones conformément à la loi.' Bien sûr, il est louable de vouloir protéger les minorités d'une éventuelle*

'dictature de la majorité', mais faut-il pour autant créer des situations acquises qui peuvent devenir des blocages à l'évolution inéluctable d'une société? La solution ne réside-t-elle pas plutôt dans l'exercice raisonné et raisonnable du pouvoir, dans la capacité des responsables à associer toutes les compétences disponibles qu'elles soient leurs origines? Il est vrai que cela ne se décide ni par un décret ni par une loi; il faut que chaque responsable le veuille. [Effort Editorial, "Associer toutes les compétences" *L'Effort Camerounais* N° 40 (1037) (10-23 février 1996), 1]

Further critique of the "autochtones-allogènes" ideology embedded in Article 57(3) is available from the very instructive 'dossier' titled "Minorités, Autochtones, Allogènes et démocratie" in *La Nouvelle Expression* (23 mai 1996). These are 28 pages of 'Dossiers & Documents' contributed by top-notch experts on the issues involved; with some of these specialists even showing President Biya not to be Camerounese, but indeed an 'allogènes' from Equatorial Guinea! One would naturally think that the biting 'Anglophone Problem' should have dominated in the 1996 Constitution. But absolutely nothing about the issue, according to Ntemfac Ofege, was in "this anti-Anglophone heathen document [that even] *forgets* to dedicate Cameroon to God" (cited in Fossungu, 2018: 151, original emphasis). According to Fohtung (1995, citing *Cameroon Post* N° 178 at 12), "Nothing in the preamble and the rest of the text even shows a remote awareness of it [i.e., the Anglophone Problem]. It has grotesquely distorted reference to the protection of minorities which instead aims at rewarding lazy land-selling natives at the expense of hard-working immigrants in industrial and urban centres. Could it be that Mr. Biya is unaware of the Cameroonian situation?" Rogers Orock has also exposed the 'indigene-settler' issue academically and held it up as 'Indications for Social (Dis)order in Cameroon';[12] with Ofege (1995b) then concluding (assuming that it was ignorance on his part: being a 'foreigner' from Equatorial Guinea) that "Mr. Biya ought to be told that the one minority recognized by international law as being in Cameroon is the Anglophone minority and it is not very hard for the state to protect the

---

[12] See Rogers Tabe Egbe Orock, "The Indigene-Settler Divide, Modernisation and the Land Question: Indications for Social (Dis)order in Cameroon" 14(1) *Nordic Journal of African Studies* (2005), 68-78.

Anglophone minority." Dr Nfi (2014) provides an excellent discussion of the problematics of the concept of 'Anglophone' in Cameroon.

The Editor of *The Herald* then firmly asserted in 1997 that it was Mr. Biya's "government [that] must be accused of encouraging ethnic violence... Why does the government... generate unrest among its different people who have learnt to live together in harmony and self-respect? Observe how everywhere in the country different ethnic groups live together happily until [no-good] politicians come in with divisive ideas to create conflict" (Forbin, 1997: 4). These newly introduced concepts of *allogènes* and of *autochtones*, according to Yondo Black, are indeed notions that subsequent Cameroonian governments must have to banish forever from the country's political discourse since ethnicity should not provide any cover behind which some officials have to hide their personal failures or inadequacies (*"Les prochains gouvernements doivent expurger[ces concepts] de notre Constitution"* because *"La tribu ne doit pas être une 'planche de secours' pour ceux qui ont échoué dans leur démarche personnelle"* [see "Un peuple qui ne renouvelle pas ses cadres est un peuple sans avenir" [- Yondo Mandengue Black], *Le Messager* (23 mai 1996), 6 & 7.]), What was the thing required to banish this regressive attitude from the Cameroons and regain national pride?

Federalism was the way to go, according to Garga Harman Adji, president of the ADD party (see Fossungu, 2025: 46 n.26). In view of rectifying and retracing its steps forward (through the institution of good governance) one of the leading opposition parties in Cameroon invited Cameroonians "regardless of your political affiliation" to understand that "the [on-going] battle for that [NESPROG] alternative is not an SDF battle but a battle for national salvation, the restoration of our lost national pride and dignity and an end to the international humiliation which the present regime has brought on this nation" (SDF, 1996: 2). To successfully salvage that lost pride, a proper federal devolution, inter alia, was very required. The institution of a responsible federal democracy in Cameroon did not then pose any threat to the country's integrity as might have been during the 1961 Foumban Conference. Circumstances have since changed and it was time to have altered the principles accordingly. Maneli (1994: 3) further emphasizes that when even one of the factors of reality changes, even through a mere lapse of time, a valid cause arises to reopen dialogue and assess the situation *ab initio*, from the very roots; concluding that during this reassessment, nothing should be regarded as sacred or established once and for all. The conditions in Cameroon in the sixties and seventies *might* thus have justified the harshness of the laws but the experts have "strongly urged that this should not be an excuse to refrain from confronting change when change is imperative." [Samgena D. Galega, "Strict Liability for Defective Products in Cameroon? Some Illuminating Lessons from Abroad" 48 *Journal of African Law* (2004), 239 at 267] That is the undemanding truth. The question remains though: Could and would the SDF really have been able to deliver the cherished goods (as Professor Gros said) with what has been characterized (in Fossungu, 2025: chapter 2) as their sour, out-of-touch and disguised mono-cultural Four-State Federation?

The message that Southern Cameroonians had been sending out seems to be this. Caricaturize our "sub-system of education" as much as you will, but do not dare think of destroying it. Since the authorities had then lost patience with piecemeal deformation and were then only bent on complete destruction, keen observers had every reason to wonder for just how long the 'Anglo-Saxon' institutions – G.C.E. Board, University of Buea (UNIBU), and University of Bamenda (UNIBA) – were to be and remain "places to be" in a *united* Cameroon. As Ndamukong (1996: 2) unambiguously pondered in the same year the 1996 Constitution was introduced:

How can the Presidency, if it is interested in the unity of this country, sit and watch an individual [Mbella Mbappe, then minister of 'National' Education] destroy part of the nation's culture? How can the Prime Minister [an Ambazonian, it must be noted] not react when a Minister disregards his orders? How can Anglophone Parliamentarians, irrespective of their political leanings be mute when a mere appointee in the name of Minister is deliberately destroying the foundations of the culture and identity of the people they represent in Parliament? Does the government of this country not know that by allowing an individual Minister to mete out shabby treatment on one part of the country, seeds of hatred, conflict and eventual disintegration are being sown? How can parents, teachers and students sit down and see a wicked individual gradually annihilating the bedrock on which their educational system and identity rest?

Honourable Joseph Wilba posed these same questions with even greater accuracy in his "When Injustice Becomes the Law, Resistance Becomes a Duty" speech in the LRC Colonial National Assembly, firmly prophesizing the inevitable breakup of the njumba cohabitation if nothing meaningful was done to ameliorate the situation. Publications like the April 1994 *Buea Peace Initiative* [for further details of this initiative for peaceful resolution, see 'Southern Cameroons Landmark Documents': http://www.southerncameroons.org/index3.htm] and old editions of the *Cameroon Post* newspaper (from February 1984) were very good at cataloguing these grievances; complaints that, according to the experts, if not properly addressed, augured badly for the integrity of Cameroon. One researcher clearly warned sixteen years before the Ambazonian War of Liberation (AWOL):

The threats of the disintegration of bilingual Cameroon are real, if we are to go by the activities of Anglophone pressure groups in Cameroon, and the radicalism of the Anglophone Diaspora in the United States, who express their 'secessionist' views on the internet in the SCNC forum. But the situation can be reversed if a genuine decentralization of power, in the direction of federalism, is introduced, and Anglophones are constitutionally guaranteed equal status with Francophones in all spheres of national life. [Nicodemus Fru Awasom, "The Reunification Question in Cameroon History: Was the Bride an Enthusiastic or Reluctant One?" 47(2) *Africa Today* (2000), 91 at 113-14.]

Having posed seventeen questions in all, the students had also made it clear fifteen long years before Dr Awasom that there was "SO MUCH UNANSWERED AND YET SO MUCH UNASKED" before concluding that,

These are not things that can be left forever unnoticed. Even the blind man when he stumbles against an obstacle here and there often shouts, or warns, or pleads so that those with whom he lives can see that such obstacles do not reoccur. We gladly accept to be the heirs of your toil and sweat. You shall know, however, that the peace of the Cameroon we are set to inherit is quite unguaranteed (Students' Letter, 1985).

I think all what these Ambazonian students were asking for was just genuineness in making them 'civilized.' Is there any justification for brutalizing these young people for wanting to be civilized? Young Ambazonian students had, since 1985, been adamantly bent – like the University Students Association of East Africa (USAEA) – on "succeed[ing] where our politicians have so far failed [in becoming civilized]" (Southall, 1974: x n.6). As Martha Bayles has also put it,

Civilization or, to say the same thing, education is the taming or domestication of the soul's raw passions – not suppressing or excising them, which could deprive the soul of its energy – but forming and informing them as art. A man [or woman] whose noblest activities are accompanied by a music that expresses them while providing a pleasure extending from the lowest bodily to the highest spiritual, is whole, and there is no tension in him [or her] between the pleasant and the good. [Martha Bayles, "Body and Soul: The Musical Miseducation of Youth" 131 *The Public Interest* (1998), 36 at 39]

I think what this expert of human rights and education is saying is simply the call for self-control in politics. The earliest and clearest of the grave concerns about the future of Cameroon as a single political entity came in 1997 from Christopher Kiloh Fai Nsahlai, then Cameroon's ambassador to the Central African Republic. "The foundation of the Cameroon nation," Ndifor's report quotes the ambassador as stating in his *Looking Up to the Mountain Top: Beyond Party Politics*, "appears to be wobbling visibly on quicksand. It is now common knowledge that a considerable portion of the Anglophone public is speaking more and more the language of secession and independence than national unity." [Asong Ndifor, "Biya's Ambassador Expresses Concern About Future of Cameroon" *The Herald* N° 428 (5-6 March 1997), 1. Also see Peterkins Manyong, "The Nsahlai Phenomenon in Cameroon Politics" *The Post* (3 September 2008); and Asong Ndifor and Michael Ndi, "Biya Bows to Progressives, Appoints Nsahlai to Head CPDM Reform Commission" *The Herald* (19 November 2003)] The ambassador, the Ndifor report continues, had equally told his boss in a letter that "by far the greatest threat to national unity is the Anglophone problem." It is hardly surprising that Dr. Nsahlai who had spoken uncomfortable truth to power suddenly died on 18 April 2008. [See Kini Nsom, "Chritopher Nsahlai Drops Dead in Yaoundé" *The Post* (21 April 2008); and Peterkins Manyong and Willibroad Nformi, "My Father's Death Was Unnatural – Nsahlai's Son" *The Post* (12 May 2009)]

> Through these discussions, you have come to know that they told a lie. We were not going to become a liability. We are going to become an asset not only to ourselves but to the people of the world. We are a great people. We should take pride in that greatness. We should invest to protect it, to project it, to sacrifice for it, and to defend it. Any other thing we think or do is suicidal. We must rededicate, recommit. We should not take the challenges we face; the problems we face to define the character of our resistance. That is far-fetched from the bravery demonstrated by General Ivo. The bravery demonstrated by General No Pity, or General Efang, General Capo, all the Generals who are fighting on the ground, the Sargarts, the Skys, the Face-to-Faces. I cannot call all their names. Generals who have given us all sorts of names. Generals No-Pity, Big Number, Craze-Man, Bitter-Kola. (Ayaba, Ngoketunjia: September 2023)

Two years before the slaughtered ambassador, a human rights activist and lawyer had made the same point by indicating that "the most important problem that must be resolved and quickly too is the Southern Cameroons problem. No admission into the Commonwealth, no media campaign will side track this basic problem. It is the resolution of this problem that will guarantee durable peace in the sub region" (cited in Fossungu, 2018: 145). As other prominent opposition politicians did even warn in 1996, "It is in the best interest of France to understand the change of climate and to react accordingly. Or else, who knows, a worse scenario than Bangui [Central African Republic] will be in the offing in Cameroon tomorrow. God forbid that should happen." [John Fru Ndi, "In the Interest of France: Trade Not Aid" *Cameroon Post* Special Edition (December 1996), 16] The list is quite lengthy. But one Newspaper Editor appears to have summarized the puzzle when he affirmed in December 1997 that "Anyone who knows of the friends of Paul Biya also knows that Anglophones are not among them. Since Biya was minister and prime minister, he has been known not to like

Anglophones. After being president for fifteen years, Biya has not cured himself of his anti-Anglophone habit of thought." [Dr Boniface Forbin, "The Anglophone Problem Again (II)" *The Herald* N° 541 (1-2 December 1997), 4.] Consequently, President Biya took zero action to face the issues, rather exhibiting his characteristic arrogance, just as he is doing now with the threats emanating from the October 2025 presidential election results. In the words of a community development expert, the Biya administration,

by avoidance of basic issues, has helped to promote the ultimate chaos that follows delay and postponement of facing up to fundamental problems, and has contributed to the deluge that comes when redress is too niggardly, when justice arrives too late. If history notices what... [this administration] has done in the past quarter-century at all, its judgment will be harsh. Posterity will [either] say it was innocent because it was too naïve to understand the consequences of what it had done, or it was guilty because it did understand, but feared the consequences of acting boldly, lacked the necessary nerve to fly into the eye of the storm. [R. Alexander Sim, "The Innocence of Community Development", in James A. Draper (ed.), *Citizen Participation: Canada* (Toronto: New Press, 1971), 171 at 171-72. The same thesis is advanced in French by Eyoum Ngangue's "Fermeture de la BIAO: une mesure tardive qui sacrifie l'épargnant" *Le Messager* (16 septembre 1996), 8.]

If the politicians were busy playing bellytics as usual, the Ambazonian students were not sitting down with folded arms. This fact would explain why many of the surviving student leaders (including Cho Ayaba, Benedict Kuah, and Ebenezer Akwanga) were abroad and highly wanted.[13] According to Taku (1995: 1), "Oppressive squads are being trained to terrorise and harass the citizenry, especially the voices of dissent. Several students, members of the student movement,

---

[13] See "We Are Going to Return Home and Continue the Struggle for Students Rights – Exiled Cameroonian Student Leaders" *The Herald* N° 389 (29 November-1 December 1996), 6. See also Francis B. Nyamnjoh, Walter Gram and Piet Konings (eds.), *University Crisis and Student Protest in Africa: The 2005-2006 University Students' Strike in Cameroon* (Bamenda: Langaa RPCIG, 2012).

Parliament, remain in exile having been banned from all universities in Cameroon and declared wanted." More on the activities of this *Parliament* is in Chapter 4. Another critic of the Yaoundé inhuman regime catalogued, for example, the invasion of university student residential quarters by both the military and the private militias of Jean Messi – then *recteur* of University of Yaoundé I – in the incredibly early hours of 14 June 1996. By the next day (15 June), at least 800 arrests had been made, with at least 100 student doors had been forcefully broken by the rector's militias with *"une violence redoubtable."* [Jean-François Channon, "Silence! On arrête, on moleste et on tue" *Le Messager* N° 516 (17 juin 1996), 8. See also Alain Bengono, "Assasinat de Betsogo Faustin: Mgr. Jean Zoa se déchaine contre la barbarie du régime de Yaoundé" *L'Expression* N° 93 (21 fevrier 1997), 10] If it were to depend, as usual, solely on Ambazonian "politicians" or 'elites', it would all have been a different story today. That is why, for instance, the Ambazonian students' first of "some pertinent questions" to their "Dear Parents" was:

> Tell us why for 25 years, the number of Francophone Cameroonians granted government scholarships yearly to study in France alone far exceeds the total number of scholarships awarded to English-speaking Cameroonians to study abroad. We have the statistics – see Cameroon Tribune of 19th and 20th August 1985. This year [1985] 8 new scholarships have been awarded to Anglophones to study in Britain, 8 in Nigeria (one of whom is a francophone), 1 in Liberia and 1 in Sierra Leone, making a total of 18. Whereas there are 1,000 (one thousand) scholarships granted to Francophone students to study in France, Belgium, etc. The Francophones will tell you that most of your children will be given scholarships after the G.C.E. "A" Level results are published. Last year [1984], 50 were granted these scholarships and even if the figures were doubled (to be doubted) that would be nothing compared to the 1,000 (Students' Letter, 1985).

To leave scholarship abroad aside, Nfi (2014) has detailed out how even in educational institutions inside Ambazonia Camerounese sort of still dominate in both staffing and student enrolment, also making the notion of "Anglophone" to virtually capture a significant population of

Camerounese, those he describes as 'New Anglophones' who 'capture' some of opportunities meant for Ambazonians. To Katerina Frantzi also, the issue of human rights abuse and advocacy advances the imperative of educating children in a democratic way for humanistic growth. John Dewey based his philosophy of education on the belief that humans and their surroundings are living in unity, within a transactional process. Alienation and dehumanization appear when people cannot see this unity in their every thought and action but set the dualisms of 'I-You', 'Us-Them'. [Katerina K Frantzi, "Human Rights Education: The United Nations Endeavour and the Importance of Childhood and Intelligent Sympathy" 5(1) *International Education Journal* (2004), 1] The Cameroon leadership was not totally ignorant of the plain fact that self-control is a necessity for liberalism and democracy. "The history of mankind", they pointed out in their political blueprint, "reminds us of the close relations which have always existed between liberalism and democracy. We see liberalism in every attempt by people to regain their freedom restricted by the feudal [and/or dictatorial] system. Liberalism is thus a political and social philosophy whose main concern is Man, better still, the individuality of Man" (Biya, 1986: 113). That is very well said. But all their declarations in this regard are meaningless or simply confusing because the same politicians making them do not only refuse to adhere to them but also starkly lack self-control.

For further illustration, the Cameroonian students (especially the English-speaking ones – Ambazonians) had been demanding nothing more than educational conditions that are "firmly rooted in their culture" (in the words of Section 5(1) of the Education Law itself) through the creation and diversification or decentralization of universities; a process that, for linguistically raven societies like Belgium, Canada, Cameroon, and Switzerland, absolutely demands the federal structure. As portrayed by the specialists, the Belgians realized the idiocy of the unitary centralized state in their case and their leaders effected change accordingly (see Fossungu, 2018: 157-58). In Africa, on the other hand, the administration's response to popular demands has, as usual, only been to utilize *la politique du gros baton* (Big Stick Politics) and the politics of decreed peace. Because of this 'Big Stick' politics, on Cameroonian university campuses, Kameni posited, one would find 'everywhere police officers, both in uniform and in civilian attire, who are permanently stationed there' ("*Partout, des policiers tant en tenue qu'en civils...qui y stationne en permanence*") [Tientcheu Kameni, "Douala: chasse à l'étudiant sur le campus" *Le Messager* (6 juin 1996), 8]. Also take note of the military brutalization and kidnapping of students (for ransom) in the Bambili branch of UNIBA in mid-May 2025. Another commentator also condemned "the type of administrative machinery put in place there" as responsible for police presence on the campus of the 'Anglo-Saxon' University of Buea. [David Acha, "Is UB Really Worth the Place to Be?" *The Herald* (12-13 February 1997), 4] The presence, on university campuses, of heavily armed gendarmes (which some have described as "*la présence des gendarmes armés jusqu'aux dents sur le campus*"[14]) obviously led some critics to the pathetic yet convincing thesis that "In Cameroon, the unique nation of advanced democracy, university students' fear of the gendarme is the beginning of wisdom. Each time there is slight disagreement between the academic authority and students, the impulse of the former is to rush to arms, to call the gendarmes with their smoking guns to *solve* problems which otherwise ought to be approached and solved in the civilized manner only academics can." [Cameroon Post Editorial, "Njeuma, Endeley, Please Eat Humble Pie" *Cameroon Post* (11-18 December 1996), 2 (emphasis is original)]

The issues also being evoked here are tied, for instance, to the question of decreeing institutions as universities but not also taking the pains to have them recognized by other similar institutions in the international community – a recognition that is strictly tied to standards of excellence. No longer can any nation still be affording not to take the education of its youths very seriously. The president and vice-chancellor of McMaster University told us without a doubt in 1996 that:

At the risk of offending some of my academic colleagues, I believe education *is* a business. Our 'business' is research, education and scholarship. Our 'product' is knowledge. And our 'customers' are the students, their parents, our graduates, business and government, Canada [or Ambazonia] and the world. They demand and deserve outstanding scholars and teachers, innovative programs, relevant research, and a commitment to excellence in everything we do. [Peter George,

---

[14] Jean-François Channon, "Université de Yaoundé I: des affrontements en perspectives" *Le Messager* (17 juin 1996), 8.

72

"The Roots of a Great University" *Canadian Business* (December 1996), 78]

Every university, no matter where found, must compete with the others on an equal footing. The scholarship and learning business, according to the Chancellor of Victoria University in British Columbia, Canada, is one that knows no peripheries because the education market functions like all other aspects of the market since "Every university is fighting on the same front line, whatever its morale. A line of defence against Soviet missiles will be out of date long before it is built, but education's line of defence is never out of date, and it runs as directly through this community as it does through every community" (Frye, 1985: 32). I wonder how Africa's universities hope to survive this market's pressures when their students' fear of the men and women in uniform has become the beginning of wisdom; and also, when there is a staggering lack of law reporting, of academic journals and well-stocked libraries.[15] Professor Anyangwe pointed out that "At the moment there is no consistent and efficient law reporting in Cameroon. There is no official policy concerning law reporting. There is no law reporting council. In a situation like this each court remains in cloistered ignorance of decisions of the other court. In these circumstances even a loose system of judicial precedent cannot properly operate" (cited in Fossungu, 2019: 97). It is simply amazing, as one expert has justifiably regretted, that, while other nations have been taking their education very seriously, "here in Cameroon we play the drunkard in a sinking boat and go to shooting the best captains sometimes at the instigation of the very opponent we have to play our [education] match against. What folly!" [Tatah H. Mbuy, "Post Synodal Reflections: Why Africa Falters (The Weevils in Our Beans)" *Cameroon Post* N° 0021 (20-26 August 1996), 11]

This craziness is also seen in the sphere of decreeing peace. As it often happens, where the smoking guns fall short of their targets most African regimes usually follow up with decreed peace, thus puzzling a lot of people as to whether peace can be decreed (see Fossungu, 2024: 132-33; & Fossungu, 2018: 158-59). Of course not! Some have even castigated the Cameroonian authority's confusing

---

[15] See Peter Ateh-Afac Fossungu, "On the Lack of Academic Journals in Cameroon: Salute to *Juridis Périodique*" *The Herald* N° 612 (27-28 May 1998), 4.

73

'peace', 'stability' and what have you, which are only too readily sold to and bought by the rest of the world. While internally, any vocal attempt to decry the process of elimination of the linguistic identity of the minority (who make up twenty-five percent of the population) has been condemned as 'subversive', a charge almost synonymous to that levied against murderers (Fonkeng, 1990: 'Preface and Thanks', paragraph 2).

The Secrecy of Population Politics in Cameroon

At 'federation' Article 60 of the Federal Constitution gave the population as 800,000 for West Cameroon and 3,200,000 for East Cameroon. But it is simply hard to take official figures in Cameroon without some considerable amount of skepticism: especially knowing the "secretive manner" (see Johnson, 1970:184; Konings and Nyamnjoh, 1997: 209-210 n.9: and Anyangwe, 1987: 129) through which the Federal Constitution (as all the others following it) came into being. Peaslee (1974: 85) estimated the entire population to be 5,736,000 in 1969. By 1970, the population of Southern Cameroonsians was estimated to constitute 20% of the entire population of close to 6 million (Tixier, 1974: 16-18; Johnson, 1970: ix). In 1990 Fonkeng (as just seen) was talking of "twenty-five percent of the population." SCFAQ (Question 16) posits that Southern Cameroonsians "make up more than 30% of the Cameroonian population, but their participation in government has never been more than 15%." The next questions that arise have to do with (1) what we are talking of twenty-five or thirty percent of, and (2) what the 'Anglophone/Francophone' categorization would mean in Cameroon and how it affects population statistics. Take the total population for now.

Because of confusion, the experts here gave a conflicting answer despite that the specialists studying the problem had up to six and more years to dig it out. In 1996, one of these painstaking findings said that the entire population was 13 million rascals (Eyoum'a Ntoh, 1996). But another expert on Cameroon politics declared it in the same year to be twelve million : "*Biya ne veut pas donner l'impression qu'il cède à quoi que ce soit même si ce sont les 12 millions de Camerounais qui lui demandent. Pour lui, le pouvoir est quelque chose qui n'obéit pas aux gens. C'est quelque chose qui obéit au ciel, à la religion*" (Eyinga, 1996: 7). Yet some other sources put the population at 14.31 million.[16] Even the CIA (Central Intelligence Agency) that is noted for being very accurate in and sure of its findings could only *estimate* the population of Cameroon in July 2000. Thus, in explicitly considering the effects of excessive mortality due to AIDS, the CIA estimated it in 2011 to be 15,421,937. This is not the same figure as *PoliSci.com*'s 15,029,433. Cameroon's population as of 1st January 2010 was said to stand at 19,406,100, a figure revealed on 15 April 2010 at the Yaoundé Hilton Hotel by Yaouba Abdoulaye (Minister Delegate at the Ministry of the Economy, Planning and Regional Development) (Achanyi, 2010). Where does one stand with these somewhat conflicting figures?

Rubin (1971: 9) appears to have summarized and settled the controversy on the country's population and size when he tersely noted that Cameroon presents unrivalled ethnic and cultural patterns "much of which is still shrouded in uncertainty." This uncertainty is compounded, of course, by the administration's tendency to twist the facts. This facts-twisting politics is responsible, as a critical document puts it, for the mystery that surrounds the actual population of Southern Cameroonsians. As SCFAQ stated it in Question 24,

Our population is far greater than that of many countries in Africa and the world. There are more Southern Cameroon[s]ians than Gabonese, Equato-Guineans, Central Africans, Congolese, Gambians, Eritreans, Lesothans, Liberians, etc., to name just a few. The real population of the Southern Cameroons has always been a mystery. The numbers have been dramatically played down by the leadership of La République du Cameroun, to make the Southern Cameroons an insignificant minority in the union. In 1961, the Ahidjo government without explanation slashed the Southern Cameroon[s]ian population from about 1.1 million to 800,000 inhabitants. Since then, population growth figures have been down-played to the extent that the Eastern and South Provinces in La République du Cameroun with less inhabitants than Bui division in the North West Province in the Southern

---

[16] See http://www.newafrica.com/profiles/profiles.asp?countryID (last visited in March 2010).

Cameroons for example, each has about triple the number of Parliamentary representatives of Bui division. If we go by United Nations approved population growth rates for our region over the past 35 years, the current population of the Southern Cameroons should be between 4.3 million and 5.0 million inhabitants. This is more than the population of a host of OAU and United Nations member countries.

Now that I am writing, the figure that is in vogue is 8 million plus. Whatever the facts-twisting, Cameroon's Southern Cameroonsian minority (whether it is the twisted official 25% of the total population) still constitutes a very sizable proportion: compared to other similar recognized cultural minorities, especially those of India and Switzerland. While the influential Muslim minority in India is 11% of the population, in Switzerland, even the 4% Italian-speaking minority is also recognized and respected just like the other more populous German-speaking and French-speaking ones (see Fossungu, 2021). French Canadians (who include a sizable proportion of non-Quebecers) are only a third of the total population of Canada. As Norman Ward has indicated in the *Preface to Fourth Edition* of a renowned treatise on the Canadian government (Dawson, 1970: vii-viii),

> Almost the whole of the earlier text could have been read without giving the reader an adequate appreciation of the third of the country that is French-speaking, and the impact of that fundamental fact of Canadian politics on the country as a whole; the book was, in short, an English-Canadian version of Canadian government, and while I cannot pretend to have made it any less so, I have where possible amended the text to include references to the rest of us.

Hodgins *et al* (1989: 507) in 1989 estimated Canada's French-speaking minority to be 33% of the population. The population of powerful Quebec (including Anglophone Quebecers) out of this figure cannot be extremely far from the 25% that was then officially the case of Southern Cameroonsians or "Anglophones" in Cameroon. Now, would the 'revealed' 1,384,286 as the population of oil-rich Debundschazone (SouthWest), for example, be referring just to people of Debundschazonian origin or to all who are resident in

Debundschazone? Revealing this population during a solemn ceremony presided by Amadou Ali (Vice Prime Minister, Minister of Justice and Keeper of the Seals), Yaouba Abdoulaye made known that "the [19.4 million given as Cameroon's] population is distributed in the ten regions [of Article 61(1)] as follows": Adamawazone, 1,015,622; Bamboutouszone (West), 1,785,285; Benouezone (North), 2,050,229; Debundschazone (South West), 1,384,286; Guinean-Savannazone (East), 801,968; Logonezone (Far North), 3,480,414; Nyongzone (South), 692,142; Sanagazone (Centre), 3,525,664; Savannazone (North West), 1,804,695; and Wourizone (Littoral), 2,865,795 (Achanyi, 2010). Once more, would the total population of both Debundschazone and Savannazone here be taken as representing people of Southern Cameroonsian origin or everyone that has taken up residence there? Reverse the argument and the question would still not be satisfactorily answered. What a messy confusion brought about by the assimilationist facts twisting!

Why was this sizable group (Southern Cameroonsians) the most marginalized and forgotten around the world? It is important to also quickly note and stress here that Canada has not always been what it is today – having been like Cameroon in the management of its ethnic minority problems "until 1965 that the power structure of this country was examined in detail. That was the year when John Porter, the Carleton University sociologist, published his monumental *Vertical Mosaic* and banished forever from the Canadian psyche the comfortable notion that this is a classless (or at any rate an entirely middle-class) country" (Newman, 1975: 386). As Newman concluded at page 390, "the Waterloo – or Vietnam – of the Canadian Establishment consisted in its failure to comprehend what had then been happening in Quebec, where a popular rage has been mistaken for a 'quiet revolution'." Yes, Canadians (English-speaking and French-speaking) realized their errors and speedily moved toward correcting them since they have always been ready to learn.

Not so in Cameroon. Konings and Nyamnjoh (1997: 229) therefore cautioned that the Government's continued denial of any 'anglophone problem' in Cameroon, and its determination to defend the unitary state by all available means, including repression, could lead to an escalation of anglophone demands past a point of no return. They were right just as my quick-thinking students were in 1985! 2017 finally got us there! One of the indelible imprints of learning in ancient Greece

77

and colonial America is American federalism that has been largely regarded as an important solution to the chronic problems of secession. As Ofege (1995b) also put it in 1995, redressing the imbroglio then in Cameroon required an effective "Re-creat[ion of] the Anglophone State... within the Cameroon polity if Anglophones are still interested in belonging." Were Southern Cameroonsians and the Cameroon State ready to sit down then and candidly talk and negotiate in the interest of the larger internationally recognized nation, bilingual and bijural Cameroon? It is obvious that they did not do so in view of the regime's unending love for absolute power, as embodied in the 1996 Constitution that specialists like Mback (2007: 63-68) have simply castigated as "The Dashed Hopes of 1996" that only came to consolidate and fortify the single-party multipartism of 1990, backed by smoking guns.

Despite the 'smoking guns' and the 'decreeing of false peace' solutions, the student *parlement* stood firm as a single force and, consequently, 'gave' Cameroon the six hurriedly decreed universities (see Chapter 4 below) largely because, as Dr. Mbangwana of the Department of English at the University of Douala is cited as ably theorizing, "you cannot speak of peace when you have not created conditions necessary to bring about such peace." [K.A. Bangsi, "Ambassador, University Don Decry Gap between Policy and Practice of Bilingualism" *The Herald* N° 446 (16-17 April 1997), 2] That is precisely the more reason why parents of the questioning Ambazonian students were compelled to provide acceptable answers to their '17 pertinent questions'. Their parents politickerized as usual with the issue. The students could not comprehend why they could not get satisfactory answers and made up their decision as to what to do.

It is for these reasons that we say that the peace of the Cameroon we are set to inherit is quite unguaranteed. For, if there is no permanent solution to the sectoral injustice and economic deprivation that we witness today, if there is no end to the assimilation destined towards us in guise of integration, we, your children, assure you that sooner or later we shall smear the homes, streets, and gardens of this nation with blood. We won't accept to be eternally stigmatized as second-class citizens, nor shall we want to be deprived of the cultural heritage which is ours and which we recognize is of greater significance around the globe. So, we shall fight for the justice we cannot otherwise have (Students' Letter, 1985).

That is unerringly how the Biya regime (like the IG-Care until recently in September 2025[17]) threw into the dustbin the true solution which is federalism within which each national group was to be able to develop and foster its own unique characteristics to the fullest, preferring to disunite by forcefully uniting. All this folly is evidence of the *Fonlon Thesis* (Anglo-Eat-Anglo) and was occurring largely because of the historyless political science that the players selfishly exhibited in 1961 in Foumban where federalism was grossly distorted. Yet the various secession and coup d'état theses claimed that a solid rights-respecting federation was therein created. The notorious 'Dashed Hopes' in Cameroon (such as the AGovC's vis-à-vis the IG-Care's) could also be seen in the 1998 Education Law that would be incessantly lip-preaching biculturalism in a serene and disciplined unitary state, claiming at the same time that the country's two inherited educational systems are different only to the extent of requiring two separate sections but not different enough to require federalism or effective decentralization. At this point, it is difficult to disagree with Canadian experts such as Newman (1968: xii) who concluded that "the country [was] being governed by fools [and not that] it [was] ungovernable." Who will genuinely argue with these experts who describe the Cameroonian administration as a bunch of idiots? These administrators are the actual problem, not the country's impressive diversity. It is instead their regressive attitude of antagonizing the people, spiced with the deliberately generated legal, constitutional, and political confusion that should be responsible for the ills in Africa. The prevailing opinion everywhere is that the only real problems in Africa, according to Franck (1968b: 187), are those in leadership non-charisma and in non-challenge

---

[17] The recent "Oslo-Kondengui Accord: A Declaration of Unity and Commitment to a Peaceful Resolution" of 22 September 2025, between the IG-Care leadership and the AGovC leadership is much lauded.

79

of historic trivia. Punctuate it with their legalization of multiple political formations.

The 1990 Multipartism Law Reinforcing the Single-Party State?

Third World leaders, Riemer's (1983: 187) argument runs, have often been pushed to instead tread their preferred road to Limbo (which is some sort of shortcut to Heaven) because of "(1) lack of an historical sense of belonging and working together; (2) the absence, often, of common language, religion, history, and custom; (3) the reality of widespread poverty and illiteracy; (4) the divisive influence of caste and tribe... and (5) the lack of instrumentalities that function to keep a nation together, such as effective national leadership, political organization, civil servants, national economic ties, and national education [the numbering has been added]." These so-called obstacles, according to Professor Riemer, "help to explain why many of the new states have often moved away from liberal or even democratic socialist ideas and toward rule by a strong charismatic leader, a single party, a disciplined military junta, and even (often reluctantly) toward authoritarian methods in order to foster primary national values" (cited in Fossungu, 2021: 22). Does this roundabout justification give enough cover to the African leadership? I do not think so because it is the absence of the first example of the fifth factor that is responsible for the existence or absence of all the others.

With the type of patriotic and charismatic people Neal Riemer of Drew University describes as being in leadership positions in the Third World, the so-called democracy 'inhibiting factors' cannot provide any excuse for regression. I must take you straight to Indonesia for the elaborate lessons in patriotism and charismatic leadership (see Fossungu, 2021) but, for now, I simply tell you that it is even untenable to employ those factors to justify the absence of the same thing (democracy) one is claiming to have in abundance. As I argued long ago,

Democracy must be nurtured and developed through channelling or curtailing those so-called 'inhibiting' factors as illiteracy, poverty, tribalism, etc. Using them to instead justify the non-institution of good and responsible governance would be clear evidence of non-charisma and absence of patriotism; not to forget that it is also philosophically untenable, especially when, at the same time, the same Cameroonians would be claiming the very democracy whose absence they appear to be justifying. *Demoncrazy* appears to be precisely what is in place in Cameroon. Illiteracy and poverty can only justify that. [Peter Ateh-Afac Fossungu, "Responsible Governance" *The Herald* N° 694 (2-3 December 1998), 10]

This whole complaint from the leadership is just total babbling (see Fossungu, 2021). What a folly called assimilation! Konings and Nyamnjoh (1997: 224 & 210) provide further illustration of the points; all pointing to the fact that genuine politicians must simply have realized that the legalization of political parties in the early 1990s in Cameroon was too good to be true and effective. Even an elementary school pupil could grasp many indicators. The first is that it is not the one-party in power that must authorize other parties to exist. There just must be a condition in the accepted constitution (such as the acquisition of a certain number or percentage of the seats in the national parliament) for recognition as a national party. Which means also that anyone can form their political parties and restrict themselves to village, city, or provincial, politics; levels that would all also have their own conditions of recognition. I must trust Ambazonians to be listening very carefully here? The Germans and Canadians have available models to show the way to those interested in learning. For instance, to eliminate splinter parties and to further the state's interest in the stability of its political system, the Basic Law (German Constitution) requires parties to win at least 5 percent of the total vote as a condition for entering the national parliament. Canada requires a minimum of not less than 12 seats in the federal parliament. The idea behind these 5% of votes & 12-seat requirements is just the opposite of what obtains always in Cameroon, with all the submarine parties, as I show below. All this is possible because it is the person who is in power who makes the rules, not the consensually drafted constitution. It is not wrong to state that only a non-human would lose a match in which he or she is also the judge or referee. Didn't it expose itself to Ni John Fru Ndi of the SDF in 1992, to Professor Maurice Kamto of the MRC in 2018, and then to 'President-Elect' Issa Tchiroma Bakary in 2025?

81

The other indicators revolve around the manner through which those parties came into existence. It is now obvious that the people that were "trying" to unseat the Cameroonian Emperor-president are just as culpable as the dictator insofar as they would not be prepared to have a system that will make it possible for others to later challenge them (should they ever get in). Could Mr. Biya then not be right in charging, as he clearly did, that all these people were not interested in effective change and were only out to take his job? Sungmini explains it better when he discusses "Mr. Paul Biya's loud cry against Mr. Fru Ndi: '*Il veut changer quoi? Il veut [seulement] ma place*'."[18] That being so how does anyone expect the incumbent administrators not to suspect that the others will ruthlessly hang them as soon as others take over? It is not speculation on my part because the 'politics of the inside' and 'outside' clearly tells the story and Biya (more than those he has been dealing with) is intelligent enough to understand it. Not surprising, having listened to the 'utilitarian calculus' of some 'politicians of the inside', an expert openly cried for the beloved country that should have been. An "honourable" parliamentarian is said to have given another rendition of the "*notre tour de bouffer politics*" (alias 'politics-of-the-inside') argument when, according to Dr. Nantang Jua, "he argued in one instance that now that from the inside they do not see anything wrong with the [Ahidjo-Biya] system... they may see something wrong with it once they become outsiders. In the face of this utilitarian calculus, I would not blame anyone who cries for the beloved country that would have been!" (Ndi Chia, 1995b: 6).

Like in the comportment of the IG-Care leadership to Ayaba's genuine nationalist proposals for joint leadership (see Fossungu, 2024: 130-33), the absence of sincerity/patriotism is thus at the heart of the difficulty of effecting genuine change (by both 'insiders' and 'outsiders') in Cameroon particularly and Africa generally. Very few are willing to

---

[18] Njemuchar Sungmini, "CPDM-UNDP Accord: What Lesson?" *The Post* N° 0040 (23 December 1997), 6. See also Ntenga (1991); Nwige Nkuku, "A Helpless Call for a True Multiparty Democracy in Cameroon" *The Herald* (3-4 March 1997), 4; Shey Wo Fonkui, "Is Cameroon a One-Party State in Disguise?" *The Herald* (13-15 September 1996), 4; T. Dibussi, "To the Leaders of the Cameroonian Opposition" *Cameroon Post* (28 December – 4 January 1991), 4; Paul Amugwa, "Wouldn't There Be Multipartism Without Arm-twisting?" *The Herald* (4-6 October 1996), 4; and M. Aleni, "Cameroon is Cracking Because of Selfishness" *The Herald* (27-29 May 1996), 4.

ask and address the right and fundamental questions. Perhaps that is what the President of the Association of Cameroon Insurance Companies (ASAC) must have realized when he advised that 'it is essential that political parties in this country exist and operate in the usual manner they do in other democracies': "*Il faudrait que les partis politiques banalisent les consultations dans ce pays pour en faire un processus normal*" (Amang, 1997). This advice must equally apply to other issues in the country, including that of the implacability and intolerability of those already in power. It will be better to say something again about the justification of the system before looking at the recent law that has come only to perpetuate this system while camouflaging political pluralism – the system's 'pluralistic democracy in an entirely democratized single-party.'

'Advanced democracy', as seen in Biya's *serene and disciplined community*, assumes one where there are simply no conflicts and discussions and compromises; as observed in the considerable length Biya (1986: 43-47) would go to justify the so-called "temporary" and "imperative" need (who decides all these?) for the perpetuation of the one-party farce he calls advanced democracy. (Note also always that the single party is incompatible with federalism and, therefore, multiculturalism.) Among such imperatives, the One-Party, Biya (1986: 43) claims, has not only spared Cameroon from the political chaos plaguing other countries in Africa[19] but, Biya rhetorically concludes, "is also necessary for the mobilization of human resources, especially intellectual resources which, though so invaluable, are still scarce in our country. *For, how could we ensure the efficient running of the State machinery if the political leanings of the few senior officials Cameroon now has, were to be torn between several opposing parties thus creating for any ruling regime an insurmountable crisis of power?*" (Biya, 1986: 44, emphasis added) The sex inevitability theory relating to conflicts must come here again.

First, why are there few senior officials? Is it not the same tribalistic Biya and gang responsible for killing or chasing away these talents? Much more importantly, the experts are quickly dismissing this as a

---

[19] Hear it from Reverend Jumban who describes these idiotickerizers. "In a nation where silliness is given a standing ovation and fools ride on royal horses, … Cameroon's false impression of greatness and self-styled portrayal as the island of peace in a sea of troubled Africa has been exposed for what it truly is" (cited in Fossungu, 2018: 152 n. 38).

nonsensical justification. In a modern age that stresses realism and political pragmatism rather than strict dogma, Professor Fombad writes, the doctrine of separation of powers facilitates unity, cohesion, and harmony within a system of checks and balances. It is clear that while the separation of powers on its own cannot guarantee constitutional democracy, he continues, where, as in Botswana (Bravo Botswana!), it exists and is allowed to work, it does so reasonably well and creates a more sustainable and feasible constitutional democracy (Fombad, 2005: 342). In addition, I must add, the doctrine of separation of powers is not meant to promote serenity and discipline but to generate said 'insurmountable crisis of power' that must then necessitate mandatory negotiation with, and compromise of, the parties concerned. That is the American Founding Fathers' idea behind the United States system with its fixed term of office and rigid checks which St. John-Stevas[20] and Loewenstein (1967: 151) say have led more to paralysis of government than anything else. These experts are here inferring the advantage of the parliamentary system. Alexis de Tocqueville would rather have this paralysis than 'peace of the graveyard' under serenity because,

The end of good government is to ensure the welfare of a people, and not merely to establish order in the midst of its misery. I am therefore led to suppose that the prosperity of the American townships and the apparent confusion of their finances, the distress of the French communes and the perfection of their budget, may be attributable to the same cause. At any rate, I am suspicious of a good that is united with so many evils, and I am not averse to an evil that is compensated by so many benefits. [Alexis Charles Henri Clerel de Tocqueville, *Democracy in America* Vol. I (New York: Alfred A. Knopf, 1945) at 91-92 n.50.]

---

[20] See Norman St. John-Stevas, "Foreword" in Humphry Berkeley, *The Power of the Prime Minister* (London: George Allen and Unwin, 1968) 7-11 at 11.

The important role of the courts that is responsible for these "so many benefits" must be highlighted (see Fossungu, 2019: chapter 3). Judicial review of the constitutionality of laws and administrative acts is largely responsible for the "so many benefits" de Tocqueville is talking about here. This power of review is something that is simply unknown in *Democratically Advanced* Cameroon. It should have been a miracle if it were since this power cannot exist amid concentration of powers. That is, in the absence of effective separation (and splitting) of power (centres). This splitting of power, by necessity, must mean having effective multiple political parties and, particularly, keeping the judiciary apart from the other branches.

In Cameroon, no iota of powers must be in any other hands other than the POR's to the extent that even 'legalized' political parties must remain mere empty shells. The 'Cameroon is Cameroon' ("*Le Cameroun c'est le Cameroun*") boastful attitude of the regime is quite understandable, for the killing or abandonment of multiparty politics is, of course, the destruction of democracy (that permits the striking of a balance between justice and order). The false impression has been given to the wider public by Ngwana (2009) that the one-party state was forced on Ambazonians: "Anglophones who were used to the multiparty system of government suddenly found themselves in a one-party system of government (the CNU monster) with its dictatorship and suppression of human rights." Falsehood! One-partism was rather precipitated by the English-speaking in the 'Federal' Republic of Cameroon through their 'unified single national party' in what some critics have lengthily described as "The Mad Rush Towards Ahidjo's Union Camerounaise" (see Zang-Atangana, 1989b: 95-119; Benjamin, 1972: 54-55; Bjornson, 1991: 112-114). Cameroon's contradictory One-Party Federation (or Advanced Democracy) was given its impetus by the Southern Cameroonsians. These momentum and inauguration had been lacking on the eastern side of the Mungo River where the opposition was seriously standing up to Ahidjo's dictatorship. Dr Konings and Dr Nyamnjoh tell the story in more straightforward and clear terms when they posit that Ahidjo looked upon federalism as an unavoidable stage in the establishment of a strong unitary state and employed various tactics to achieve this objective. After becoming President of the Federal Republic of Cameroon in October 1961, he played Anglophone political factions off against each other, eventually persuading them to join the *Union nationale camerounaise* (UNC), the single party formed in September 1966, and was able to penalise any anglophone leader like Prime Minister Jua who remained committed to federalism (Konings and Nyamnjoh, 1997: 210).

This One-Party federation of theirs the regime is fortifying under the name of national unity, order, and tranquility. This is just as nonsensical as their single-party advanced democracy and experts on Democratic Federalism have all stiffly challenged it. I draw attention to Dawson (1970: 415) who thinks there must be the existence of parties in the plural, for it is obvious that democratic government as it is understood and practised in Canada cannot function without the aid of more than one party; the communist and fascist idea of a single party and the rigid suppression of all dissenters has clearly no place in a democracy. The question is: Has the situation changed today in Cameroon with the law on multipartism? Could there be an effective Opposition party (let alone strong third parties) in Cameroon: with the selfish and corrupt attitude of Cameroonians? Put differently, can Garga Harman Adji's Alliance for Democracy and Development (ADD), for instance, effectively ensure that the government's programme incorporates ADD's federalism contribution (which appears to threaten West-Central African political geography and peace)?

Deconstructing the Multipartism Law's Threats to West-Central African Political Geography: Federating for Security in Cameroon?

Trager (1968: x) has posed some important questions that, inter alia, do help in deciphering the invisible hand of federalism. What is federalism, and why do federations form and fail? In other words, what are the prerequisites, if any, for a successful federation? Can one discern factors that make for success or failure? What role, for example, is played by the constitution itself, its formula for dividing power between the centre and the units? What relative importance should be attached to the non-constitutional factors? Most of these issues have already been touched in the previous Chapter; this section being devoted mostly to some of the forces pushing for and against federalism. There are some six factors that almost every writer on federalism has cited as being responsible for entities federating. These factors, constituting the bases of successful federations as set out by Wheare (1963) and cited by Southall (1974: 138) and Eleazu (1977: 17) are:

A sense of military insecurity and the consequent need for common defence, a desire to be independent of foreign powers, and a realization that only through union could independence be secured; a hope of economic advantage from union; some political association of the communities concerned prior to their federal union; geographical neighbourhood; and similarity of political institutions....

How many of these factors (if any) do apply to Cameroon's experience? Stevenson (1989: 13) has answered by opining that it may be that no single factor can explain every instance of the formation of a federal union, and even in a particular case, as the Cameroonian here, a variety of factors may contribute. A critically balanced analysis of the FRC and other recent proposals for federalism provides ample evidence that both the Ambazonia and Cameroun political elites involved used the 1961 Foumban Conference merely to something else and not for the sake of what federalism is usually adopted to achieve: special human rights protection. Thus, the invisible hand of federalism in Cameroon would come nowhere near those of other federations, explaining in part or in full what I see as its funny multiculturalism and definition of culture that does not encapsulate history. It also explicates the insecurity (rather than security) that the people were dragged into.

The search or desire for security has certainly also played an enormous role in the formation of many great federations. H.W. Springer, according to Stevenson (1989: 13), has categorized all the security factors into two main groups of "predisposing conditions" and "inducements". Discussing R.D. Dikshit's *The Political Geography of Federalism* (1975), Stevenson (1989: 13) points out that he has instead distinguished factors leading to union from those leading to the retention of some degree of regional autonomy; indicating that a preponderance of the first will lead to the formation of a unitary state, while a preponderance of the second will prevent any union from taking place. Only a balance between the two will lead to federalism and only if the balance is maintained. On the other hand, Trager (1968: xiv) has summarized everything and come out with two compelling forces pushing for federalism, namely, (1) affording the necessary force for aggregating territory, and (2) readiness against some impending military-diplomatic threat or opportunity. This factor would explain why the Canadian Fathers of Confederation indicated that they were federating to escape "our impending misfortune" (Newman, 1968: 299; Hogg, 1996: 100-101). It is thus very important that all the federating entities perceive the problem; otherwise, there is a problem.

Security will thus not be a credible factor if some of the entities are not feeling insecure. This is seen in the Caribbean Federation which de Smith (1964: 280) says hinged tremulously on, "about to be bereft of its most important members", largely because Castro's communist Cuba which might have fostered West Indian unity was not considered enough threat especially by the Jamaicans who constituted the most important entity. ECOWAS and their Western-backed threats of invasion of Niger (and BKF & MAL subsequently, of course) fostered the AES formation. The impending misfortune (security reasons) in Canada can scarcely be captured by anything in the case of Cameroon, not even by the much-sung Igbo factor, discussed in Fossungu (2025) in the context of the 'Kamerun Idea'. This Igbo Factor (which obviously floated so well in the Ambazonian walking-out-of-Enugu waters) cannot float in the Rivers of Foumban. It is thus to be conveniently discarded as not being common to both prospective federating entities in Foumban, since Camerounese were not under its impulse. As Stevenson (1989: 13) has tersely noted, security motives are somewhat harder to discern, although not entirely absent, in other cases, "such as those of Australia, post-war Germany, and Cameroon." So, why is it necessary to call anything federation there (in Cameroon): except for the calculated use of the word as a trap into insecurity or state terrorism?

Were it otherwise (as claimed by 'Ambazonian elites' in Cameroon), then there would have been no need for Dr Anyangwe's Tiger-DNA

88

Theory that follows, since the federal principle is necessarily an appropriate dose or medication for fencing or controlling that DNA.

I submit to you that federation no longer commends itself to us. The freedoms we cherish, seek and desire cannot be achieved in the context of any form of political arrangement or co-existence with French Cameroun as one polity. The untold massive atrocities, injuries, sufferings and political, economic, social and cultural emasculation that French Cameroun has inflicted on us over the past six decades are just too profound, wide, and visible to be swept under the carpet for any form of political cohabitation with that country. The colonial oppressor has shown no remorse or contrition for those atrocities. In fact, he has not even acknowledged these crimes, let alone committed himself to atone for them and to turn over a new leaf. Quite the contrary. He behaves like the repeat psychopathic offender. He laughs and boasts about his crimes, his cunning, his fraud, his treachery, his violence and his duplicity. He is fundamentally evil and untrustworthy. Even in the unlikely event of France ordering him to commit to something, he cannot be trusted to respect his plighted word or written commitments. A tiger never changes its spots. No amount of rain and detergent can remove those spots because they are part and parcel of the tiger's DNA. We should therefore be wise and not make another monumental mistake, this time an eternally fatal one (cited in Fossungu, 2019: 121-22).

All what is theorized in the above passage (and the others like it in chapters 1) would only go to clearly show that there was no federation formed in Foumban at all; also, only obliquely (rather than openly) indicating that France is the real coloniser of Ambazonia to be ordering, not Cameroun that they are openly crediting with that status. Failing to straightforwardly call a spade a spade can only give good and very comfortable cover to the unnamed spade. It must be noted with

Eleazu (1977: 17) that most of the security factors now have relatively no meaning because of the changed international environment and technological advancement. Does such advancement also affect the geographical factor? And did geography and patriotism push for federalism in Cameroon?

Most probably not; and the mere act of "federating" then is to be largely decried because, before the window-dressing exercise in Foumban, the key figures of the delegations of both "federating" states (to be accurate, two political parties – see Johnson, 1970, chapter 7; Zang-Atangana, 1989b; and Benjamin, 1972: 147) knew pretty well that they were looking at the federation issue from different sides of what some see as 'the deepest gulf between us and them.' This alone should, however, not be taken as saying that the parties at both extremes of the state-form spectrum cannot federate. They perfectly can do so because we have learned from the experts that federalism is necessarily a compromise solution for the extremes of separatism and of the unitary form. What is rather being deplored here is the fact that "federation" is camouflaged even when no agreement of minds to achieve practical and reasonable ends has been reached, thus leaving us with only what Maneli (1994: 32) has castigated as a *Gleichschaltung* of minds. Yet, the intellectuals have been presenting a different picture. The politics of academic discussion obviously does not constrain agreement from the participants, but it does not also give the participants the right to deliberately confuse or confiscate the issues. So, does the Cameroon law on political parties threaten political geography in the region?

I would like to aid you answer the question through a detailed look at Cameroon's one-party multipartism. Very briefly then, I would say NO; because the regime is indeed still the One-Party System which is clearly the synonym for dictatorship, defined by Pearson and Rochester (1984: 593) as a closed, authoritarian governmental system in which the free expression and flow of ideas is severely curtailed and political opposition severely restricted. This definition also captures the "paper system" because multipartism can clearly not be effective where there are simply empty shells called parties, most of them with no platform or issues except the insatiable filling of the belly. The 'platformlessness' or 'issuelessness' of the myriads of 'opposition' political parties in Cameroon was, *inter alia*, well-orchestrated by the unilingual 1990 Parties Law (*Loi N° 90/056 du 19 décembre 1990 relative aux parties politiques*), carefully designed by the incumbent president (Paul Biya) who was very desirous of preserving himself as life Emperor of the U.K. (Unconstitutional Kingdom-republic) of Cameroon. No doubt that one Nigerian comedian (4Fun Mamimiya) recently calls him 'the Igwe of Cameroon' and 'Emperor Biya the First',

The stark reality is simply that Cameroon was only silently legalizing hundreds of paper parties. In Cameroon (which copies from France but not its effective multipartism and unique divided executive), there is hardly any separation. There is only fusion to a degree that even political parties must remain mere shadows. Thus, as Canada and others are *Legalizing Politics* [see Michael Mandel, *The Charter of Rights and the Legalization of Politics in Canada* (Toronto: Wall and Thompson, 1989)], Cameroon was only silently legalizing myriads of empty shells called political parties. If that about covers it, the critics have questioned, then why invent a concept called multipartism that does not exist? Why do so except for confusion and assimilation? An elaborate examination of the sham creation of the multiparty concept itself will help the experts' charge. By the Parties Law, a person can create political parties by first having a *dossier complet* or complete file or application. The completeness of the application necessitates (I will indent them so that they can stand out):

(1) a stamped application that indicates the names, addresses, as well as the complete identity, profession and residence of those to be at the helm of the party; (2) a certificate of non-conviction of the prospective leaders; (3) three copies of *le procés verbal de l'assemblée constitutive;* (4) three copies of the statutes; (5) written, signed and legalized undertaking to respect or abide by the enumerated principles of Article 9 below [to be seen later]; (6) *un mémorandum sur le projet de société ou le programme politique du parti;* and (7) an indication of party headquarters (Article 5(1)).

The law is, as it was usual in Biya's Cameroon, only in French and I have cautiously avoided translating where the sense/effect will be lost. By Article 5(2), any change or modification in any of the above requirements must be communicated to the governor's office concerned (*gouverneur territorialement compétent*). The complete application is then filed with the Minister of Territorial Administration through the said governor's office (Article 4(1)), the said governor then has to issue, to the depositing party, *"Une décharge mentionnant le numéro et la date d'enregistrement du dossier"* (Article 4(2)); also having *"quinze (15) jours francs"* within which to forward the same to the said minister (Article 6); with this minister being the only competent person to decide on and authorize the existence of the party being requested (Article 7(1)).

How does one know if the minister has legalized the requested party in Cameroon? It is very silently simple indeed, by Article 7(2): *"En cas de silence gardé pendant trois (3) mois à compter de la date de dépôt du dossier auprès des services du gouverneur territorialement compétent, le parti est réputé exister légalement."* This provision is simply saying that no news is good news. Hence, three months of silence from the date the complete application is submitted to the concerned governor's office signifies that the requested party has been legalized. Unlike in the toilet where 'yes' means occupied and, therefore, 'You can't come in', this time it is silence that means yes. The *silent* nature of this Article 7(2) of the Parties Law is effectively the commencement of the *sous-marins* (submarines) strategy that is just one of the several methods that were carefully designed solely to flush effective multiparty politics down the drain, where it appears, in the estimation of the Biya regime, to properly belong. Who in Biya's position would voluntarily give up the unrestrained powers he enjoys? President-Elect Issa Tchiroma Bakary, are you real?

Success in the strategy of perpetuating his iron-fisted rule was greatly guaranteed by the greed of Cameroon "politicians". The submarines are political parties with no agenda or following (headed by 'former' CPDM stalwarts) that the ruling CPDM silently legalizes to conveniently dilute and stultify any effective opposition. There is absolutely no obligation on this minister to publish all the parties that he has 'legalized.' Who then said Biya could be besieged by the opposition? According to an un-authored piece in 32(15) *Africa Confidential* of 26 July 1991 titled "Cameroon: Biya Besieged", these silently created parties are known as submarines, "because they dive underwater to torpedo the big ships." But that is not the only potent arm because, where those big ships cannot be sunken in that fashion, there is another more potent weapon. According to Article 17(1) of the Parties Law, the territorial administration minister can, for reasons of *"l'ordre public"*, suspend the activities of any of these parties; with possibility of his decision being taken to court by the person concerned as per Article 8 of the Parties Law (Article 17(2)). The minister can, in equivalent manner, also dissolve these parties, with such dissolution not barring legal proceedings against their leaders (Articles 18-20).

All this, I am inclined to think, should have clearly led anyone genuinely desirous of change in Cameroon to pose questions. For instance, by Article 5(2) of the 1996 Constitution (which is just the continuation of previous ones since the federal, as seen earlier) the Cameroonian president "is the symbol of national unity" – with this becoming even more disastrous when that president alone (by this same provision) decides/defines what that elusive concept entails; ensures respect for the Constitution; is the guarantor of the independence of the Nation and of its territorial integrity; etc. This should unmistakably and inevitably signify to anyone with the slightest number of brains that *anything* that tends towards unseating this president must simply become a threat to "national unity." The Gen-Zs of Cameroun are just out there now (October 2025) burning 'national unity' down or do they indeed have any change at changing the UK of Cameroon? Not sure change is possible without the barrel. That being the case, the ultimate question that any of the so-called opposition party leaders (if they are/were out to fix Cameroon for their children) should have been posing, rather than madly rushing to create shadow parties, is this. Just how can anyone ever unseat the incumbent, without threatening "national unity"? This question should have as goal the unconditional call for a complete clean slate to begin with, as happened in most other francophone African countries, notably Benin, with national conferences that laid down new ground rules [see Filip Reyntjens, "The Wind of Change: Political and Constitutional Evolution in Francophone Africa, 1990-1991" 35 *Journal of African Law* (1990), 43–55].

The question is even more especially important as these same opposition leaders must have also initially undertaken in the Parties Law's Article 5(1) that has been set out above to respect the principles of Article 9 of the Parties Law by which: 'No legalization would be allowed for any political party that: - threatens the state's territorial integrity, national unity, the republican nature of the state, national sovereignty, and national integration, especially by way of any kind of discrimination, be it based on ethnicity, province of origin, linguistic group or religious belief; - leans towards violence or envisages having a military or paramilitary organization; - receives foreign financial support or whose leaders (one or all) reside(s) abroad; - favours internal strife or war with other nations.'[21] This would effectively mean in Canada, if the same model of legalizing parties is adopted there, that the government in Ottawa would have been crazy to have legalized the Bloc Quebecois. Brought back to Cameroon, could this law be representative of the confluence of, or war between, dictatorship and democracy in the preservation of international peace and frontiers? I ask the question because it is not exactly clear what the ADD president means by Ahidjo's enlargement of the federal system in 1972 in Cameroon (see Fossungu, 2025: 46 n.26).

This point is the most intriguing of anything I have so far encountered in regard of all the talk of federalism in Cameroon. Yes, indeed! From all the debates the great question has not been that of whether, but that of how, Cameroon should have gone federal. This is where the SDF's role in thwarting the people's wishes becomes graphical to the corrupt and corrupting Biya regime. 'Langa-Throat' Ambazonians, as AGovC Spokesman Asu has recently called them in October 2025, with reference to Issa Tchiroma's federalism bait. Could the ADD president be referring to the realization of the *Kamerun Idea*? That is, was he alluding to the regaining of former German Kamerun by reuniting all its severed parts, including British Northern Cameroons (that is now part of Nigeria) and other territories that France had ceded to its adjoining colonies of Gabon and of Central African Republic? Or was the ADD president instead alluding to Ahidjo's rumoured annexation of Spanish-speaking Equatorial Guinea in the late 1960s to form a trilingual federation, as Rubin (1971: 192) has suggested? Which of the two possibilities could be the enlargement of Cameroon's federation in 1972 that Garga Harman Adji was referring to? Could he be having both situations in mind?

Either or both ways would clearly still involve the redrawing of West-Central African political geography as well as affecting

---

[21] *Ne peut être autorisé, tout parti politique qui:*
- *porte atteinte à l'intégrité territoriale, à l'unité nationale, à la forme républicaine de l'Etat, à la souveraineté nationale et à l'intégration nationale, notamment par toute sortes de discriminations basées sur les tribus, les provinces, les groupes linguistiques ou les confessions religieuses;*
- *prône le recours à la violence ou envisage la mise sur pied d'une organisation militaire ou para-militaire;*
- *recoit les subsides de l'étranger ou dont l'un des dirigeants statuaires réside à l'étranger; favorise la belligérance entre les composantes de la Nation ou entre des pays.*

international peace, all of which Biya's dictator-perpetuating law here seems to have excluded. In other words, Articles 9 and 17-20 (requiring dissolution for reasons of "*l'ordre public*") of the internal dictatorial multipartism law in Cameroon would appear to have served to avoid the implementation of the ADD federation enlargement agenda because that would involve "threatening" not only "the [Cameroon] state's territorial integrity" (through incorporating 'new' territories) but also those of neighbours (Central African Republic, Gabon, Nigeria, and Equatorial Guinea); thus necessitating the application of the nullifying dissolution arm of that Parties Law. Is there any court in the country to which the ADD can then turn for umpiring on the issue? Yes. That court is judge and party – President Biya in his Constitutional Council. Is President-Elect Professor Maurice Kamto not still there to vouch for it? Should the international law and community begin to ignore this real problem because of the wars and the like that Terrorist Dictator Biya has (inadvertently) taken care of, then I would like to invite them to this other side of the coin. Imagine Biya being the one with the *Kamerun Idea* agenda like Hitler was, who or what organ is there in Cameroon to put a break on his war-mongering agenda? The Bakassi War (Nigeria/Cameroon) and the most recent and ongoing Ambazonia/Cameroun War declared by Biya from the tarmac of an airport are exceptionally clean cases to this issue of undemocratic administrations making themselves the synonyms of the state. The hypocrites are all out there condemning and fighting against Putin's Russia 'for invading to annex Ukraine' (not to plunge into NATO's provocation of Russia into it); but not only annexation proper but also genocide have been on the Ambazonian people for close to nine years now by France/LRC: without any coughing from the same international community. Hypocrisy! Hear them threatening to remove and kill Captain Ibrahim Traoré because "he is a dictator" but not a word at all about Paul Biya who has been there for eternity! Dr Ayaba, please, do lecture them a bit for us.

We are doing our international work, we are taking our international obligation seriously, making sure we introduce Ambazonia correctly, not as a victim but as a potential to our friends, our future partners. I don't want the world to continue to look at Ambazonia from a position of pity. They should see us as the warriors who gave LRC political asylum, as the warriors who have, through their creativity, their ingenuity, their hard work, supported LRC with 60% of their GDP. They should see us like the generation that rose up from the ashes of near destruction with bare hands, Dane guns, and fought valiantly. Our stories should be told like the stories of the people who fought in the trenches in World War I; in the tunnels in Prague, and all those who fought to defend Norway, to defend western democracies. The warriors who are taking over in Africa, we should be seen as a generation of the braves. We cannot continue to market pity. We should market opportunities. Ambazonia is a state whose time has come. And the world must know that we have an electricity power grid that can provide energy in West Africa. That we have the highest peak in West Africa. That we have potentials in Ngoketunjia for the culture is a place for the craftsmen and craftswomen that should attract tourists. That on the hills of Lebialem will be the Alps of Ambazonia where you can hop from one high hill to the next as a holiday destination. That the opportunities in Ndian in Rio de Rey alone, the oil beneath the soil if extracted and marketed at 100$ per barrel, will provide for each Ambazonian 2,500$ US. That is only about two wells (Ayaba, Ngoketunjia: September 2023).

Whatever the case, the attitude of Cameroonian politicians who formed (and are still creating) all the shadow political parties is even more incomprehensible especially as the one-party-perpetuating Parties Law itself very clearly states in Article 8(2) that 'in case of disagreement the person seeking the legalization of a political party can sue the authorities refusing such legalization in the administrative branch of the Supreme Court in accordance with the laws in place.' One of such laws is specifically the much-regulated Ordinance regulating the Cameroon Supreme Court (*Ordonnance N° 72/6 du 26 août 1972 fixant l'organisation de la Cour suprême*). The story of the dependence of the 'apex' court in Cameroon is shortened considerably by the manner the country's Supreme Court has itself been brutally regulated, as seen in said Ordonnance, which provides the 'appetizer to the confusing story of amendments in Cameroon' (see Fossungu, 2019: chapter 3). Could a court like this one be able to say a decision taken by the executive agent (the minister of territorial administration) must be reversed and the solicited party legalized, or that the party-legalization process in Cameroon be changed? By Article 8(3) of the Parties Law, certain provisions of this 1972 Supreme Court Ordinance have been set aside (*"Par dérogation aux dispositions..."*) to permit those whose envisaged political parties have been refused legalization to have recourse to court action 'by simply presenting a request for a determination before the president of the administrative branch of the Supreme Court.' Professor Anyangwe (1996: 824-25) has pithily shown that administrative justice in Cameroon is a total sham; being tied to the dependent status of the court.

Ignorant Democrats Prop Up Dictatorship

As I have already asked in Fossungu (2019: 72), shouldn't any right-thinking person have first made sure that this un-supreme court became effectively supreme before launching into creating a political party? Where are the likes of Honourable Daniel Kemajou (who would rather die in dignity than live in slavery and dishonour) in this country? Have *pleins pouvoirs* slaughtered all the authentic democrats of this country, leaving only Laski's ignorant democrats? As Laski has competently explained their attitude, ignorant democrats simply cannot defend democratic principles because (like the Kondengui Interim-Government of Sisiko Ayuk Tabe) they usually only know what they have lost after they have lost it, at which time it is too late to halt, let alone eliminate the dictatorship. [*"Des démocrates ignorants ne pourront défendre la démocratie, tout simplement parce qu'ils sauront trop tard ce qu'ils auront perdu"* Harold-J. Laski, *Le gouvernement parlementaire en Angleterre* [Translated by Jacque Cadart and Jacqueline Prélot] (Paris : P.U.F., 1950) at 323]. And where are the 'Anglophones' that boasted so profusely (before the Foumban drama) about teaching their French-speaking 'brothers' across the Mungo River the essentials of responsible governance? What is responsible government but another name for one marked by separation of powers and constitutionalism? Is it the problem of their poor colonial education?

97

The query is apt because of the endless talk of the guarantee of quality education to children in Cameroon. The Cameroon state, according to Section 2(2) and (3), guaranteed quality education to Cameroon's children by providing it to them with the assistance of private sector partners. The critical issue to resolve relates to who should be at the forefront and with whom as assistant in the guarantee and provision of this essential cultural service, especially in a bicultural state. For instance, while education was generally a private-sector affair in English-speaking West Cameroon, it was the reverse in French-speaking East Cameroon. Now, how does one properly integrate two opposite or divergent views like these? Canada's Prime Minister Pierre-Elliott Trudeau, as already seen above, would think it cannot be done in any other way except through genuine federalism, a device which permits each national group to fully develop its unique national characteristics within the larger state. There is even research that reveals a worrisome fiscal crisis in state-supported education in Cameroon. This fact, Boyle (1996: 617) has indicated, has now meant "greater parental involvement in the finance and management of most schools, and the near sudden appearance of private education. If such changes are not surprising, their existence suggests that education in Cameroon has entered a new phase that merits further examination." This important further inspection must also entail delineating the appropriate domain to which education should belong in a multicultural society. This is a job that I will do next through examining (1) the constitution and the education domain, an inquiry that enormously aids the comprehension of the philosophy or design of the Education Law (Chapter 3); and (2) the subtle prevention of biculturalism using *epsi* (Chapter 4).

Chapter 3

The Constitution and the Education Domain: The Assimilationist Philosophy of the Education Law under the Equality Microscope

Education is key. The knowledge you acquire would determine whether you live a free person or live as a slave. And all the intoxication that we went through made us perfect slaves to LRC. Not only was our history distorted. We were taught things that were totally irrelevant to our own existence, estranged to our own realities. Never taught to see our Land as a place where we were going to thrive in. Go to western capitals and see how they have designed curriculum of education that reflects the opportunities in their own country, and even in other countries because of their colonial history (Ayaba, Ngoketunjia: September 2023).

Confusion is so deeply embedded in the Education Law that would be superficially preaching educational dualism that it was solely out to prevent or efface. By educational dualism, I am merely referring to the existence and effective 'near-independent' operation of two educational systems in the same social field or country; a description that draws largely from Section 15 of Cameroon's 1998 Education Law. As I have noted above, the real purpose of this law is not the one that is stated; it was the destruction of any remaining traces of cultural dualism in Cameroon – a strategy that did not augur well with what Reverend Tatah Mbuy saw as Cameroon's 'entrusted and confirmed' spiritual and legendary continental direction (see Fossungu, 2025: 38-39). To concretize this thesis, Parts II and III of said law (portions that deal with organization, management and financing of education) will need to be carefully studied; matters that would first require a digging into the issue of whether education is a national or regional domain in bicultural societies.

The relationship between the status of a country's government and its constitutional scholarship is not a very difficult one to establish. The global view I have adopted in this study appears to somehow combine and overshadow Arthurs Report's (1983: 65-66) research classification into conventional, legal theory, law reform, or fundamental: which it respectively defines as (1) one designed to collect and organize data, to expound legal rules, and to explicate or offer exegesis upon authoritative legal sources; (2) one designed to yield a unifying theory or perspective by which rules may be understood, and their application in particular cases evaluated and controlled – usually including scholarly commentary on civil law known as *doctrine*; (3) one that aims at accomplishing change in the law, whether to eliminate anomalies, to enhance effectiveness, or to secure a change in direction; and (4) the type designed to secure a deeper understanding of the law as a social phenomenon, including research on the historical, philosophical, linguistic, economic, social or political implications of law. Some researchers have also distinguished legal sociology from lawyers' internal perspective of law.

Any academic worth the name cannot but be very critical of the way most of the scholars in Africa generally but particularly pre-2017 Cameroon twist plain facts. The facts-twisting is especially accentuated in regard of the 1961 Foumban Federation or Constitution about which there are numerous confusing theses on separation of powers, human rights guarantee, full citizen participation, etc. It is even doubtful if one should continue referring to the facts-twisters as intellectuals since, by definition, intellectuals are supposed to be shedding light on the issues, not emasculating them. Earlier, we saw the youths wanting to know if the Foumban actors were ignorant of existing federations when they crated theirs. In addressing this issue, Enonchong (1967: xii-xiii) told the questioning youths that ignorance on the architects' part was clearly out of the question "because the framers of the [Cameroon Federal] Constitution frequently adverted to these constitutions [of the United States, Canada, France and Great Britain] at the Foumban Constituent Assembly. This is particularly true of the principles of federalism and judicial review which have been closely modelled, knowingly or unknowingly, on the American idea." The authenticity in most of these issues concerning Cameroon's 'fascinating federalism' is coming to light as I am examining the theory and practice regarding the formation of, among others, the two federal unions whose constitutions have just been alluded to.

The content and quality of education provided in any society are largely, if not entirely, coloured by the country's education politics. That of Cameroon would seem to see no necessity for federalization and/or decentralization of educational matters. In a federal or decentralized state that is characterized by linguistic differences, according to Shapiro, "education, inexorably linked with the survival of language and hence culture, assumes great significance. Among Canadian experiences, we could recall the history of the Manitoba School Question or the more recent controversy over educational language restriction in Quebec" (Shapiro, 1995: 67 n.255). As Green (1999) has stressed, in Canada (as in most proper federations or effectively decentralized multicultural polities) "education is subject to provincial jurisdiction." This has been so in Canada since the 1867 *British North America Act* whose section 93, Green again emphasizes, permits provincial legislatures to exclusively make Laws in relation to education, including the language of instruction (Green, 1999: 453 & 454). This Canadian arrangement is just another version of the Swiss geographic language principle which has been explained to mean that there if you cannot or do not want to speak or use the language of a canton the only option is for you to move on (Fossungu, 2021: 11). Yes, National unity is not turning diversity into *monosity* or what is generally known as assimilation.

The book, *Distribution of Powers and Responsibilities in Federal Countries*, presents what Majeed (2008: 3) describes as an objective and balanced description and analysis of the distribution of powers and responsibilities in the federal constitution and actual practice of eleven countries: Australia, Belgium, Brazil, Canada, Germany, India, Mexico, Nigeria, Spain, Switzerland, and the United States. For each federation there is an in-depth examination of such themes as (1) the distribution of governmental, political, monetary, fiscal, administrative, and policy responsibilities; (2) symmetry and asymmetry in the distribution of responsibilities; (3) the reasons and ways in which powers and responsibilities are explicitly and implicitly exclusive, concurrent, or shared in the constitution; (4) the reasons and ways in which responsibilities become divided and shared in actual governmental practice; (5) current controversies over the division and/or sharing of powers and responsibilities; and (6) assessments of the exclusive and concurrent exercise of powers and responsibilities. Is there any home for the 'true federation' logic in Cameroon? This query is another way of saying that it is not clear that Cameroonians have, since 1961, ever known and practised local government, a system of governance that the country's current 1996 Constitution is also bragging about in its Part X (Articles 55-62). The intellectuals do claim that there were, contrary to what I am saying, a lot of power-sharing in the FRC, marked particularly by judicial review. Can there really be judicial review without separation of powers? And was there such separation of powers in Foumban?

Inventing Federalism from Nowhere: Power Sharing in Foumban?

My response, of course, is no. Of course, as Ngwana (2009) rightly points out, "A Federation is the only way by which any multinational and culturally diverse communion has the opportunity for variation in laws, existences, dispensations, that take into account of the motley sensibilities and accordingly concede reasonable autonomy to the constituting units." But I think all these things cannot happen without that 'Federation' being marked by separation of powers both in theory and practice.

It is here that this study asks how different jurisdictions interact with one another. Their relationships may be characterized by hierarchy, mutual dependence, asymmetrical dependence, or relative independence. To understand these distinctions, one has to understand both the formal and informal institutions of the country in question. In addition, any discussion about the distribution of powers and responsibilities must encompass the constitutional mechanisms that have been used for that end. Structural changes have been introduced in many federal countries, and any debate on a distribution of responsibility and of resources remains incomplete if the constitutional provision of the federal structure remains blurred (Majeed, 2008: 5).

Some Ambazonian intellectuals insist however that there was a great deal of multiplicity of power centres in the FRC; and this involved all levels and branches. To Gorji-Dinka (1991: 5), for instance, the 1961 Foumban Constitution "shared power: (a) territorially, i.e., between the states and the centre; (b) institutionally, i.e., between the executive, the judiciary and legislature [and] (c) personally-wise, i.e., the Executive power was shared by the President and the State Prime Ministers; while legislative power was shared by State Deputies and Federal Deputies." This theory is then claiming, first, a clear demarcation of federal-provincial domains; implying that there was "politics of intergovernmental relations". Further discussion of this indispensable federal-state cooperation has been provided, for instance, by Shapiro (1995: 26-35: cooperative federalism in Germany, & 71-73: cooperative federalism in Belgium); Hogg (1996: 129-131: cooperative federalism in Canada); and Hodgins et al (1989). This is an aspect which Eleazu (1977: 267) says "today from the viewpoint of the states and localities is (1) a right to be heard in the design of programmes and (2) a right to share in the implementation of programmes." In the second place, Gorji-Dinka (1991) claims what Schneider (2008: 130-133) prefers to describe as "Horizontal Division of Powers: The Three Branches of Government", a principle that has been widely adopted because the liberty of the individual lies in the separation of powers – that is, in such an arrangement of the various institutions of government that each should prevent the other from having sufficient power to act tyrannically.[22]

Gorji-Dinka's claim of "The Constitutional Distribution of Powers" (Simon and Papillion, 2008: 97-100) in the FRC has been confirmed by Enonchong (1967: 22) who declares that "The general feature at the national level is, therefore, that the [Foumban]

---

[22] H. Finer, *The Theory and Practice of Modern Government* revised edition (New York: Holt, 1949) at 84. See also W.B. Gwyn, *The Meaning of Separation of Powers: An Analysis of the Doctrine from its Origin to the Adoption of the United States Constitution* (The Hague: Martinus Nijhoff, 1965); Loewenstein (1967: x-xi); and Brian Dickson, *The Rule of Law: Judicial Independence and the Separation of Powers* (Address to the Canadian Bar Association, August 21, 1985) at 9 & 22-23.

Constitution seeks to separate powers between the executive, legislative and judiciary, with the set purpose that each can be an expert in its own field. The federal legislature is identified with making legislation, the executive with implementing it, and the judiciary with interpreting the rules where necessary." Gorji-Dinka (1991: 5) then concludes that "In this way the guarantee of security for the individual was institutionalised." Enonchong (1967: chapter 7) also discusses the FRC's 'Civil Liberties and Constitutional Guarantees'. The theses on the institutionalization of individual freedoms are highly erroneous or manipulative and would appear to have been inspired by Enonchong (1967: xi-xii) who seems to have led the others to their baseless positions when he posited in 1967 that "Undoubtedly the [Foumban] constitutional instrument had allocated powers to the federal and federated state authorities and among the three governmental bodies, namely, the Executive, the Legislature and the Judiciary."

I must highlight over and over that these are confusioncratic (confusing and manipulative) theses, as I am elaborately showing; and that they are coming from intellectuals (mostly lawyers and jurists) who, rather than tell the truth ('and nothing but the truth, so help me God') to the people who are looking up to them, will be busy inventing facts where none exists to further compound and emasculate the people's real situation. I would simply think that all the unfounded claims about the FRC (if not deliberate confusioncracy) could then be purely the result of what Ntenga (1997) vehemently condemns as the "cow dung journalism [and intellectualism]." It is surely cow dung, as Ntenga (1997) explains it, because it will not "Take up the spade of the journalist [and intellectual] and go into the field and dig out the root causes of those events and also draw from history" and then "get down to analytical, incisive and objective reporting." Ntenga is right; and this correctness applies as well to Ntenga's own Solid Edifice Theory discussed above. "Once more," another press critic has questioned, "it becomes necessary to question who in Cameroon may be termed a journalist. Is it the young man who can write good sentences in very colourful language or persons trained in activities as well as the ethics of this privileged profession?"[23] Answer with the gender of patriotism and equality.

The Sex of Patriotism and Equality: Gender Politics in Cameroon via the 1997 Legislative and Presidential Elections

Since all the Foumban players were all males, observers now believe and pray that God bless African mothers and sisters who might have given the country something better in the place of chop-broke-potist Paul Biya and his gang of bellyticians. Thus, although a minority of them would clearly not see why and how that should be,[24] the majority of writers have forcefully suggested that women would likely do better where men have woefully failed in Cameroon/Africa and enjoining the latter to cede place to the former – not to completely ignore though Pascal Bruckner's thesis that "it's well known since Nazism that women who possess power don't behave better than men" (cited in Fossungu, 2023: 316). For instance, writing for the Association for the Fight against Violence on Women (ALVF), Chinje (1997) posited that "After [more than] forty years of reign by the men and despite the fact that the women have shown proof of exceptional qualities, no female candidate ran for president [of Cameroon in 1997]." [See also Bernadette Wendi, "Women are Naturally Good Managers" *The Herald* N° 452 (30 April-1 May 1997), 11; Veronica Morfaw, "Men Have Failed in Leadership" *The Herald* N° 441 (4-6 April 1997), 11; & M.L. Lokanga, "Cameroon's Next President: A Dark Horse?" *Le Messager* N° 029 (18 July 1991), 5]

---

[23] Tadoh Ndikum Munji, "Save the Profession from Hijackers" *The Post* (Limbe, 24 October 1997), 4. Instructive also are the following who catalogue instances of sensational and unhelpful journalism: James Fallows, "The Most Famous Journalist in America", in Charles Peters and Nicholas Lemann (eds,), *Inside the System* 4th edition (New York: Holt, Rinehart and Winston, 1979), 246-66; J. Konana, "Journalists Urged to Avoid Journalism of Excess and Innuendoes" *Cameroon Post* N° 0028 (8-14 October 1996), 4; & Jude Waindim, "Laughing at the Press" *Cameroon Post* N° 0274 (11-18 December 1995), 9.

[24] E.g., Napoleon Viban, "The Campaign by Women for Emancipation is Unnecessary" *The Herald* N° 427 (3-4 March 1997), 11; and Takwa Suifon, "The Future of Feminism" *The Herald* N° 508 (10-11 September 1997), 6.

As I must indicate, Cameroon's Advanced Democracy is known to resist such proposals with all its French-backed genocidal might. The brutality on Cameroonians generally and Ambazonians particularly is carried out, according to the terrorist regime, because "for the sense of patriotism of every Cameroonian really interested in the future of *his* country," the ruling party, "[t]he CPDM, therefore, remains an irreplaceable instrument in the medium term for national unity" (Biya, 1986: 43, my emphasis). Two essential theories stand out here, namely, (1) the patriotism/equality of females and (2) the matchlessness of the party in power, thus making the ruling CPDM irreplaceable in 1986, long before the arrival of "paper" multipartism in 1990. Cameroon's system of advanced democracy (if I must keep the word 'democracy' alive) can only be best described as 'inverted democracy.' The inversion reflects easily in those who can have equality or be patriotic in it. Females constitute about 52% of Cameroon's population but Chinje's (1997) report holds that they have been excluded by the same 'pre-multiparty' "discriminatory provisions in the laws of the land" from being patriotically interested in the country's past, present, and future, as can be seen in another good instance of particularly sexing equality at the same time as one is 'advocating' equality. To Biya (1986: 37), "It is necessary to make every Cameroonian feel that he is fundamentally equal to all other Cameroonians." Several researchers have studied the important but not well-articulated role that women have played in the liberation movements in Africa generally, but especially in British Southern Cameroons (now Ambazonia); largely regretting the visible neglect women have had to know in 'post-independence' participation in public life (see Adams, 2006; & Kah, 2011), leading to the further calls from Canada for "Rethinking Equality and Citizenship."[25]

---

[25] Susan Jackel, "Rethinking Equality and Citizenship" in David Schneidermann (ed.), *Conversations Among Friends* << >> *Entre Amies: Proceedings of an Interdisciplinary Conference on Women and Constitutional Reform* (Edmonton: Centre for Constitutional Studies, 1992), 43. Also see A. Nzangou, "Municipal '96: les femmes ne sont pas sorties du ghetto" *Dikalo* N° 196 (29 juin 1998), 9; & Diane Lamoureaux, "Une majorité Encore oubliée", in David Schneidermann (ed.), *Conversations Among Friends* << >> *Entre Amies: Proceedings of an Interdisciplinary Conference on Women and Constitutional Reform* (Edmonton: Centre for Constitutional Studies, 1992), 58.

An interesting report in April 1997 indicated that about 37 women were expected to be in parliament after the May 1997 legislative elections as opposed to the last parliament's 23 females out of the 180 parliamentarians (as per Article 15(1) of 1996 Constitution). For the said May election, the report continued, the ruling CPDM had about 15 substantive and 40 alternate female candidates, the Social Democratic Front (SDF) 15 substantive and 16 alternate candidates, while the National Union for Development and Progress (UNDP) had 8 substantive and 12 alternate candidates. Yet, after that election, the number of women in parliament dropped from the 23 before it to just 10 [See "Female Representation" (*The Herald* N° 446), 3]. Some experts have also reported how Yaou Aissatou, then minister of Women's Affair, lamented that "From the 23 female deputies in the 1992-1997 parliamentary mandate here we are today reduced to only 10 women" (Muabe, 1997). This lack of gender awareness amid the singing of gender equality does not only end in parliament.

But (like the Ambazonian students in Chapter 2) the women and other interest groups have not been sitting back and waiting on the other sex to grant them their equal rights anyway. The ALVF is an association that has, since 1991, embarked on a permanent national sensitization and public education campaign for more effective participation of women in the public and political life of Cameroon. According to N.E. Ndoumbe, ALVF principally targets women, organized women's groups, political parties and the public and private media: with its programme being "to strengthen the capacity of the female Cameroonian citizen to participate effectively as a voter and candidate at the various elections since 1992." [Ngobo Ekotto Ndoumbe, "ALVF and the Cameroonian Woman in the Electoral Process" *The Herald* N° 521 (10-12 October 1997), 7] Another insightful report titled "Cameroon Female Politicians" (*The Herald* N° 624 of 24-25 June 1998, p. 6) tells us that, claiming to be aiming at "a more just, balanced and harmonious society", female ministers and parliamentarians therefore met at the Yaoundé Conference Centre on 20 June 1998 and formed an association called *Le Commité des femmes ministres et parlementaires du Cameroun* (CFEMP). Was that creation to confront the problem?

One cannot exactly tell; but among the assorted reasons advanced for this phenomenon (block to women's political growth in Cameroon), Muabe (1997) has identified "women who were enemies to their fellow women [and] Political parties and men." The fact of well-placed Cameroonian women only paying lip service to female empowerment and of women being the real enemy of women[26] might explain why Mrs. Garga of the Alliance for Democracy and Development (ADD), in making a critical examination of the situation of the woman in Cameroon then, according to Chinje (1997), "even went further to condemn the newly created CAUCUS of women as being a white elephant, empty of substance." Others see illiteracy as also contributing. Thus, a journalist from Conakry in Guinea, who was one of the coordinators of the Forum for African Women Educationalists (FAWE), lamented that two-thirds of Africa's illiterate population are women; and urged men especially "to look at women as unique beings and to give the girl-child the same type of education given to boys."[27]

As far as concerns the role of political parties, there is much that Chinje (1997) decries regarding "the role the woman has played within political parties, serving [only] as dancers and cooks for occasions." This ALVF report took note of the programs envisaged by each of the nine 1997 presidential candidates for the betterment of the Cameroonian woman. It began by lauding all the candidates for admitting that the Cameroonian woman faces peculiar problems that require special attention. But it expressed regrets (1) that none of the

---

[26] See Peterkins Manyong, "Well-Placed Cameroonian Women Only Pay Lip Service to Female Empowerment – Aseh Dorothy, College Proprietress" *The Herald* N° 597 (20-21 April 1998), 14; and Rositta Fualem, "The Real Enemy of the Woman is the Woman" *The Herald* N° 419 (12-13 February 1997), 11.

[27] Peter Ngea Beng, "People Should Look at Women as Unique Human Beings – Madelein Kaba, Guinean Female Activist" *The Herald* N° 631 (10-12 July 1998), 13. Also see Diane Acha Morfaw, "Women are Transformed into Workers Right from Childhood" *The Herald* N° 449 (23-24 April 1997), 11; and Yinusa, Muhammed A., Joseph A. Oluyemi and Raji Abdullateef, "Children, Women, Development and Fundamental Human Rights in Some African Societies", in Munyaradzi Mawere (ed.), *The Political Economy of Poverty, Vulnerability and Disaster Risk Management: Building Bridges of Resilience, Entrepreneurship and Development in Africa's 21ˢᵗ Century* (Bamenda: Langaa RPCIG, 2018), 279-308.

candidates' wives gave them a helping hand in the campaigns; and (2) that none of them put forward any concrete, practical programme even for the growth of the woman, "who all of them used as mere pawns to read out their respective programmes for the woman" (Chinje, 1997). The report gives cases to illuminate this point. For the CPDM, for example, it was Dr Mrs. Dorothy Njeuma (then Vice-Chancellor of the UNIBU) who spoke on behalf of her candidate, claiming that the incumbent has done very much for the promotion of the woman since his accession to power in 1982. To illustrate this, Chinje pursued, Dr Njeuma said President Biya created a ministry to take care of women's issues as far back as 1984 and that for the past 15 years women have held responsible positions in the administration. She also said that there were forty women in the CPDM central committee with four in the political bureau. But either by design or by error, the ALVF report concluded, "Mrs. Njeuma did not say what these figures really represent. I therefore feel that her failure to provide a complete data to back her claims is only meant to mislead people" (Chinje, 1997). Mr. Paul Ndemhiyembe, another CPDM speaker claimed that if re-elected their candidate was going to "improve on the situation of the woman." But the word 'improve,' to Chinje (1997), "can be taken to mean that this candidate is yet to realize that men and women need to participate fully as equal partners in ensuring effective economic growth."

There is another poignant illustration that soundly corroborates the whole rhetoric of equality and of people's rule in Cameroon. As one researcher on the NGOs (non-governmental organizations) in Cameroon also discovered, echoed in every development project is the word *gender*. Given that women make up a substantial proportion of Cameroon's population (as I said earlier over 52%), there is need for gender-balanced development, the study recommended. It is for this reason and others, the research proceeded, that NGOs have cropped up to cater for gender issues in development. Paradoxically, the findings posited, these NGOs that advocate gender-balanced development are gender biased. This is the case of Helvetas and the Women's Information and Co-ordination Office (AWICO) in Bamenda. Though directly involved in gender and development issues, Ms. Jane Frances Mufua concluded in her report, they are neither gender sensitive nor gender aware; for there is only one female worker in Helvetas and no male worker in AWICO which clearly shows that there is an imbalance. [Jane Frances N. Mufua, "Creating Gender Awareness" *The Post* (24

October 1997), 6] This imbalance does heavily exist in the political arena to better facilitate assimilation.

That is why the ALVF writer therefore called on "all Cameroonians and gender-sensitive men as well as women, in particular," "to examine their consciences and vote only the candidate who proved prepared to address their most cherished demands with commitment" (Chinje, 1997). The conclusion of this incisive report is that women feel strongly that the current practices of making them dancers and cooks for parties continue to tarnish their image. The ultimate ambition is to eventually have the woman integrated as an equal partner in development, for persistent inequality between women and men constrains a society's productivity and slows its growth. Women have the competence and should fully participate in the running of "The Republic of Cameroon [that] shall be a decentralized unitary State. It shall be one and indivisible, secular, democratic and dedicated to social service" (1996 Constitution, Article 1(2)).

Let us now find out what the education-domain situation is like in Cameroon. From the Article 1(2) constitutional provision I would naturally expect to see a lot of powers and responsibilities (especially those revolving around cultural issues like education) devolved to the regions or provinces. That is the usual thing to expect, the more so with the firm approval of Mback (2007: 74): "Indeed, like democratization, decentralization is a process involving the sharing of powers; therefore, it involves a civilized management of the sociopolitical contradictions within the state." But that is only dashed hope or unfulfilled expectation because the same 'decentralizing' constitution has exhaustively listed matters reserved for the national/central parliament in Article 26(2) to most significantly include "The system of education"; this provision even being just the re-written version of federal Article 24. According to Article 24 of the Federal Constitution, "The following matters shall be within the sphere of Federal Law, within the framework of the powers specified in Articles 5 and 6:

(1) The fundamental guarantees and obligations of the citizen: protection of the freedom of the individual; public liberties; labour and trade-union legislation; the duties and obligations of the citizen in respect of national defence.

(2) The law of persons and property; nationality and personal status; the law of personal property and real property; the law of civil and commercial obligations.

(3) Political, administrative and judicial organisation with respect to: the electoral system of the Federal Assembly; the general rules relating to the organisation of national defence; the definitions of crimes and offences and the establishment of penalties of any kind, criminal procedure, means of enforcement, amnesty, and the creation of new orders of jurisdiction.

(4) The following questions of finance and property: the currency issue system; the Federal Budget; the institution, assessment and rates of federal taxes and dues of any kind; legislation relating to State lands.

(5) The aims of economic and social action within the framework of the laws relating to economic and social policy.

(6) The Educational system.

To reiterate the point, the system of education apart, most of the matters captured by Article 26(2) are obviously not to be central government matters. A quick visit to Canada, Belgium and Switzerland would furnish confirmation that the federal or national parliament is usually clothed only with residual legislative domain or "*le pouvoir législative résiduaire*" (Bissonnette, 1963: xiii). What is even more interesting, and which must be highlighted for the plain case of assimilation is the fact that nowhere in that federal document is there any convincing talk of state domains, a position that stands unaltered till date. From the 1996 Constitution's Article-26 list (a mere rewritten version of the Federal Constitution's Article 24), it is doubtful that there is anything at all left for the regional authorities. The 1996 list of the domains of the national parliament is all-embracing and very catastrophic for any effective decentralization and local government – the viable vehicles for multiculturalism. Mback (2007: 64-66) has already extensively exposed 'The Ambiguities of the Constitutional Principles of Free Administration of Local Government', with Fossungu (2019: 129-35) also divulging the 'Illegality of the Suspension and Termination of the Regional and Local Authorities'.

111

Now, not to just leave the Foumban matter hanging confusingly in the air like the 'intellectuals in politics' in Cameroon, the Foumban Constitution which is based on lies to the populace put all or most of the matters of grave concern to Ambazonians at the altar of the 'Federal' Authorities. Articles 5 and 6 of the Foumban document (that is being acclaimed for having shared power) simply made all matters relating to justice administration, education and other unique cultural aspects exclusive federal matters. This, to say the least, is like taking all such matters from Quebec's jurisdiction and burying them deep down into Ottawa's graveyard and yet be claiming fuller freedom, self-government and the like for Quebec. For a graphic illustration, the Foumban document in Article 5 lengthily enumerated the powers of the "Federal Authorities" to "embrace the following matters":

Nationality; the status of aliens; regulations concerning conflicts of laws; national defence; foreign affairs; the internal and external security of the Federal State, emigration and immigration; development planning, guidance of the economy, statistics, the control and organisation of credit, external economic relations (including trade agreements); the monetary system, the preparation of the Federal Budget and the establishment of taxes and revenue of all kinds to meet federal expenditure; higher education and scientific research; information services and radio; foreign technical and financial assistance; postal services and telecommunications; aviation and meteorology, mining and geological research and the geographical cover of the national territory; regulation governing the Federal Civil Service and the Judiciary; the organisation and functioning of the Federal Court of Justice; the territorial boundaries of the Federated States; [and] organisation of services pertaining to these matters.

Quite a list that must obviously leave anyone with the slightest amount of education (intellectual in political science or not) wondering about much. "Indeed, by claiming for itself nearly all the most important functions of state business, the federal government ensured the redundancy of the governments of the federated states and denied them any *raison d'être*, except a political one" (Konings, 1999: 298). Most of these matters are clearly not to be in the federal domain especially for a multicultural state. Tremblay (1967) has ably managed the position in Canada, while that of Belgium has been handled by Shapiro (1995: 57 & 60) and Dumont *et al* (2008: 38-49). Legal education, according to Professor Allott, refers to the experiences and training that help different kinds of people to understand and use the law in society (Ojwang and Salter, 1989: 78). This means that one does not necessarily need to be a *lawyer* or *law* student to interest oneself with the law and especially with the Constitution and its issues (Gold, 1985: 496-98). As intellectuals (lawyers and jurists or not) we simply cannot escape from the issues, if we must retain those descriptions given us since, by definition, "the task of any intellectual inquiry is to raise people (the oppressed) to a level of 'true consciousness' because only when they truly appreciate how oppressed they are, can they act to transform the world."[28] The Ambazonia Governing Council (AGovC) Team, don't the experts hear you well? The contrary is what largely holds true for Cameroon with the rampant confusioncracy, thus making it almost impossible for the oppressed to 'act to transform the world' since they cannot 'truly appreciate how oppressed they are'. They thus continue to scramble for bread and sardine from their oppressors till date.

The German Basic Law in its most current form in Chapter VII (Federal Legislation – Articles 70-82) and Chapter II (The Federation and the Länder – Articles 20-37) more clearly divides domains and responsibilities between the two levels before calling on the two to co-operate in certain matters in Chapter VIIIa (Joint Responsibilities – Articles 91a & 91b). Schneider has examined "The Logic of the Constitutional Distribution of Powers and Responsibilities" (2008: 136-38) as well as "Cooperation between the Governments (2008: 142-44) of this German system. These are some models for Africans to examine

---

[28] Egon C. Guba, "The Alternative Paradigm Dialog", in E.C. Guba (ed.), *The Paradigm Dialog* (Sage Publications, 1990), 17-27 at 24; also see Richard L. Abel, "From the Editor" *African Law Studies* N° 14 (1977), 1.

and emulate. But will they want to do so? Jamais! Therefrom War becomes the only option for redress.

So, whatever you think about this war, we must conclude that the trial-and-error from 1961, where we thought they were our brothers, we should trust them and give them a blank cheque, and they would be nice. We watched them dismantled our institutions, we said nothing. They crumbled Cameroon Bank, looted 75 or 78 billion Amba, we said nothing. They used our money to build an oil refinery, carried all their people and put in there, it pays its taxes into Douala, we said nothing. We had our own Powercam, the Menchum Falls with 12,000-megawatt production against three LRC grids of 780-megawatt. They neglected our own for theirs. We have our Ndop rice fields that could be expanded and developed to feed our people. No. They abandoned it to allow you to import rice from China, from Thailand through their ports at exorbitant prices. That is your fate, that is the warning Endeley gave us. We cannot say we didn't know. I am re-echoing that message of Endeley today. However you dream about LRC, it should be a neighbour as far as possible. Whatever you think about this war, it should be victory at all costs. Our survival as a people depends on the outcome of this war. It would take just 100,000 Ambazonians in the Diaspora to give us enough money to handle two states in a sustainable defensive and even offensive posture. This is not rocketing science. This is arithmetic. I invite each one of you, if you have not paid your tax and you are in the Diaspora, go on http://www.atla.africa (Ayaba, Ngoketunjia: September 2023).

As if the Cameroonian Article-5 list was not already devastating enough to the Foumban Intellectuals, the next provision (Article 6) came in with these further centralizing and damaging anti-federalism powers:

114

The powers of the Federal Authorities shall also embrace the following: Public liberties; the law of persons and of property; the law of obligations and contracts in civil and commercial matters; judicial organization, including the rules of procedure and jurisdiction of all courts (with the exception of Customary Courts of West Cameroon, save as regards appeals from the decisions of such Courts); criminal law; transport of federal importance (roads, railways, rivers, maritime and air transport) and ports; prison administration; legislation relating to State lands; labour legislation; public health; secondary and technical education; administrative organization; weights and measures.

What then was not a "federal" matter to those Intellectuals in Politics (that was to be reserved for the Federated States)? In other words, what would be the Article-38 "Matters other than those specified in Articles 5 and 6 and other than those which under the present Constitution are to be the subject of a federal law [that] shall lie exclusively within the competence of the Federated States"? Perhaps the intellectuals of Ambazonia pinned all their hopes on a certain hoodwinking portion of Article 6? Said portion (with my emphasis) stipulates that "So far as concerns the matters enumerated in this article the authorities of the Federated States may continue to enact laws and to direct the corresponding administrative services *until such time as the Federal National Assembly or the President of the Federal Republic, as the case may be, shall decide to exercise the powers vested in them respectively."*

This Article-6 provision is described as deluding because it does not at all meet the requirements of federalism despite Professor Bernard Nsokika Fonlon's confusioncratic justification that it is not unique to Cameroon federalism (see Fossungu, 2019: 124). It was not even long before the said "federal authorities" began 'federalizing' most of those matters in 1962-1963. By 1964, according to Benjamin (1972: 13), only penitentiary services remained; being solely because of a clash of jurisdiction over it between two federal ministries. As early as 1963, he concludes, there were even open attempts to abolish altogether the so-called federal form. The only problem that even delayed the issue until

115

1972 was that of what to do with the numerous secretaries (appellation for non-federal ministers[29]) of LRC. Could this be taken as the origin of the inflation of ministerial portfolios that is characteristic of this country? And where are the towering IQs that understand the world with unusual perspicacity? It is not clear how the Cameroon people can be taught the rules of democracy and of federalism (as requested by Biya, 1986: 127) by those whose knowledge of what is to be imparted and learnt cannot be distinguished from that of the students meant to be instructed. Thank you, Simon Nkwenti, Executive Secretary of the Cameroon Anglophone Teachers' Union (CATU), for the information.

This has truly not failed, of course, to leave the road wide open for the second classing of some citizens and the like of gross human rights violations in Cameroon without the court being able to say anything. "No one coming from a system in which parliamentary sovereignty has stultified creative legal thinking", Ackerman has declared, "can fail to be moved intellectually and otherwise by the unfolding history of the American Constitution." [L.W.H. Ackerman, "Constitutional Protection of Human Rights: Judicial Review" 21(1) *Columbia Human Rights Law Review* (1989), 59 at 70] The said constitution, no doubt, has been able to be what it has been, is, and will be, doing so solely because the judges have made it so. These American judicial officials, I think, could not have done so if they were not independent and influential. They could not have been that independent without public support. Public support can hardly be forthcoming if the citizenry is not politically aware and active. In view of this fact, Frye (1986: 21) therefore thinks that teaching the humanities is a militant activity: it has constantly to fight for the freedom that the critical faculty represents against passivity and uncritical acceptance. Explaining why the constant lecture to Ambazonians is,

---

[29] By Article 39 of the Federal Constitution (which is now the equivalent of Article 58 of the 1996 Constitution), "The President of the Federal Republic shall appoint the Prime Minister of each Federated State, who must be confirmed in office by simple majority vote of the Legislative Assembly of the State concerned. The President shall appoint the Secretaries of State [who are] members of the [Federated State] Government on the proposal of the Prime Minister confirmed in office. He [the President] may relieve them of office under the same condition." Is there any sense in talking of two levels of government here?

We cannot allow this enemy state to continue to butcher our people. Our soldiers are brave. We are watching them daily, and I know you are praying for them daily. What has held us back is sustainable commitment to the War of Liberation. All the squabbling, political positioning, is irrelevant. All those things will happen in an independent Ambazonia when people have formed their political parties, they want to run to become the mayor of a city like Ndop, they want to become representatives in the state parliament, they want to become representatives in the federal parliament. And they would be arguing who is the better candidate, staking their claim to that position with their policies, with their ideas. At this stage, it is war. The only argument we should be having is the number of rifles that should be in the hands of our soldiers, the number of bullets that they should have, the sophistication of the armament that we give them. We are watching people deploying drones. We should have a drone fleet that can be deployed into Yaoundé. Oh yes. We have a comrade who has committed to that. We must make the investment that is required by a people who are facing a threat like the one we are facing from LRC. So, everything we can do to end LRC's rampage, we should. We should not be limited in the 21st century by the means. We have availed ourselves to different forms of technology on how to defeat enemies. Our forces have been making rocket launchers. They have been producing all forms of IEDs. We should improve on the quality, on the range, on the quantity, and would end this war in the shortest time possible. Because the more we delay in making this commitment, the longer the war, the longer the suffering. Complaining will not change our fate. Hoping that there is a return to negative peace will not change our fate. Hoping that there should be some negotiations with LRC, considering its history of negotiations, would not change our fate. Dreaming about some form of coexistence with LRC is only a nightmare. You will get up to remain a slave in your own Land. French

117

systems don't coexist. They only dominate. That is the history of all Francophone systems. They don't federate; they only have central governments that are designed to rule with impunity and power. French systems don't cohabitate; they dominate (Ayaba, Ngoketunjia: September 2023).

To sustain the charges, I will then solely talk about the domain-listing provisions. Articles 23 and 47 of the Federal Constitution made legislation-making to belong equally to the President of the Federal Republic and the Deputies of the FNA. Replacing the federal, the 1972 (Unitary) Constitution, in "allocating" legislation-making domains, listed the legislature's domains in Article 20 and matters reserved for executive decrees in Article 22. Its Article 21 (being successor to Federal Articles 23 and 47) then said "the National Assembly may empower the President of the Republic to legislate by way of ordinance for a limited period and for given purposes" on the Article-20 matters usually when the National Assembly is not in session. Anyangwe (1987: 207-211) has more extensively discussed these three Unitary Articles (20-22). The 'limited period' and 'for given purposes' authorization had since become the usual method of law-making in Cameroon because National Assembly sessions were shortly thereafter made more infrequent by the POR through one of such Article-21 *laws*.

The same strategy applies to date; hence, the alluded disaster to the 1996 Constitution's local government. The long list of matters reserved to the central "legislature" in Article 26(2) is not all that makes the disaster. It is most especially capped by the fact that the matters (if any at all) that are not enumerated in the Article-26 list become the exclusive prerogative of the POR (1996 Constitution, Article 27), and not of the regional and local authorities. In addition, the POR does also legislate on the Article-26 matters and, when he does so, his legislation on these Article-26 subjects "shall enter into force on the date of their publication" irrespective of whether the National Assembly and Senate have ratified them (1996 Constitution, Article 28(2) & (3)). The 1998 Education Law is an apt example of the president's laws that 'enter into force on the date of their publication' whether ratified by the two chambers of parliament. This knowledge gleaned from the constitutions is very helpful in comprehending the philosophy of the Education Law.

Grasping the Designs of the Education Law

The Education Law is composed of 42 Sections that fall under five parts. Part I gives the General Provisions (Sections 1-10) while Part II deals with the Formation and Implementation of Education Policy and Financing of Education (Sections 11-13). Part III has two chapters (Section 14-31). The first chapter, running through Sections 14-29, governs Organization of the Educational System, while the other chapter, of two brief Sections, talks about Evaluation of the Educational System and Research in Education. Part IV is devoted to the Educational Community and has three Chapters (Sections 32-39). Chapter I (Sections 32-33) defines The Concept of Educational Community; chapter II (Sections 34-36) outlines Students' Rights and Obligations while chapter III (Sections 37-39) enumerates the Rights of Teachers. The final Part concerns Miscellaneous and Final Provisions (Sections 40-42). Being an apt example of the lack of self-control in this country, it is not very surprising then that one finds, for instance, that it is the central state (and not the regions) that will "formulate and implement educational policy with the assistance of regional and local authorities, families as well as public and private institutions" (Education Law, Section 11). I am inclined to think that in a situation of genuine biculturalism and decentralization the arrangement was to be the other way round. That is, the regional governments, including public and private institutions, were to be those to formulate and implement their respective educational policies (within a national constitutional context) with the national or central government instead being the *assistant*. As it was otherwise, one cleanly had to stop talking of decentralization and educational dualism.

As Merle Wallace and Raymon Athamesara have theorized in support, while it is possible to develop multicultural education programs by adding modules about various ethnic and minority groups to existing curricula, or even finding texts that include multiple points of view, "we have found that having communities and schools write their own texts and pull together their own curricula create processes of participation that have far more potential to encourage and help develop the cultural and emotional imaginations of teachers, students

119

and community members." [Merle Wallace and Raynou Athamesara "The Thai Community Curriculum as a Model for Multicultural Education" 5(1) *International Education Journal* (2004), 50 at 51] The untoward absences of processes of participation probably account for Barry Fohtung's explanation that Cameroon school children were being grudgingly taught by teachers whose "visible pain, desperation, estrangement and their hypocrisy reminds a regular churchgoer about Bible stories of the Israelites in the wilderness separating them from the distant and receding Promised Land" (cited in Fossungu, 2019: 80). Partly explaining the desperation of its teachers is the fact that not an iota of these things would happen in Cameroon, with or without the Education Law: since it is even well known from Mback (2007: 74) that the Cameroon "government, hesitant to undertake any true democratization, [would not] subscribe to a significant decentralization." That being the case, what then was the Education Law generally and its Section 11 particularly actually after?

The goal was the subtle destruction of Anglo-Saxon institutions that had that far not been demolished. In this enterprise the power of subvention played a very vital role. The purse-pulling strategy of the ultra-centralized government in Yaoundé was being constantly enhanced; with the G.C.E. Board and the two 'Anglo-Saxon' universities (UNIBU & UNIBA) being obvious targets of the strategy. The falling status of Anglo-Saxon institutions in Cameroon has been largely attributed, inter alia, to drastically reduced (or no) government subvention. As Ndamukong (1996) put it, "[t]he meagre amount of 160 million francs in the first year of the [G.C.E.] Board's creation and 40 million francs in the second year and nothing in the third year is nothing compared to the 3.5 billion francs which were spent on the same [G.C.E.] examinations yearly when they were conducted by the Ministry of Education." As a result of these deep cuts, there were very serious problems, especially with honouring engagements with the teachers who marked the examinations [see Kum Set Ewi, "1998 G.C.E.: Marking Begins as Teachers Receive Half Claims for Last Year" *The Herald* N° 632 (13-14 July 1998), 2]. Researchers like Boyle (1996: 618) found out that the beginning of the same kinds of delays in the payment of salaries for teachers since 1993 "demonstrates the extent to which public and state-supported denominational schools faced a virtually identical set of problems created by the penury of public resources (despite their allocation on paper), and exacerbated by the rapid expansion of the [school] population." The more reason why Ambazonians are fighting to have

An indigenous Ambazonian education system with a curriculum designed to reflect the standard, the opportunities, the weaknesses of our socio-economic and political landscape. And that any school that continues to enable, to give comfort, to perpetuate an illegal education system, we will dig it from the foundation, right from the foundation upside-down. Don't send your children to any school associated with LRC (Ayaba, Lebialem: 29 August 2023).

There was a general and heightened lack of transparency in the way things were done in Cameroon. For instance, just look at the October 2025 presidential election whose official results would not be available even after weeks after voting day (12 October) because the incumbent administration is still arranging the rigging. On education specifically, Azebaze discussed and condemned the education minister's unpublished inter-ministerial orders that imposed school fees in public schools, together with some other illegal provisions that were geared towards benefitting the partisan clan (the National Education minister's *"arrêté interministériel non publié généralisant les frais de scolarité dans les établissement publics"* and several *"des actes illégaux"* *"au service de la clientèle partisane."*) [Alex Gustave Azebaze, "Gestion financière des établissements scolaires publics : Mbella Mbappe dupe parents d'élèves, communes et... le MINFI" *Le Messager* N° 543 (16 septembre 1996) 11]. What else would anyone be expecting from the education minister whose boss, the POR, could simply get out of bed any morning and, for no stated or clear reason, just sign one of those his decrees or laws imposing fees on students at state-run universities? In view of this generalized absence of transparency, it might be hard not to believe the charges against the Yaoundé regime regarding subvention to the G.C.E. Board that is based in Buea, the capital of Ambazonia. All this because of the desire to prevent the rise of Ambazonia, according to

some cheap rats in LRC, money doublers, scavengers, thieves that we worship today, scammers we are hailing them. And then you want to kill General Efang. You killed General Ivo.

You know, you want to butcher the Sagarts, the Vultures, the Capos. You call them 'Amba Boys'. You watch US movies, war movies of their heroes. You see how the Americans romanticize their own fighters, whether they bomb Iraq to the ground or massacre people in Afghanistan. They are coming home to great reception. You are tarnishing the image of your own warriors. You are attacking them for the interest of the occupier. Hahaha. Hahaha. Hahaha. *Eh! On the last day when Amba go came oh, whether you be Chiroma, you must go. On the last day when Amba go came oh, whether you be enabler, you must bow.* They would bow to the indomitable, unquenchable, no blinking generation. Yes. Shoot the hell you want. Do what you want, you will leave our country. We would make Ndian an Eldorado and its finest son, DDC Horace, and his people would define the laws that govern Ndian. And would be able to use its resources for the interest of its people, for humanity. Not loot, store in private bank accounts and reciprocate with torture, torment, environmental degradation, and abuse. The people of Ndian would be able to have flyovers, why not heliports, airports, where they hop from one place to another like taxis. Yes. Because they are rich, they can afford it. But to get there, pay your Liberation Tax and we would show the enemy the exit door. We would show the enemy the exit door. You can trust every word I utter. Because if experience is anything to go by, we have done better (Ayaba, Ndian: 27 August 2023).

But the same transparency logic must keep one on guard. In other words, I am saying that you should embrace some of the charges from Buea against Yaoundé with some scepticism. For instance, there is the somewhat contrary account of a former Chairman of the G.C.E. Board. Sylvester Dioh indicated that the G.C.E. Board management in Buea should not be shifting the blame to the wrong quarters but rather "Accept full responsibility for the fate that has befallen you and your Board." According to Dioh, this Board was failing because the Chief Executive of the Board had personified everything (in the same way as the POR), turning the Board into his private property, and by-passing

122

its regulations, etc. Dioh documented his claims so well with rules and regulations and instances of this and that: it is simply hard not to believe him. Above all, he pointed out how the Board's personified executive had been feeding the gullible private press with wrong information about the true state of affairs because the MINEDUC had been sending in the subvention money as usual: until the MINEDUC discovered what had actually been happening to the money. [Sylvester N. Dioh, "G.C.E. Board: Anglophones are not Responsible for the Mess, But the Management" *The Herald* N° 471 (13-15 June 1997), 4] But could it just have been the allocation of subvention money on paper only, as earlier seen?

Whatever the actual position of subvention could be, it is certain that one will remain in the dark if the centralized and personified system persists. Beware then of Issa Tchiroma's Federalism Bait, Langa-Throat Ambazonians, says Asu Lucas; because Francophones and the French NEVER federate, they only assimilate, says Dr Lucas Cho Ayaba. Ambazonia is blessed with these Lucases who are real Hisofeans! Meanwhile LRC is cursed with Pauls (Biya, Atanga Nji, Tasong, the other one calling himself mayor of Abakwa, etc). The persistence of the system easily finds a comfortable haven in the politics of the purse or what some experts would want to describe as 'The [Assimilationist] Economics of Education'. [See Tafah Edokat, J.U. Umo and R.E. Ubogu, "The Economics of Education: Evaluation of the Determinants of Primary School Performance in Cameroon" 2(2) *Zimbabwe Journal of Educational Research* (1990), 93-110] This purse-politics was overwhelmingly decisive in the assimilation strategy of the Education Law under review. The politics of this law was aimed at largely and doubly confusing to easily reign and assimilate unchallenged. For instance, it purports to be "lay[ing] down the general legal framework of education in Cameroon" in Section 1(1), but curiously (at the same time) does not apply to university education; only "apply[ing] to nursery, primary, secondary grammar and technical education, as well as to teacher-training" in Section 1(2). (The French text seems to exclude the points following when it states: *Elle s'applique aux enseignements maternel, primaire, secondaire général et technique, ainsi qu'à l'enseignement normal.* Does "*enseignement normal*" mean 'university education'? Or are universities sufficiently covered by 'technical education' and 'teacher training'?) So, where does one stand at this point as far as university education was concerned? No one could correctly divine that until some 13 kilo-Sections away, a distance after which most scrutinizers' enthusiasm and critical eyes would have waned or tired out. At that time and point, Section 14 then makes clear that "The organisation and control of education at all levels shall be the bounden duty of the [central] state." Is the limitation in Section 1(2) then necessary?

The answer principally depends on what 'necessary' is taken to mean to the 'intention'; but, according to the law that this much faraway now applies to all levels of education (including university), while the responsibilities of the regional and local authorities in the implementation and financing of the education policy shall be defined by a separate law from the POR (Section 13), the financing of education shall be by: budgetary allocations from the state; contributions from education partners; budgetary appropriations from regional and local authorities; donations and legacies; all other contributions provided for by the [POR's] law (Section 12). What then has indeed been decentralized in Cameroon since 1996 (or 1961)? To cloth the assimilation points being made, the entire Section 11 ought to be scrutinized. "To that end" (of the regions *assisting* the central state rather than the other way round), it pursues, the Cameroon State shall:

- set the objectives and general guidelines for national teaching and training syllabuses in conjunction with all the sectors of national life in order to make education more professional;
- ensure the constant adaptation of the educational system to national economic and socio-cultural realities, and also to the international environment, especially through the promotion of bilingualism and the teaching of national languages;
- lay down the conditions for the creation, opening and running of government and private educational establishments and control them;
- define standards for the construction and equipment of public and private educational establishments and control them; [and]
- draw and update the school location map.
  (2) The state shall realise the above objectives with the assistance of an advisory body, the National Education Board whose organisation, duties and functioning shall be laid down by decree of the President of the Republic.

There is much that can be said about this entire Section 11. For example, it is not clear whether the authorities in Cameroon do in fact comprehend what "Guidelines" (in the title of the law) would signify. That meaning-confusion alone can furnish enough material for a book of its own from linguistic experts. I am not venturing there though. To buttress the doubt being cast on Cameroon's educational dualism, I will here simply comment on Section 11(2). This important comment turns on (1) the question of whether Cameroonians really needed a National Education Board (NEB) and (2) the consequences on then existing G.C.E. Board.

The National Education Board and/or the PROBAC Board: The Ministerial Duplication Story Evidencing Education as Top Priority?

My reasoning was that Cameroon did not need a NEB which was obviously superfluous: assuming that this country was then factually and legally bicultural. If multiculturalism or cultural dualism was the rule in Cameroon, as the authorities claimed, then this is the suggestion of what I told them they could have done, since they seemed to be so urgently in need of something to create. They should rather have decreed only a *Probatoire/Baccalauréat* (PROBAC) Board to cater for Cameroon's "French-speaking sub-system" of education because there was already a G.C.E. Board that handled the country's "English-speaking sub-system". This suggestion or interpretation of mine was quite sane, being crushingly supported by several factors. But before then, hear the result of the neglect of sane counsel.

An adviser of mine called me today and said, CIC, you are a Man-Boy, eh. And I was laughing. And he said he has dedicated his life for Ambazonia; and he said to me that he is a self-styled Tax Collector, going around and making sure that everyone pays their Liberation Tax. [30] Then he said

---

[30] "ADF Logistics Chief, Pascal Kiki, and ADF Mama Wally (OGC – Overall Ground Coordinator) have explained and emphasized the issue and

something which was very fantastic. That he doesn't know what else would be without Ambazonia. It would be a misery. For him, Ambazonia is his hope. What other cause would be right? To go to work and come back? Is that exactly the essence of your existence? So, every day wherever you are, whatever you are doing, remind yourself of the thousands of our people who are dying because of Ambazonia. Remind yourself of those who are in jail, living in squalor, because of our Homeland. And remind yourself of where you live, especially those in exile, and how men and women battled it out to make sure that they established a place within which you can live in peace and pursue your dreams (Ayaba, Manyu: 14 September 2024).

To begin with, I must indicate that I have had to simply talk of the Ministry of Education (MINEDUC) in this book in order not to further complicate a lengthily incomprehensible duplication matter. There was in fact no ministry of education in Cameroon then, but about seven ministries that dealt with education: ministry of basic education, ministry of primary education, ministry of secondary education, ministry of higher education, ministry of scientific research and innovation, ministry of sports and physical education, and ministry of employment and professional and technical training. Puzzled foreign-resident experts have even recommended that "The post of ministers in charge of [unknown] *special duties* should be scrapped. What makes the situation very alarming is the fact that most of the citizens whose tax money is used in paying these people do not know *what these special duties are*. Is it going out for CPDM campaigns? Does it entail transferring public revenue from Cameroon to private accounts in the Swiss Banks?" [Lord W. Degaulle, "Retrench Ministers to Fight Economic Crisis" *The Herald* N° 356 (13-15 September 1996), 4 (emphasis added)]

---

how to pay at http//www.atla.africa more than enough for anyone to still be claiming ignorance about it now. Spokesman Lucas Asu (whose official contact points are public information) is also always available to guide anyone not able to use the online portal, especially on GZ and other such places, on how to pay their Liberation Tax. It is currently the authentic passport/ID card for Ambazonians. HAVE YOU PAID?" (Fossungu, 2024: 151)

Lord Degaulle's theory does many things. First, it explains what is behind the burgeoning and astronomical number of ministers and rank-of-minister portfolios in this small triangular West-Central African country. Despite the suggestions for reduction, they would rather be creating more ministries and more posts in them [see Fidèle Muabe, "Biya Restructures Government to Compensate CPDM Hawks, Contrary to Advice" *The Herald* N° 545 (9-11 December 1997), 8; Denis Nkwebo, "Le Sud, L'Est et Centre: l'argument tribal faussera le partage" *Le Quotidien* (27 octobre 1997), 3; & *Decret N° 98/043 du 13 mars 1998 portant nomination des secrétaires généraux de certains ministères*]. This finds roots in the federal arrangements as seen above. As I would keep saying, the Foumban Constitution is so confusing that many experts, even well-groomed ones, do easily fall prey to its traps; believing, for instance, that there were functionally three legislatures in the FRC. [See Barry B. Fohtung, "Parliamentary History in Cameroon 3: The One-Party State" *The Herald* N° 446 (16-17 April 1997), 6] That is, of course, the impression given but there are some doubts since it is highly disbelieving why and how Cameroun or LRC could have had twice as many deputies than the entire Federation which had only 50. Was the constitution being respected? As I continue to say throughout, most of these issues continue to largely baffle most black-letter lawyers and academics who cling on to a single constitutional provision, without considering the entire document as a package. By Article 40 of the Foumban Constitution, "The number of representatives in the Legislative Assembly of East Cameroon [LRC] shall be one hundred; in the Legislative Assembly of West Cameroon [Ambazonia], thirty-seven." By the same constitution's principle of representation, as already seen, we have 1 deputy to 80,000 inhabitants (Article 16); and its population ratio tells us that there were 800,000 West Cameroonians and 3,200,000 East Cameroonians (Article 60). The important question to answer now is: How was the Federal Article 16 principle respected, to be able to also have 37 deputies for the West Cameroon House? Is this another version of 'two cubes of sugar in Cameroon growing into thirteen cubes of sugar in Ambazonia' (Fossungu, 2025: chapter 2)? The query for the FRC is more especially significant because Enonchong (1967: 164 *et seq*) has very elaborately indicated how 'Federal Law [epitomized by the Federal Constitution] Governs Federated State Institutions'. Is this the normal arrangement in a true federation? If so, then why do the experts like Hogg (1996: chapter 5) bother about discussing the essential requirement of "coordination" of both levels?

Second, Lord Degaulle's theory tells us that citizens and businesses pay too many taxes but do not get services in return. Confusion is very unhealthy for progress of any kind, except progress in regression; and businesses love certainty and time well used. In addition to the mosaic confusion in this country that is very time consuming,[31] there is also an avalanche of excessive taxes that come down hard on businesses (*"une quarantaine d'impôts frappent les enterprises"*[32]) in Cameroon. As there are no roads and other necessary infrastructures to propel economic development, what are all these taxes even used for, except for the unknown missions of the POR's personal appointees? The nature of the role of these appointed chiefs in Cameroon has left people wondering about much. In fact, as earlier said, foreigners residing in the country have been particularly appalled not only by the arbitrary nature of regulating their stay;[33] but also, by the dubiety of missions and the ever-growing ministerial portfolios whose competence the taxpayers hardly even know. Corruption has eaten so much into the Cameroonian fabric that citizens are even wondering why they should still be paying taxes which would only end up in individual overseas bank accounts especially. Rogers Orock and Oben Mbuagbo are two university lecturers in Cameroon who have thus explored how Cameroonians view the payment of taxes to the state in the backdrop of the pervasive corruption and the dismal levels of social service provision characterising public governance in the country since the early 1990s;

---

[31] That is quite right since researchers have discovered that Cameroon's legal arsenal is a mosaic confusion which no doubt "leaves the foreign investor who is coming to Cameroon for the first time wanting and confused since he cannot lay hands on this legislation within a reasonable time. Also, administrative bottlenecks and the constant referring to other legislative texts which might not be easily handy, makes the entire process cumbersome and time consuming." Isaac Fru Zama, "Legal Guarantee of Environmental Protection within the Industrial Free Trade Zone in Cameroon" 9 *Juridis Info (Revue de Legislation et de Jurisprudence Camerounaises)* (1992), 43–45 at 43.

[32] Laurent Marcaillou, "Patrice Mandeng Ambassa, ministre camerounais du Développement industriel, « Le Cameroun aidera l'Afrique du Sud – Confidences: propos recueillis par Laurent Marcaillou »" *Jeune Afrique* (18-24 mars 1993), 33; also see Tixier (1974: 44-45, 50-53, & 59-61).

[33] See *Loi N° 97/012 du 10 janvier 1997 fixant les conditions d'entrée, de séjour et de sortie des étrangers au Cameroun.*

coming to the conclusion that such negative perceptions about taxation illustrate the challenges confronting African states if they seek to expand their capacity for domestic resource mobilisation through taxation (Fossungu, 2019: 87-88). Ambazonians, on the other hand, are willingly paying the Liberation Tax because the AGovC matches it with management, accountability, and reciprocity (see Fossungu, 2025: 41-44).

Perhaps the unnecessary multiplicity or duplication of education ministries also could have been the government's unique way of selling the idea that it was making education "a top priority of the Cameroon State" as per Section 2(1) of the Education Law. Is this a sellable idea? Not sure it is. Whatever the case, I think

> The importance of this lockdown to the foundation of our economic development, was the foundation of our value system. Whether tomorrow we would exercise tolerance and compromise, would be informed by the foundation of our education. Whether tomorrow we would learn to live together, work together, fight together, together be free, and go to jail together, would be informed by the foundation of our education. So, we cannot accept that, all through our existence, we were told a lie about our own history. We were told a lie about our own potentials. And that we were forced at gunpoint to see our relevance in the image of our oppressor. And that, for us, being Cho wasn't good enough. Being Mbakwa wasn't good enough. And that we had to change our identity to fit in (Ayaba, Manyu: 14 September 2024). [See also Peter Ateh-Afac Fossungu, "From Peter to Pierre: Même Chose?" *The Herald* N° 547 (15-16 December 1997), 4]

I do not think that the 'top priority' claim could easily sell. Education could simply not be a top priority of the Cameroon State when, according to data published in *Cameroon Tribune* of 13 March 1991 and cited by Boyle (1996: 610 n.3), up to 40% of Cameroonians over the age of 11 were illiterate; the situation being aggravated by what Boyle (1996: 616 n33) castigates as a significant drop in funds allocated to education by the centralized administration from earlier levels of 20-

30% to just 12% in the 1986-90 period. Ambazonia is treating it differently because

We have also issued an executive order on the issue of education, and I have spoken about this several times. Independence means independence. And that means the foundational pillars of our society need to be structured in a way that reflects the notion of independence. Whether it is the army, the education system, the legal system that is being gradually developed through public acts, different codes, and practices. These would become the foundation of the Ambazonian legal system. The processes that we engage in developing these acts and codes and practices would also be very useful in developing a due process approach in the way that we deal with issues of conflict in the Ambazonian society. The foundation of the occupation of our country, apart from the military takeover, was the curriculum of education imposed on us. And we all know today that the foundation of this phase of our resistance in the past 7 years has been because teachers rose up and said this foundation is inconsistent with our way of life and needed changing (Ayaba, Ngoketunjia: September 2023).

Education could indeed not therefore be a top priority of the Cameroon State when it is also well known from Johnson-Hanks (2006: 125) that "Not only the economy, but also Cameroon's instructional system is in [serious] crisis." Ambzonia explains it better. 'I know people are always worried because we have been so dependent on LRC, we have been so dependent on the international system, because the way we were designed, the way we were taught is that you need to get a certificate so that you can use it somewhere. That is the way we have been designed. But I can assure you that sometimes the certificates you acquire without any experience will take you nowhere. Certifications are simply attestation of enrolment and outcomes. What we are putting in place are packages, certifications and skills. There are many Ambazonians who live out here, men and women. They cannot change the tyre of their cars. They don't understand anything basic about the cars they drive. There are so many things we came out here and we didn't know how to do. You have a problem with your window. You have basically no carpentry skills. Nothing. We have no skills. We look like buffoons. And we must understand the relevance of skills in our survival. All these certificates you have acquired through the LRC education system is/are zero. I can assure you that it is zero' (Ayaba, Ngoketunjia: September 2023).

Education basically could not have been the Cameroon state's main goal when there was the well-known distressing story of some teachers from "the dubious 'Ecoles Normales'" (as Fohtung, 1996: 8, put it) who always abandoned school children for weeks and months in order to make the usual 'pilgrimage' to the 'supermarket ministry of finance' in Yaoundé in view of "bribing and 'screwing' their way to integration in Yaoundé's civil service or towards their meagre salaries." Talking of dubious 'Ecoles Normales' and student-abandonment let's hear a tydoning (tying down) case from a first hander. Most of you from the West following this eye-opening or HISOFE lecture would discover some "innovations" of Cameroonians to beat the worrisome socio-economic-educational bog. When graduating student Mpako talked to me in 1998 of a colourful graduation and other aspects of the UNIBU, he stated just a minute portion of the entire Cameroonian Quagmaticking Show, directly consequent on *The Grand Master Plan of Assimilation.*

Stephen Fomeche of the Quaqmaticking School has neatened and authenticated it with a lot of survival strategies employed even by the citizens already working (civil servants, including teachers from the dubious ENS) to attempt 'beating Cameroon is Cameroon' – thus confirming its everlasting place as an 'undeveloping' "developing nation" – as you also peruse his 1999 letter to "Dear Power". Opening with "Happy New Year!", Fomeche went on to give "Many thanks for the beautiful card to us and the kind wishes contained therein. Hope you are fine and studies on progress. We are fine for now and life is just bearable." He then plunged into the matter, beginning in paragraph 3, with:

> I thought of several possibilities when I got this opening to come to E.N.S. Yaoundé. Many colleagues who come in as civil servants usually disappear between the ministry and school to pursue their interest. Some use it for private business; meanwhile others go out for further studies. The advantage here is that while in school, you earn salary and secondly you

are not under any authority of your ministry. In this way you undertake whatsoever interest of yours without fear of query from a boss. Since all the possibilities to go out of the country did not work out well, I am open only to business. For now, I am poised to embark on some little things, no matter how mean. Primarily, I thought of running a taxi of my own, myself as the driver, but the initial amount needed for the purpose gets more than a third of the previewed cost. If God permits, I will become a broker for state contracts. I have already got the headway. I just need some money to start.

We were at Schola's graduation. It was the first time I was attending an occasion of the Buea University. The crowd I saw was the first of its kind – colourful, thick, joyous and promising. It helped me, Power, to forget about my struggles, failures and disappointments of life. So many young promising Cameroonians who may have had the sky as their limits are compelled to soar and join the market of jobseekers. We are indeed in Cameroon. That notwithstanding, our occasion was good. We feasted with your kinsmen from Douala and Muyuka.

I will write a more detailed letter next time. I just hope I will get you on the line when next I call. Accept the love and wishes of Jacinta, Yeye and Zisuh. Bye! It's Fomeche Stephen Z. signed [cited in Peter Ateh-Afac Fossungu, *The Expibasketics and Intrigues of Love* (Bamenda: Langaa RPCIG, 2016) at 73-74].

The sure handiwork of the unbending drive to assimilate, isn't it? Ex hypothesi, there is no other convincing reason, absent forceful assimilation, why this administration was willing to create those many ministries to cater for education but would not entertain the idea of having two (through then forming only the PROBAC) boards to, respectively, handle the country's two educational sub-systems under the auspices of an Education Ministry. Or why not even create two ministries such as (a) Ministry of Anglophone Education and (b) Ministry of Francophone Education? That would appear to be the logical thing to do since creating ministries would seem to have been easier than creating examinations boards in Cameroon. Two education ministerial departments like these would still have been in order, if educational dualism was in fact the rule.

Furthermore, the education law itself (if it is not confusion of assimilation but anything to seriously go by) talked of Cameroon's educational system as being "organised into two sub-systems: the English-speaking sub-system and the French-speaking sub-system, thereby reaffirming our national option for biculturalism" (Section 15(1)). In addition, it further stressed in Section 15(2) that "The above-mentioned educational sub-systems shall co-exist, each preserving its specific method of evaluation and award of certificates." That being the case indeed, then the third point follows, namely, that creating a NEB then was not only needlessly duplicating the MINEDUC but, above all else, was very loudly denying the avowed biculturalism by re-assimilating the G.C.E. Board that had not been easy in bringing into existence in the first place.

Cementing Assimilation with PROBAC/GCE Differentiation: The Obliteration of the G.C.E. Board?

The answer is YES. The creation of the G.C.E. Board to manage the English-speaking "sub-system" of education, according to Abanda (1996), was itself the result of the determination of various groups which galvanized and channelled public opinion to "resist cultural assimilation." At the launching of a book on the G.C.E. Board (*The Cameroon GCE Crisis: Test of Anglophone Solidarity*), Archbishop Verdzekov of Bamenda is reported by Abanda to have decried "An unwritten policy of absorption and assimilation" existing in Cameroon where "one could have to be Frenchified in order to be accepted." Hence, resisting Frenchification quickly turned Ambazonians into *les enemies dans la maison* called Cameroon. Referring to the leakage in the 1996 G.C.E., Abanda reports, the archbishop declared that "Recent events seem to indicate that the forces of evil and of darkness have not been disarmed. They are deploying their lethal arms to destroy the credibility which the G.C.E. Board has established through great sacrifice" (Abanda, 1996). Similarly, Julius Afoni reports that Reverend Dr. Betene (the National Catholic Education Secretary) also talked of there being "a massive attempt this year [1996] ... to make the good work of the G.C.E. Board fail." [Julius Afoni, "Forces of Darkness Blamed for G.C.E. Board Crisis" *Cameroon Post* N° 0028 (8-14 October

1996), 3] Both clergymen were accurate in their predictions/suspicions because two years later the 1998 Education Law was there to spell the end of the G.C.E. system, not just its failure. Necessitating the war of survival, therefore.

> Alright, so, the lockdown has been very important. Apart from the issue of school, it has been very important. It has come to remind every one of us that there are more than 4,000 of our people locked in jail because of Ambazonia, because of us. It also reminded us that there are more than 20,000 of our people in the grave because of an ideal for freedom. And we should never forget, we should never forget that Mamie Appih never really, really had a chance to be given a befitting burial. She was burnt in her sleep in her home. We must be reminded that Baby Martha never lived to ever get to walk to the altar and say I do. She never lived to bear her own child. We should be reminded of how Sam Sawyer died. We should be reminded of the thousands of our forces who lost their lives. And I don't know what you think. But, for me, every day is Amba until death or freedom. Every day is Amba. I cannot, I cannot betray those who have died. I cannot betray the sacrifices of those whose liberty has been taken away from them. I cannot betray the thousands of our people who lost their homes because we told them this ideal of freedom was sacrosanct. I cannot sit back and pursue my own path, forgetting the millions who don't have a chance. It would be a travesty; it would be an affront to my generation and the generations behind it if one day I even think, even in my sleep, to spare one second without thinking about the freedom of Ambazonia. It is Ambazonia or death (Ayaba, Manyu: 14 September 2024).

Quite apart from the negative official attitude toward the G.C.E. and its Board that has already been largely catalogued in the literature already cited in this book, the fact that assimilation was its real goal is very evident even in two Sections of Part III of the Education Law that deal with the organization and evaluation of each 'sub-system'. According to Section 16 that purportedly organizes the English-speaking 'sub-system',

(1) The English-speaking sub-system shall be organised into cycles and fields of study as follows: nursery education with a duration of two years; primary education with a duration of six years; secondary education with a duration of seven years; post-primary education with a duration of two years; teacher training with a duration of two or three years.

(2) Secondary education shall comprise: a first cycle of five years having an observation sub-cycle of two years with a common-core syllabus and an orientation sub-cycle of three years of general or technical education; a second cycle of two years of general or technical education.

(3) In addition to general education, practical training shall be provided to students in vocational colleges and high schools, on the basis of the courses they choose.

By Section 17 that is meant to deal with the French-speaking 'sub-system',

(1) The French-speaking sub-system shall be organised into cycles and fields of study as follows: nursery education with a duration of two years; primary education with duration of six years; secondary education with a duration of seven years; post-primary education with a duration of two years; teacher training with a duration of two or three years.

(2) Secondary education shall comprise: a first cycle of five years having an observation sub-cycle of two years with a common-core syllabus and an orientation sub-cycle of three years of general or technical education; a second cycle of two years of general or technical education.

(3) In addition to general education, practical training shall be provided to students in vocational colleges and high schools, on the basis of the courses they choose.

Tell me frankly here what the difference is to the government's 1983 order modifying the G.C.E. examination (see Konings and Nyamnjoh, 1997: 213) that I have discussed above. Only in their degree of force, this 1998 one being a law while the other in 1983 was just an order. From a simple reading and re-reading of the two sections of the

135

law here, the only difference between these two different 'sub-systems' would be just the two hyphenated terms "English-speaking" and "French-speaking". There is already a detailed review by Anyangwe (1989: 198-200) of some of the differences in cycles and other disparities (before this law) that are rooted in the pre-university academic programmes in both educational "sub-systems". Kanyongo (2005) provides more information on the issue, regarding Anglophone Africa generally. Hence, to the Yaoundé regime, the systems were different (only to the extent of meriting separate sections) but not at all different. Nothing could be as far from the truth as this.

An expert on Cameroon constitutional law has poignantly indicated that the "differences between the French-trained lawyer and the English-trained lawyer in what is and what is not constitutional law are not trivial [because] They range from the form to content of the entire spectrum of constitutional law" (cited in Fossungu, 2018: 135-36). This sharp contrast in perspectives, according to Dr Enonchong, would thus turn the issue of 'What Cameroon Constitutional Law is' into one which "is certainly a difficult question to answer because it bristles with a multiplicity of complex problems which are of historical origin" (Fossungu, 2018: 136). Justice Nyo'Wakai's 2008 book (*Under the Broken Scale of Justice: The Law and My Times*) also neatly demonstrated how the conflict of judicial concepts, procedures and usages have led to the Francophone judicial system trying to impose itself on the Anglophone judicial system in Cameroon. Often reduced to toothless bulldogs by new constitutional dispensations informed only by the French colonial legacy and Francophone realities. According to the Supreme Court justice, Anglophones have bemoaned the independence of the Judiciary identified with their Anglo-Saxon heritage [see http://www.langaa-rpcig.net/Under-The-Broken-Scale-of-Justice.html (last visited in February 2021)].

A complicated historical question or not, the well-couched strategy of fanning the differences (while refusing their existence rather than trying to bridge them) took the form of unfettered appointments of the less qualified Camerounese to positions where they boss over the more qualified Ambazonians, punitive transfers, unjustified promotions/demotions, etc. (see Fossungu, 2019: 80). The G.C.E. Examination (representing the "English-speaking sub-system") principally provided the root/explanation of the differences in those lawyers' education. There is little doubt that the lawyers and judges

136

being talked about above would all have generally earned a university law degree – the *licence en droit* or LL.B. But overall, looking at their pre-university education, there is research showing that Ambazonian students were better well-prepared to embark on the study of law than most of their Camerounese counterparts (see Anyangwe, 1989: chapter 11).

The G.C.E. model which was responsible for this better preparation is envied enormously by Francophone/Camerounese students for a host of reasons (including the absence of the failure-instigating *moyen general* and the capricious *tirage* system). Thus, explaining why this G.C.E. system was being targeted by the regime. Another educator brings out one of the advantages as follows: "One contrast between the *Brevet* and *Bac* examinations on the one hand, and the G.C.E. O' & A' Level examinations, on the other hand, is that in the former, in order to obtain a certificate the candidate need only score an average of 50% on the aggregate of the marks for the subjects taken; whereas in the G.C.E. he must score at least 50% in each of the required number of subjects" (cited in Fossungu, 2024: 205). Even at the then unique UNIYAO's Law and Economics Faculty where both cultural candidates studied for the LL.B. degree (better called *Licence en Droit*), their respective workloads would also reveal a significant difference (see Fossungu, 2019: 90-93). To Dr Anyangwe, the UNIYAO's *tirage* system, "of course, is examination by ambush [and] No one has been able to explain convincingly the rationale of a system as capricious as this one" (Fossungu, 2019: 93). These *tirage* subjects (including the oral interviews[34]) and *moyen général* are concepts that most Ambazonian students met for the first time only at the then 'one and only' UNIYOA. The University of Yaoundé II at Soa (former UNIYAO's Faculty of Laws and Economics) and all the other 'East Cameroon' universities (Douala, Dschang, Ngaoundéré, Yaoundé I), of course, are continuing with the same practices. This strange educational arrangement is one of the numerous factors accounting for the fact that, by 1990, according to Boyle (1996: 616), Cameroon's educational

---

[34] "Furthermore, given the fact that the teacher conducts the interview alone, it is extremely doubtful that these interviews are completely objective and that all the marks given adequately reflect the performance of the candidates. Indeed, there have been cries not altogether unfounded, of favouritism and victimization by the teachers during oral examinations" (Anyangwe, 1989: 207).

"system was plagued by high costs and drop-out rates, as well as by its ambiguous value for economic development." The decried "capricious *tirage* system" is one of the several hurdles that, until the advent of the UNIBU in 1992, had stiffly stood in the way of Ambazonian students at the UNIYAO, since they were accustomed to the G.C.E. model that gives no room for examination by ambush or the *moyen général*.

Yet, this was the faulty system that must be imposed on everyone while brandishing biculturalism to the rest of the world. Again, I cannot help but wonder with you again what the difference in the two 'sub-systems' was to the authorities: except the two hyphenated words of "English-speaking" and "French-speaking". Contrary to the biculturalism postulates of the Education Law, this could be precisely what has too often been described by Benjamin (1972: 126) as 'Being Bilingual in French' and/or by Fossungu (2018) as living in a 'common Civil-Law Country'. Furthermore, what exactly do the specific things that are to be preserved by each sub-system in Section 15(2) consist of? There is absolutely nothing of the sort especially as the same law commands a little afterwards in Section 18(3) that the certificates issued by each sub-system of the educational system shall be determined by decree of the POR. Assimilation! Assimilation! Assimilation! That is what was written all over this law. All this happened largely because the Foumban gathering did not occupy itself at all with guaranteeing the rights and institutions of Cameroonians generally and the Ambazonians particularly.

So, in a western school they are teaching children about mining. In their country there might be no mining, while in our country where you can do mining you are never taught anything about mining. And so, we have done our best to design our own curriculum of education, and it is going to be brick by brick. We are going to stumble. That is fine. But we are going to perfect it with time. And I am proud of what our Department of Education has been doing. A phenomenal job. And now every Ambazonian, wherever you may be, can enrol in our program and study practical skills, as I said the other day, that can help you. So, if you are a farmer and you want to improve on your yields, you can enrol in a program and study how to multiply your yields and to improve on your lot. We must be practical in our approach. Because all the theories we have learnt, though important for interpretation, for understanding basic things, but they are not tailored in a way that can make us an asset to our Homeland, and we must alter that (Ayaba, Ngoketunjia: September 2023).

The biggest problem and irony though concerns some of the Ambazonian "intellectuals in politics" who, when given the golden chance to do so, never even tried to correct things. For example, I have already reported how the then minister of higher education (incidentally an 'Ambazonian') visited Canada in 1996 and met with the Cameroonian community at the Université de Montréal. During that Montreal meeting, the minister was all through only talking in 'French' and only about the French-speaking sub-system of education (*Baccalauréat* and *Probatoire*). When asked specifically by a participant (in English) whether he was higher education minister for both brands of educational settings in the country or only for the Francophone one, the minister (who studied in the USA) responded in 'French' that "There was nothing like Anglo-Saxon education in Cameroon." [Peter Ateh-Afac Fossungu, "Paradoxes of Cameroon's Intellectuals" *The Herald* N° 559 (16-18 January 1998), 4] This was not coming from just any person; it was coming from President Biya's minister of higher education.

Yet we were being told in its Section 6 that the Education Law has guaranteed the right of every child, without distinction, to education (in accordance especially with Articles 2(1) and 28(1) of the United Nations Convention on the Rights of the Child). The higher education minister undoubtedly told us the only kind of education that was available, with the same Education Law itself telling us in Section 37 that the teacher is the "principal guarantor of the quality of education." It is then not hard to know the kind and quality of education that Ambazonian children were guaranteed in Cameroon because it is perfectly reflected in the quality of Cameroon's teacher-training institutions and the trained teachers. Running nose civil servants, as the critics call them. That is exactly how the Cameroon state had (according to Section 2(2) and (3) of the Education Law) guaranteed low quality mono-cultural education to Cameroon's bicultural children by providing it to them with the assistance of private sector partners, as evidently reinforced by Section 18(3) and others.

In view of Section 18(3) of the Education Law (president's decree determining the certificates to be issued by the educational system) you must wonder what to make of the much-sung administrative autonomy of the regional authorities in Article 55 of the 1996 Constitution. The 1998 Education Law was a sure part of the new subtle strategy in Cameroon of obliterating anything Anglo-Saxon there but still camouflaging biculturalism. The unmistakable targets were the so-called 'Anglo-Saxon' universities and the G.C.E. System and Board. The continued existence of these institutions in a united Cameroon was then greatly in question, thanks to improper management. For proper governance of radically diverse polities like Cameroon, federalism was the most cogent form or structure. Belgium would easily testify here and there and here, having successfully moved from the unitary form to the federal. If it worked for Belgium, there was no reason why it would not have worked for others, absent confusion and manipulation that are rooted in the absence of patriotic leadership. Let's further strengthen the hypothesis with epsi and the objectives of education in the next Chapter.

Chapter 4

Deciphering the Subtle Prevention of Biculturalism: Epsitologizing the Purpose and Objectives of Education in Cameroon and Ambazonia

So, the last two weeks have reminded us of our obligation to the common call for a freed Homeland. The last two weeks have reminded us that there are thousands of men and women still carrying rifles. They have no schools to go to, no clubs to go to, no beer parlours to sit in. They carry rifles in the name of Ambazonia, to defend the Flag and territorial integrity and the freedom of our people. We must remind ourselves daily of the reason why we fight (Ayaba, Manyu: 14 September 2024).

This Chapter generally critiques the country's education politics, using *epsi* or *bourse* ('scholarship') to further demonstrate that the real purpose of the law on education was not the one that is stated but that of assimilation of the Ambazonian minority. As I said earlier, in countries like Cameroon and Canada, bilingualism and bijuralism often link not only one to the other but as well to the system of education. That should already also tell the tragic story of the educational systems passing through *epsi*'s critical assimilationist role. The Chapter demonstrates that the laudable purpose and objectives of education in the law are only political gimmicks as the practice to date of Ambazonia's departure portrays a different story; also debunking the regime's somewhat 'benevolent' administrative devices such as *epsi* that might have been employed solely in preventing the establishment of a genuine bicultural educational base; illustrating how the 1998 Education Law came only to camouflage assimilation for multiculturalism. I will first examine the purpose of education before its objectives.

On the Purpose of Education in Cameroun: Addressing the Dog-Breeders

The sphere of education very well makes the point on pointless biculturalism and camouflaged national unity in Cameroon for two interconnected reasons. First, the burning human rights issues of bilingualism and bijuralism (in countries like Cameroon and Canada) do radiate out of education. Second, as shown in previous sections, education has been the only stronghold of Southern Cameroonsian resistance to outright assimilation and, therefore, what gravely threatened Cameroon's fake national unity. The reasoning then was that what brute force had till then failed to completely achieve, could easily be attained through the law. (Remember President Biya complaining vehemently to the French in Paris how they have brutally done everything possible to completely assimilate the Anglos, but to no avail?). So, it was then time to employ alluring terminologies (such as educational dualism and bilingualism) in the very laws specifically geared toward obliterating those very conceptions.

Like the AGovCists, Sheri Wisnowski also sees education as an undisputed "key factor of life." [Sheri Wisnowski, "Letter to Editor" 44 *Canadian Business* (December 1996), 11] It is so vital to development in all its connotations that nations that are truly desirous of advancement have not spared any effort in taking the education of their youths very seriously. Gospel also according to Saint-Captain-President Traoré. This accounts for Kanyongo's (2005: 65) indication that, soon after independence, most governments of developing countries like Zimbabwe reformed their educational systems to align them with new national goals. Cameroon, unlike Zimbabwe, is not one of such countries that have embarked on massive reforms of their education system to reflect and/or incorporate 'new' national realities. Cameroon's education politics did not augur well for development of any kind and must leave multiculturalism experts with more than enough to negatively talk about. Legal education must, of course, be topmost in any society. As I have already pointed out, Anyangwe (1989: chapter 11 – 'Legal Education in Cameroon') has offered a general discussion and critique of the sorrowful state of legal education in Cameroon. In Ambazonia, by contrast,

Our e-learning program is very important. I know that people have been asking how we are going to do with internet. Ambazonians have phones they communicate with widely, and we have the e-learning that gives you access to all forms of skills that you can acquire. There are skills on how to improve your yields, how to do a lot of things. I encourage Ambazonians to sign up to our e-learning program and acquire skills. We all went to schools, acquired certificates, but had no skills. And the AGovC, through the Education Department and the Board of Education, is rolling out massive programs that would help our children of different age ranges to acquire the skills that they need to survive within the neighbourhood. This is the future. Out here is the same. Going to university is good. But, with a 6-month skill program, you acquire the knowledge to earn a lot. We have, within the AGovC, the VP of the AGovC who is providing skills in IT; you have the Secretary for Human Rights and Humanitarian Affairs who is also providing skills in cybersecurity. So, you must understand the way that the world is moving. All this sitting in classroom for 15 years, getting general knowledge and getting out of there and sharing a pair of shoes with your dad is becoming outdated. We must catch up; we must fit into what is working. And I think the e-learning program the AGovC is offering is not for Ambazonians only. Go on our e-learning site and you are going to find out amazing programs that can be beneficial for your children (Ayaba, Manyu: 14 September 2024).

Education, according to President Nelson Mandela, a great and respected African human rights activist, is the great engine of personal development. It is through education that the daughter of a peasant can become a doctor, that the son of a mineworker can become the head of the mine; that a child of farm workers can become the president of a great nation. It is what we make out of what we have, not what we are given, that separates one person from another (cited in Fossungu, 2024: 180). Mandela really knows what he was talking about. It is trite then that it was only through its judicious handling of its education politics that Cameroon could have become the leader of the multicultural continent of Africa. It is truly what Cameroon could have made from the two dominant foreign cultures it inherited, and not what any of those foreign powers was instructing it to do, that would have separated success from failure. So how did Cameroon fare in the domain of purposeful education?

The given impression is that its 1998 Education Law came to rectify things. This law in its Section 4 sees the general purpose of education in Cameroon to be to train Cameroon's children for their intellectual, physical, civic, and moral development and their smooth integration into society bearing in mind the prevailing economic, socio-cultural, political, and moral factors. Had this law then come to correct the situation that had been prevailing in Cameroon's institutions of higher education before it? For instance, Anyangwe (1987: xv) thinks "It is amazing, though by no means surprising, how much many of our law students and legal practitioners know of English and French law but only little [or nothing] of that of their own country. We here in the [Yaoundé University] Law Faculty are partly responsible for perpetuating this mischief.... this unacceptable situation." Ayaba has variously pointed that out in other spheres and disciplines. The UNIYAO law professor is not exaggerating because it is well known that most lecturers of the then unique Yaoundé University (to be specific, its Faculty of Laws and Economics that Dr Anyangwe was reproaching), often, if not always, prefaced their lectures with: *Je sais très bien que les anglos aiment bien la politique; mais je vous avertis que mes cours ne donnent aucune occasion pour la politique.* This in English translates as meaning: 'I am aware of the fact that you, Anglophones, are very fond of politics but I must warn that my classes do not provide any platform for any non-legal or political discussion or commentary.'

Thus, politics and history, for instance, according to these lecturers, must completely dissociate themselves from legal education. Is that instruction correct and consonant with the job of teaching people about knowing and firmly assuming their rights? Is the Ambazonia Education Board (AEB) listening with awareness here? Yes, of course!

In 2025 we would be altering our school calendar. We would begin in January. No longer September. We depart completely from LRC. That is how it was before. It is the

144

practice by so many African countries. African education calendar was simply tailored to match up with the colonial system. We would alter and depart completely from what looks, sounds, waxes, and screams like LRC. And we would make it on our own. So, let us all prepare ourselves towards this. I encourage you, for us to speed this up, you must pay your Liberation Tax. Pay your Liberation Tax. I am encouraged especially by GZ. I am encouraged by what our people are doing. They are asking how to pay. I listened to an audio from a lady asking: How can I pay my Liberation Tax? Would I be issued a receipt? And would there be any proof? And we said, yes, you would be issued a receipt, not only a receipt. It is emblematic, it is captivating, it is powerful, it is a statement of intent. Once you receive your certificate of payment, you can enlarge it, frame it and put it on your wall as a badge of honour. And I tell you, some years down the line the prisoners who would be freed would be proud of you. Those from exile who return home would know they did so because of you (Ayaba, Manyu: 14 September 2024).

Cameroon might not be alone here; but Pirie (1987:580) has answered in the negative because he considers it to be a 'dog-breeding' modus which, while effectively "sharpen[ing] the mind by narrowing it", can only aid in furthering the "false legitimacy to existing social and power relations." Pirie is not alone in condemning the strategy since Suifon (1997) also declared that,

Opinion is divided whether the role of the University of Buea [UNIBU] as the citadel of Anglo-Saxon cultural heritage has so far been fulfilled since its inception in 1993. One fear which ought to be haunting Anglophone Cameroonians, but which doesn't seem to be the case is the fact that UNIBU appears to be judiciously following the example of the then University of Yaoundé which for years churned out stereotypes into the job market who are unable to prove that rather than pass through the university, the Buea University passed through them.

145

The dog-breeders that the UNIYAO had as lecturers, would partly, if not entirely, explain why some critics like Mvondo have posited that many graduates pass through the UNIYAO without the University passing through them since "a graduate of law," for example, "knows little or nothing outside law. He is a big illiterate in computer science, etc. The science graduate is no better as he knows little outside botany, geology, and zoology." [J.M. Mvondo, "On Graduating from the University of Yaoundé" *Cameroon Post* (12-19 August 1991), 6.] Absolutely correct, Mvondo is. The University of Alberta is still there for the expibasketization. Imagine my gigantic embarrassment and difficult shock arriving at the University of Alberta, Canada, for graduate studies in law without having ever used a typewriter, talk less of a computer! The challenge was astounding, especially as I needed to make use of the computer even just to locate a book in the library. Indeed, it was not at all pleasant looking like a buffoon, but I am an adaptive learner. There seems to be disagreement with Mvondo and me though as the UNIYOA-trained lawyers, as some of its teachers say, have broader objectives than just the practice of law because the institution's Bachelor of Laws (LL.B.) degree "aims at broader objectives than just the practice of law. Which is why in addition to courses of a more strictly legal nature, courses in the political and social sciences are also taught: sociology, political ideas, political regimes, civil liberties, political economy, general economics, financial institutions, and introduction to accounting" (Anyangwe, 1989: 201). Whatever the case,

The AGovC is not simply talking about independence in its abstract. We, at this moment, have built an army that you could see providing education, you could see providing public health services, skills that are necessary for both our kids and all of us who are old. So, this is the beauty of becoming part of the AGovC. And this is the future that we look forward to offering our country once all these institutions are put in place. So, I encourage each of you, it doesn't matter your age, you know. Acquire a particular skill, be an expert in something. And you are going to see the reward. Don't always quantify the reward only in terms of money. Also quantify the reward in terms of

146

liberty. Just being confident that you have the skill. Just being able to fill something in your CV as having acquired a skill. I always tell AGovCists who hold positions that skill acquisition, as president, I have a role. I am providing leadership. It is a skill that I have acquired through functionalism. So, it is not simply standing by the side and shouting independence, and a draft report is sent for people to review and add their own ideas, and you say, well, that is not my call. And you wonder tomorrow why when they ask for skill during a job interview if you have acquired any skills in editing papers or reviewing papers. Basically, you say no, whereas you had that opportunity working within the community of the AGovC or any other movement to acquire that skill. So, our education system is skill oriented. There is, of course, general education simply for knowledge. There are specialized areas where you can improve, you can develop on the skills that you have to meet up the demands of society. So, I encourage each of you to look forward to what we are offering. Our children would be displaying during the celebration of our Independence Day; we have seen a lot of videos of their practice. You would be proud to see our children in dealing with education (Ayaba, Manyu: 14 September 2024).

The Anyangwe-position in the UNIYAO would clearly differ from Kenya's LL.B. which Ojwang and Salter (1989: 90) say does not incorporate a "more societal perspective." Marc Gold would think this has also been the case in Canada (outside Quebec) where legal scholars by and large "lack rigorous training in anything but law [and] This training tends to incline the academic lawyer towards an identification with the bench and bar, in part as a way to rationalize what the academic lawyer can do best" (Gold, 1985b: 498 n.11). Pirie (1987: 579) also regrets "the failure of legal education [in Canada] to include important political perspectives in the curriculum." This may largely explain why, for instance, Canadian law journals and other publishers are fond of refusing to extend publication to interdisciplinary manuscripts such as this one for reasons such as: "it deals with an issue that may not be well known by our Canadian readership" [so, when will they ever know until they begin somewhere and somehow?]; "The manuscript assumes a detailed knowledge of Cameroonian affairs which our readership would not possess, and its main disciplinary links seem to be more with political science than law"; "the Editorial Board was uncomfortable at times with the tone of the article. The Board thought this is partly due to the author's strong understanding of the subject, which can have the result of alienating a reader who is less familiar with the subject. One solution could be to provide more context for the reader who is unfamiliar with Cameroon politics";[35] "While it can add colour to the article, the Editorial Board felt that the author should avoid overly using familiar language"; etc. The important question would thus become that of knowing why the Cameroonian intellectuals, especially the lawyers (with all the wider scope and the like), unlike their Canadian and Kenyan counterparts, would be such "societal illiterates" and be very sheepish. Is this due to other factors or to the decried educational dog-breeding?

Liberator Lucas Cho Ayaba thinks he also can help us with the answer here after I have given you a little background. You find the Cameroun regime, for instance, telling the Ambazonian 'Boyses in the Bushes' who are defending themselves against Biya's Genocidal Machine, to drop their guns without simultaneously declaring a ceasefire (or disarming their own brutal military and militia). And you find those calling themselves lawyers sitting on Equinox Television and stupidly castigating these freedom fighters for not laying down their guns. And these buffoons always insist on being addressed as "Senior Barrister" X! I hand over to the accomplished orator and fossungupaligist. Hear their distressing back-stabbing tale from the AWOL leader as discussed in Fossungu (2023: 226-28). Lawyers indeed! Talking of 'making sacrifices and investment in the efforts of those on the ground fighting' I would here repeat my utmost appeal to all Ambazonians (see Fossungu, 2023: 325-26). No dog-breeding to be tolerated in Ambazonia!

---

[35] As Nancy Whistance-Smith (of Edmonton, Alberta, Canada) also put it in her letter of 25 September 2001, "Peter, you have a passion for your country and, as far as I can tell, a realistic view of the greater world as well."

The future is our kids and we parents must look at what our kids are learning. We have the tendency of always regurgitating the same nonsense that we were fed with, then wonder after 20 years why our kids are at the same spot as we have been in the past 50 years. So, there must be a change in the way we perceive the future. We must be revolutionary. We must be aggressive. The AGovC, through different networks of skill providers, has also been offering AGovCists different IT skills through which they can improve in their wealth, they can be able to support the struggle, and they can also be able to support their families in a meaningful way (Ayaba, Manyu: 14 September 2024).

The 'dog-breeding' strategy in Cameroon's educational institutions may also largely explicate why many of the students eventually get to public or political positions without knowing how the political game is supposed to function, principally because they were never groomed to know, for example, that in politics, self-control is a necessity. This lack of self-control is exhibited in various ways, including, for instance, in the training or recruitment for the civil service; with teachers (of all people in society), according to Damien Bodo's report, passing the *concours* or competitive examinations into the infamous ENS (*École Normale Supérieure*) where they are trained: without even having sent in their candidature, let alone sat for the examinations (see Fossungu, 2019: 88-89). Simon Nkwenti, the Executive Secretary of the CATU, also lamented about this awful situation: "Look at the breed of teachers passing out of ENS today. ENS is virtually being sold at Mokolo market, Melen market, just anywhere. The result is that we have fake teachers sneaking into the profession. By all standards, ENS has been transformed into a comprehensive college. It is no longer a teachers' college. And what do you expect? A breed of teachers no better than the students they're sent to teach! The dividing line between the knowledge of teachers and students is so thin."[36]

---

[36] "Admission into ENS Can Now Be Bought at Mokolo Market – Nkwenti Simon" *The Herald* N° 508 (10-11 September 1997), 6. See also Peter Fon, "Scandal in E.N.S Admissions" *The Focus* N° 0021 (22-26 September 1997), 1 & 2; & Akem Etang, "Teaching Has Become an Adventure in Cameroon, Says Headmaster" *The Herald* N° 590 (30-31 March 1998), 11.

According to Fohtung (1996, omission is as in original), "Since 'Ecole Normale' is the only professional institution admitting and churning out young students into the civil service, we can argue that a good number of these running-nose civil servants are the teachers...of our children!". The simple truth is that, with such a glaring "Scandal in E.N.S Admissions," "Teaching Has Simply Become an Adventure in Cameroon." How can any civil service or government department that is filled to the brim with people of this sort be able to know how laws must be properly enacted, and be general and neutral in application? Is that not explaining why Atubah has said "our parliament up to now is full of people who haven't the least idea of the law" to "enact laws suitable to our own society"? [Awutah Philip Atubah, "The Legal Implications of Sections 11 and 15 of the Southern Cameroons High Court Law 1955" *The Herald* N° 430 (10-11 March 1997), 4] Here then would lay the heart and philosophy of *Developing through Confusing and Incomplete Rules & Laws*

The Roots of Developing through Confusing and Incomplete Rules and Laws

Cameroon's economic decline can also be plainly seen in the administration's ill-conceived Objectives. Of the nine (out of the 'Thirty Objectives for Cameroon') that are devoted to the Economy (Objectives 10-18), only two merely refer to 'power production' 'aimed at achieving [economic] autonomy'; one mentions the credit and banking system (Objective 12).[37] Another one (Objective 11) sparingly talks of the tertiary sector ('distribution'). Meanwhile, the remaining FIVE Objectives do harp on agriculture to make sure "that no effort is

---

[37] An estimation of the frightful situation of the banking sector in Cameroon is furnished by Tiani Kéou: "Les entreprises face aux banques dans le contexte actuel au Cameroun" 6 *Juridis Info (Revue de Legislation et de Jurisprudence Camerounaises)* (1991), 71 (being the integral text of a 'séminaire sur le droit et le redressement des entreprises en difficulté'); "La crise des banques au Cameroun: une crise profonde" 4 *Juridis Info (Revue de Legislation et de Jurisprudence Camerounaises)* (1990), 51; "La crise des banques au Cameroun" 1 *Juridis Info (Revue de Legislation et de Jurisprudence Camerounaises)* (1990), 53; & J.M. Nyama, "Reflexion sur la responsabilité du banquier" 9 *Juridis Info (Revue de Legislation et de Jurisprudence Camerounaises)* (1992), 33.

spared in bringing agriculture… to remain the mainstay of Cameroon's economy" (Fossungu, 2025: 107 n.66). Indeed, as Protais Ayangma Amang (President of Association of Cameroon Insurance Companies, ASAC), declared in 1997 in an interview with Michel Eclador Pokoua, there is every indication that the Cameroon administration is doing everything to prevent the existence of strong private initiatives in boosting an industrial economy in this country: "I am of the opinion that the Cameroon government does not want to see the emergence of a strong private sector in this country" ("*J'ai le sentiment que le gouvernement [Camerounais] ne veut pas d'un secteur privé fort*" (Amang, 1997: 6)). Confusion facilitates oppression; and it is promoted through the policy book and laws, as well as using poverty and agriculture.

The whole philosophy in Cameroon that is geared toward confusing and compounding (to prevent industrialization that is required for authentic democracy) can also be seen in the policy book as well as in some pieces of legislation. Cameroon's policy book has gone on, for instance, to indicate that, in "order to be relatively independent Cameroon's economy will have to rely more on the private dynamism of Cameroonians than on foreign capital and undertakings" (Biya, 1986: 129 – Objective 12). But this seems to remain the contrary policy and on paper because, according to informed and prospective national business circles,

> [laws by way of presidential decrees] to *arbitrarily* increase and fix the minimum level of the capital of banks from CFA 300 million to CFA 1 billion will have the effect of discouraging, stifling and blocking the entry or establishment of new banks by nationals….In the spirit of liberalizing the economy, if a citizen wants to start a bank and limit his activities just to one province or just his village, he should not be saddled by a law which requires him to come up with a minimum capital of CFA 1 billion which he does not need. [Lawrence L. Tasha, "Re: Capital of Banks" 0 *Juridis Info (Revue de Legislation et de Jurisprudence Camerounaises)* (1989), 38 at 39 (emphasis added)]

More understanding comes from Asenoh who has cited Arthur N. Nwankwo doubting in his *Can Nigeria Survive?*, with "Can a country be truly independent while its banking and insurance systems, distribution networks, manufacturing sectors, indeed nearly every facet of its

151

commercial life, are controlled by foreign nationals?" [A.B. Asenoh, "Who Chooses the Leader?" *West Africa* (6-26 April 1998), 400] In view of the confusion here one might want to know who the Cameroonians in Objective 10 are: "Cameroonians have to preserve the prerogative of initiative in the running of Cameroon's economy by determining priorities and expressing the real needs of the nation. In this regard, it is important to ensure that our planning is democratized and not subordinated to foreign interests, with our sole motivation being the general interest of Cameroonians" (Biya, 1986: 128). If this is not confusion, what is it? *Qu'est-ce qu'il faut alors faire?* Put differently, how do we reverse the trend to regain lost national pride?

It is hard to see how there can be national pride in a country "Choked full of poverty in all its ramifications; right and left, up and down, east and west, north and south! (Fossungu, 2018: 169) But as a solution some critics have suggested the restructuring of certain sectors of the economy, marked by a drastic cut in the size of government. Some of these critics like Amang (1997: 6) think, for example, that 'the restructuring of the insurance sector would not cost even a tenth of the amount required for restructuring the banking sector' (*"La restructuration du secteur des assurances ne coûtera pas le dixième des dépenses de la restructuration du secteur bancaire"*). In the eyes of other analysts, this is no solution because it is not so much the restructuring sector-by-sector that should matter; it is that of the ground rules of the entire legal and political system or edifice that is required. To support their stance, these critics like Bambou have poignantly pointed out, for example, that the government (through then Minister of Economy and Finance, Justin Ndioro) made known its policy of the restructuring of the financial sector on September 12, 1986. But six years after its first dose of restructuring in 1989, it was like everything needed to be done all over again – *"tout semblait encore à refaire."* Bambou went on wanting to know just when and how this futile exercise could end the problem. *"D'une restructuration à l'autre, le système bancaire a connu toutes sortes d'intervention supposées le remettre à flot. Si la mise en œuvre respective de mesures de toilettage est étonnante du fait que l'héritage de Paul Biya était sain et prospère, force est de reconnaitre que les résultats laissent à désirer. Les assurances ont connu le même marasme."* [F. Bambou, "Sous le renouveau: échec de la restructuration" *L'Expression* (22 septembre 1997), 2] As I have already indicated, it is truly a question of refashioning the ground rules of the entire legal and political system. Long term and strategic planning are not Cameroonian, of course.

And while we are building our foundation, we need the support of our population. You must have faith in what we are doing, and don't only think about yourself in the moment. Think about 20 years from now. What would be the effect if we continue the same path with the system that we have been in for the last 60 years without any results. The results you see are potholes everywhere, dilapidated buildings. For instance, in Ngoketunjia, the UNVDA [Upper Noun Valley Development Authority[38]] alone enrolled thousands and thousands of farmers, dug roads, farm to market roads. Today what has happened? Are we going forward or we are going backward? Why have all those things collapsed? Because we lack faith in ourselves and in our Homeland. Because our own mindset was altered by LRC to make us to believe in them rather than in ourselves. And this is our journey. This is our journey to alter that history once and for all, and to give back to our people faith in themselves and in our country. With that faith, we would be able to turn water into wine. [[39]] We would be able to transform our society in a way that we would take pride in, and our children would inherit a better place (Ayaba, Ngoketunjia: September 2023).

The critics could be quite right. No one in their right senses can argue that an economy like the one being propagated in Cameroon could never produce anything for advancement, except advancement in

---

[38] For more on which, see Patience Eshankeh Chindong, *Information Circulation in Rice Production: The Case of UNVDA and Ndop Rice Farmers, Cameroon* (MSc. Thesis, Sept. 2008, Wageningen, The Netherlands).

[39] "Manyu people are one of the greatest intellectuals you have in Ambazonia. Very smart people. Highly educated. The foundation of education in Ambazonia is from Manyu, in Tali. That is where you find some of these criminals who are enablers. That is where they were produced, in Tali. So, apart from the knowledge to be able to turn water into wine that exists in Manyu, you have the water also, right?" (Ayaba, Manyu: 14 September 2024).

regression as can also be seen in the following pieces of confusing, incomplete and weird 'restructuring' legislation on both insurance and banking: *Loi N° 90/019 du 11 août 1990 modifiant certaines dispositions de l'ordonnance N° 85/002 du 31 août 1985 relative à l'exercice de l'activité des établissements de crédit*; *Loi N° 90/025 du 10 août 1990 modifiant certaines dispositions de l'ordonnance N° 85/003 du 31 août 1985 relative à l'exercice de l'activité d'assurance; Ordonnance N° 90/005 du 19 septembre 1990 modifiant et* <u>*complétant*</u> *les dispositions de l'ordonnance N° 003 du 27 avril 1990 fixant les conditions de liquidation de banques*[40] (Underlining has been added to draw attention to the fact that this administration had been applying incomplete legislation for six months); *Ordonnance N° 003 du 27 avril 1990 modifiant et* <u>*complétant*</u> *les dispositions de l'ordonnance N° 85/002 du 31 août 1985 relative à l'exercice de l'activité de crédit* (same underlining and comment as above); *Décret N° 89/1283 du 18 août 1989 portant création de la Société de Recouvrement de Créance du Cameroun;* and *Loi N° 89/021 du 29 décembre 1989 fixant une procédure* <u>*simplifiée*</u> *de recouvrement de créances.* The underlining has been added to this last law: What was the need to first complicate things for four months before now simplifying? What was also the use for promoting agriculture before but now abandoning it completely?

The modus operandi of this country's administrators would seem to furnish the real inner meaning of the motto of 'Peace-Work-Fatherland' in the 1996 Constitution's Article 1(4) and in the Federal Constitution's Article 1. In other words, doesn't 'Peace-Work-Fatherland' in Cameroon mean "Remain forever on the Farms" and stay poor? The role that agriculture, poverty and confusion must play in the calculated process of frightening Cameroonians away from the normal type of democracy is thus evident. This is especially so for two reasons. The first has to do with the lectures of some Canadian experts called Rob McKenzie and Yvon Gasse. According to the time-tested thesis of these experts, "When you're a farmer… you develop a good tolerance for uncertainty." And this seemingly endless tolerance of a person, Director Gasse further explains, is true especially if you're one of the dozen or so children of families of double-digit broods. [Rob McKenzie, "Vivre la difference" *Canadian Business* (December 1996), 44 at 47, quoting Director Yvon Gasse of the Entrepreneurship Center at

---

[40] There is commentary on this law by Paul-Gerard Pougoué in 4 *Juridis Info (Revue de Legislation et de Jurisprudence Camerounaises)* (1990) 35-36.

Université Laval] Here then can be the haven wherein Cameroonian irrational pride and ridiculous democracy are relaxing in Perfect Peace rather than in irredeemable pieces. Cameroonians, according to J.T. Ayeh, "pride themselves of many things which, on the basis of existing evidence, are genuine for the most part; but if, by some remote coincidence, rationality is one of them, it raises an eyebrow for a people who easily consume myths" (cited in Fossungu, 2018: 141). Anyone doubting Ayeh's & Gasse's theories, should better explain Zuhmboshi's pride to me, please.

> Notwithstanding the fact that my origin [Cameroon] is a land whose people are victims of unfair and inhuman treatment I, beyond all doubts, have an admiration for it as it is a magnet for tourists...[who] flow into the land like butterflies visiting a hibiscus to enjoy the beautiful Savannah scenery. Furthermore, it is a cemetery for Heroes. These corpses endowed with veneration, wisdom and probity do manure the earth (of my origin) and act as undying inspiration for upcoming Heroes. The diligence of the people (when it comes to farming) is undeniable. [Eric Nsuh Zuhmboshi, "Pride in Dying for a Just Cause" *The Herald* N° 446 (16-17 April 1997), 4]

The second factor concerns the glories surrounding agriculture that suddenly disappeared from the scene in the early 1990s when the moves toward Western democracy began, culminating in the Parties Law studied above. A UNIBU lecturer would tell this story exceedingly well:

> Government's commitment to ensure the future of agricultural development until the 1990s has been consistent. The agricultural show schemes and best farm competitions served as additional incentives to farmers. The creation of zones *d'action communautaire et culturelle* and community development in the former East and West Cameroons respectively were all signs of government interests in agricultural development. These realizations were further extended to the development of agro-pastoral infrastructure. One can cite the examples of schools, agricultural research centres (e.g. IRZ and IRAD in Ekona, Bambui, Mankon),

155

agricultural training institutions and credit schemes that serve both regional and national interests. All these investments in agriculture and the rural economy produced far-reaching results in the domain of population and political stability, as well as economic growth.

However, this has not lasted for ever as the situation has changed in recent times [with the unexpected arrival of the quest for Western-type multi-party democracy]. There has been a systematic neglect of the agricultural sector and its infrastructure while, at the same time, a lot of lip-service is paid for its importance. Such abandonment of the nerve centre on which the Cameroonian economy revolves has opened the way for poverty, rural exodus, hunger, crimes, etc., to gradually but steadily infest a country of great economic potentials. Economic development has generally slowed down and the living standards of the population in most localities are deplorable. Although many are quick to attribute this situation to the economic crisis of the mid 80s and the harsh structural adjustment measures that followed in the 90s, the central issue remains that the deteriorating state of agro-pastoral infrastructure in Cameroon is a call for concern. [otsmart N. Fonjong, "Changing Fortunes of Government Policies and its Implications on the Application of Agricultural Innovations in Cameroon" 13(1) *Nordic Journal of African Studies* (2004), 13 at 14 (note omitted)]

Can you not see a parallel trend with UNIYAO *epsi* here? As Fonjong explains in the missing footnote, IRZ is the Institute of Zoo-technical Research and IRAD the Institute for Agricultural Research and Development. To properly address that concern, local government (I must keep repeating) was the way to go for developing states since it is in a sense the science of the second best because a municipal government expert has pointed out that it is not always the question of what is the most desirable or *serene* way of meeting a problem, but what is the best of the practices which will secure court approval and not be held unconstitutional (Kneier, 1939: preface). In putting development into perspective, Magstadt (1991: 60) has also indicated that 'the science of the second best' is "a key concept in nearly all the natural and social sciences." One of such sciences is local government which is furthered federalism or decentralization. What states of the Third World need therefore as the right path to national integration would be decent education, rigorous training and clear-cut recruitment procedures for/of the citizenry and the national bureaucracy. Since only authentic education is the key for awakening the people, the need for effective civic education is simply axiomatic. Just as the only real solution to social problems is moral education,[41] the only real solution to political problems is sound civic and legal education – a type of education that cannot be divorced from the people's authentic history or culture. Genuine multiculturalism thus becomes inevitable. The centralized unitary state is incompatible with this, Gospel according to *St. Ambazonia vis-à-vis LRC 'One-Cube-Of Sugar' (OCOS) Genocidal War*. The different perspectives of these two states involve even those on agriculture and the treatment of farmers.

> So, if Singapore that is not even primary base, Singapore is not an indigenous land to produce palm oil, it can make 11.5 billion dollars while LRC's budget is just 6 billion FCFA. And Singapore has not even ended there. It is using the derivatives to make margarine. So, each time you are swiping margarine on your bread, it is what you call *mbanga* grown in Lebialem that the COS told me is barren. Lebialem, *allalay*? We would turn it into an oasis. Since you people have moved to Fako, you would not move back alone. You would move back with the people of Fako, because there would be enough. We would dignify mass production of our resources. We would not live in a society where farmers are treated with disdain and scorn, as though they have nothing to offer. The people who feed the world! (Ayaba, Lebialem: 29 August 2023)

How do the dog-breed students in Cameroon know that educational opportunities should be available to citizens not based on

---

[41] Earl Rubington and Martin S. Weinberg, "Social Pathology", in Earl Rubington and Martin S. Weinberg (eds.), *The Study of Social Problems: Five Perspectives* 3rd edition (New York: Oxford University Press, 1981), 15 at 21. See also Richard L. Henshel, and Anne-Marie Henshel, *Perspectives on Social Problems* 2nd edition (Don Mills, Ontario: Academic Press Canada, 1973) chapter 3.

unnecessary discriminatory criteria[42] but be open to all who qualify without exception? Those 'lawyers' on TV running their watery mouths for chicken change from the regime, do they even know what the job of a lawyer entails? There is no doubt then, according to Stark (1976: 441), that "The West Cameroon elites who arranged 'federation' were badly advised, had little experience or education, and were confused by the ... [translator]." No justice, I think, would be done to the Foumban federalism enterprise in Cameroon without a clear call for an end to the seemingly ceaseless emasculation of the translator's impeccable anti-federalism role in the Foumban Enterprise. Translators in any society are, in a lot of ways, like teachers and lawyers who often abuse their unique 'key to knowledge': "You teachers of the law... are really in for trouble! You carry the key to the door of knowledge.... But you never get in, and you keep others from getting in" (Luke 11: 52; also see Williams, 1987: 401-403 – the Meta-Story). Once the lawyers of Ambazonia (selfishly?) rose up in 2016, there was unstoppable 'Ambazonia Rising' from then forward. The 'key to knowledge' of translators/interpreters enormously surpasses that of lawyers because it is translation that "opens the window, to let in the light, that breaks the shell, that we may eat the kernel, that puts aside the curtain, that we may look into the most holy place, that removes the cover of the well, that we may come by the water" [see "The Translators to the Reader", King James Version 1611, as cited in *The Contemporary English Version*, Canadian Bible Society (1995) at) vii]. The shoddy doings of Mosé Yeyap are a living concrete case of what translators' power of abuse can amount to. I do not need to set out here the details of the unfortunate events created by this Foumban man (Mosé Yeyap) and their lasting effects on the Bamum traditional court [see Christraud M. Geary, *Things of the Palace: A Catalogue of the Bamum Palace Museum in Foumban (Cameroon)* (Wiesbaden, Germany: Franz Steiner Verlag GMBH) at 15]. One may not even need to peruse all that Bamum history to comprehend translators/interpreters who are largely known to "impose themselves upon their world" [Roderick A. Macdonald, "Legal Bilingualism" 42 *McGill Law Journal* (1997), 119 at 141].

Professor Stark is obviously right on his education thesis, but people could be astonished to hear this talk of 'little experience or

---

[42] See Fidèle Muabe, "Bamileke Students Petition Biya for Educational Discrimination" *The Herald* N° 334 (16-18 August 1996), 3.

education' especially as the leader of that delegation is/was being addressed as Dr. John Ngu Foncha. How some of these titles (including Dr. Paul Biya) have come about will only go to mystify the mystery that is/was Cameroon. Impossibility is/was truly not Cameroonian? "Oh Afrika! This biggytitlemania again and again! It makes me to always reflect on Nancy Whistance-Smith's eye-opening counsel in 2000 that 'God never had a PhD.' Yet he is the one who created the world, including those having the PhDs plus!" (Fossungu, 2021: 66). Patriotic Ambazonians now also understand PhD to mean 'Pull Him Down'. Is the current LRC colonial prime minister (Dion Ngute) not also a PhD in law?

> All what we have produced and prescribed from the AGovC is based on a deep understanding of the flaws and strengths of our enemy. You empower our people mentally, you make our people to accept their identity, you make our people to believe in their own Land, you are 80% free. Once the thieves know that their location is identified, it is just a matter of time. They can use Dion Ngute. The other day I was listening, oh, what a disgrace! What a disgrace! A whole man who calls himself prime minister is on video begging the slave to remain a slave in the hands of their abductors and kidnappers. Confused about what to say. Whether he should beg but the mama, we should pray to God, to Allah, or we should do what? Just for him to be in the good books of a man who, I am sure, is senile enough not to even know who Dion Ngute is. I thought they had won the war. Now we still control the suburbs. Well, thank you all for being part of this interactive conversation (Ayaba, Lebialem: 29 August 2023).

It was also perhaps to eschew the discriminatory situation and several others that the Education Law in Section 7 also placed on the Cameroon state the duty to guarantee or ensure equal opportunities for education to all, without discrimination as to gender, political, philosophical or religious opinion, or social, cultural, linguistic or geographical origin. There is a lengthy discussion of the requirements of this provision by Brunnell (2005); and Adams (2006: 4-8). It also makes clear that education is not only a top priority of the Cameroon State (Section 2(1)), but must also be apolitical (Section 8), with the state firmly guaranteeing that public education be compulsory at primary level (Section 9) and secular, neutral and independent vis-à-vis all religions (Section 10). These are very commendable policies except that they are just French photocopies that do not only not reflect national realities but also end only on paper. For example, Cameroon's claim to secularity has been held to be just another instance of blind copying "from Metropolitan France" because "it is a contradiction in terms to what prevails in this country." [Bonny Kfua, "What Does Being Secular Mean?" *The Herald* (4-6 October 1996), 4]

Therefore, the 1996 'anti-Anglophone heathen document', like the Education Law, did contradict beliefs in Ambazonia, with Reverend Jumban ably stepping in to tell them what they do not know about Ambazonians:

I wish to let you know something of the people of the Southern Cameroons which many French Speaking Cameroonians seem to be ignorant of. They are people who do not distinguish between their love of country and their love of the Church. They love those two things with their whole hearts. Their patriotism is ethical, concrete, and religiously dutiful – reason why your brother bishops of Southern Cameroons (in the example of that pragmatic culture) have spoken for their subjugated and dispossessed people against such a stinking political tyranny as Biya's. That is why though many from East Cameroon are comfortable with the atheistic political system glorifyingly baptized laïcité, it has been scandal of the highest order to the religious sensitivity of Southern Cameroons who, like true Africans (and tinged by Anglicanism's reverence for God and respect for the Monarch), believe that without God and indigenous culture life is impossible. We know very well that this atheism we see in Cameroon politics is not from your own ancestors, but it is borrowed from France. The people East of the Mungo have been educated in Gallican opinions. We of the West have been educated in Anglican opinions. The respect of each other's opinions from those educational systems have been what La République du Cameroun has deprived us of, and it pains us to the marrow. That is why our teachers and lawyers took to the streets to peacefully demonstrate their anger and protest

160

against an evil system. They were met with an autocratic response by a government you fear to criticize (cited in Fossungu, 2019: 74).

Yes, Ambazonians are God-fearing and God-loving; a fact that is undebatable as the Ambazonian Anthem (which also stands tall in the matter of originality and straightforwardness) says it in incomparable terms (see Fossungu, 2025: 59). The 1996 Constitution therefore obviously abused Ambazonians' religiosity and patriotism plentifully. But more importantly, the document, true to its description, did not only reaffirm and consolidate the contested 1984 name-change in its Article 1(1). This constitution also apparently went ahead to confuse and side-step the issue by rewarding laziness at the expense of hard work (contrary to what the 1998 Education Law, coming two years after it, would be saying in Section 5(6), namely, that one of the objectives of education in Cameroon was to "cultivate the love of effort and work well done, the quest for excellence and team spirit").

The regime could also not be right in saying that education in Cameroon is apolitical when experts attribute the current laughing-stock status of the UNIBU to factors that principally include the

political inclination of the top brass of UNIBU and the consequent squelching of the politically non-conformist lecturers; the suppression of an elected students' union body; the victimisation of its leaders, some of whom were simply dismissed; the avoidable tragedy resulting from the politicisation of the university by the authorities and the accompanying tribal cleavages [which] created a sense of betrayal especially as some of the indigen[ous people] perceived the university as nothing short of a tribal estate (Suifon, 1997).

This must not be surprising to anyone who understands just how the Cameroonian POR himself deals with the country as one would do with one's private property. Why should anyone expect the plethora of his personal appointees to behave any differently? It is thus clear that the 1998 Education Law would not have made any difference since the practices are continuing despite its laudable objectives of education; praiseworthy only in the name of confusion of assimilation for multiculturalism, as I will next demonstrate further with *epsitology*.

Epsitologizing the Objectives of Education: Parlement and the Golden Lessons of Unity of Purpose

Desirous of success in the domain of leading Africa out of the dungeon, it would seem, the Cameroon administration took steps to enact the 1998 Education Law geared towards "reaffirming our national option for biculturalism" in its Section 15(1). Using *epsi* or *bourse* in the demonstration, this study however shows, through an informed and critical inspection of its objectives of education, that the reaffirmation of "our national option for biculturalism" is extremely far indeed from being the aim of that law. Just as the creation of an Interim Government (IG) did not have liberation and independence of Ambazonia as the objective or goal. Section 5 specifies the objectives of education in Cameroon as being to:

(1) train citizens who are firmly rooted in their culture, but open to the world and respectful of the general interest and the common weal;

(2) inculcate the major universal ethical values which are dignity and honour, honesty and integrity, as well as a sense of discipline into pupils and students;

(3) promote family life;

(4) promote national languages;

(5) provide an instruction to the democratic culture and practice, respect for human rights and freedoms, justice and tolerance, the fight against all forms of discrimination, the love of peace and dialogue, civic responsibility and promotion of regional and sub-regional integration;

(6) cultivate the love of effort and work well done, the quest for excellence and team spirit;

(7) develop creativity, a sense of initiative and spirit of enterprise;

(8) provide physical, sports, artistic and cultural training for the child; [and]

(9) promote hygiene and health education.

These are noble objectives indeed, but it is not clear if the authorities are genuine about them. I do not think they are for a couple of simple reasons that tie themselves to *Epsi*. It is the student-invented milieu name for the monthly grant that the Cameroon administration had been spending in the name of *bourse* to UNIYAO students for no other reason than just to make unthinking drunkards out of them and, therefore, avoid facing and tackling the important issues of an authentic bicultural educational base. This *epsi* strategy would seem to have taken its toll on the Ambazonian students who were also largely frustrated by the UNIYAO educational language politics that is popularly known as Ngoalingualism (see Fossungu, 2021: 71). *Epsi* and *Ngoalingualism* (the first attracting them to the second) obviously imposed their exacting levy on Ambazonians to an extent that the following statement (in Njangawatok or Ambatok) had become very commonplace: *"Massa, leave man withi politics. If one beer dey, tell me I go follow you."* This is Ambatok for: 'I am not a politician and do not want to bother anymore about what the politicians are doing; if you have something else to offer, for example, a bottle of beer, then I am all yours.' Fonkeng (1990: 20 & passim) furnishes other familiar forms of this 'Massa leave man' talk: "How we go do now?", "Dokta, weti man go do noh?" That is exactly what *epsi* might have been meant to achieve. Attract them with *epsi* and then frustrate them with *Ngoalingualism* as much as possible so that heroes are never born out of any of them. As one expert has confirmed and elucidated:

> Heroes build nations. Nations admire, encourage, and revere their heroes, but in Cameroon, we ridicule, frustrate, imprison, and kill heroes or chase them into exile…. Do we have such people in Cameroon? Yes! But they are all 'locked up in themselves.' They do not set the example we expect. They have become frustrated beings, drunks, con men, lecherous fornicators, adulterers, white-collar thieves, blatant liars, and occult worshippers. These are the people our children are supposed to emulate. These are our heroes. This is our future. [Marian Chia, "Our Heroes" *Cameroon Post* (11-18 December 1995), 10]

Epsi was in CFA francs per month as follows: 60,000 (*doctorat* students), 50,000 (*maîtrise* students), 40,000 (third year *licence* students), and 30,000 (first- and second-year *licence* students). In view of the university population then the amount of money dished out as *epsi* in just five years, for instance, could be more than enough money to have built at least two well-equipped and high-quality universities in Cameroon (including or excluding the UNIYAO). But rather than confront the problems while they were still easily solvable, the authorities had thought that *epsi* was the 'magic portion.' Indeed, to think that *epsi* was the 'magic fix-all' was brainless enough because it does not take any great amount of intelligence to see that *epsi* was to instead precipitate and aggravate the issues. Since its links with the congestion at the UNIYAO (which brought forth *Parlement*) is plain enough. The overpopulation and the accompanying ills that gave birth to *Parlement* would not be hard in coming because of the discovery that "Every year hundreds of [high school] students register in the [Yaoundé] University *without any serious intention of studying but simply to acquire the status of University student and to receive the monthly grant which they consider as a kind of unemployment benefit*" (Anyangwe, 1989: 199 n.7, emphasis added). If the students get this *epsi* money and drink their unemployment and frustrations to death, there will be no problem. That was the administration's line of thinking, which is perfectly normal for one that is well known for its policy dubbed *navigation à vue* (visionless policy). The only vision traitors ever have is traitoriality (it is the HISOFE terminology for 'traitor mentality').

It is hard to gainsay that human rights (including those to good health and authentic education) are the invisible hand behind any meaningful development or nation-building. It pays to emphasize here again that bona fide "Education is the highway that propels America, driving its businesses, delivering opportunity, and fueling its political, social, and moral conscience" (Brunnell, 2005: 343). The thesis on history obliteration (assimilation) would explain why other French neo-colonies (and even France itself) but without the 'Anglophone Equation' are having advantages over Cameroon notwithstanding that the latter far outweighs the others in terms of natural and other resources. Take *epsi* as a simple illustration. Just imagine only the astronomical sums of money spent over years as *epsi* to UNIYAO students in an unrelenting effort to assimilate the English-speaking, and you would have grasped the point very well. Côte d'Ivoire or Chad or Botswana, for instance, during that same time (that Cameroon is paying out *epsi* and creating lots of all sorts of confusion) would be putting just

164

one-tenth of said sums to more progressive developmental use. *Capiche?* Got it? It is this argument that can duly account for the differences between countries like Cameroon and, say, Ghana – to leave out South-East Asia's Indonesia where, according to Canadian Ambassador Gary Smith, "You can get stinking rich in a hurry." [Quoted in Satya Das, "Playing by the Rules in Indonesia: A Little Homework Goes a Long Way for Investors" *The Edmonton Journal* (26 December 1996), E1] This Indonesian case is getting rich without being *voyou* or *véreux* like in Cameroon – as has been elaborately catalogued by Eyoum'a Ntoh (1996) and others. The honour in the Indonesian case, of course, not only results from being able to do business "playing by the rules," but also by rules which are known beforehand by (and encourage full realization of potentials, rights and obligations of) the parties involved: foreign or national (see de Jorge, 1993; & others[43]).

It is plainly doubtful therefore that the Cameroonian authorities were serious about the stated objectives when it is no longer a secret that teaching has become a dangerous adventure in Cameroon due to the very corrupt demeanours of school administrators and most teachers who are members of the educational community that is defined in Section 32 as follows: "(1) The Educational Community shall comprise all individuals and corporate bodies that contribute towards the functioning, development and prestige of a school. (2) It shall comprise the following members: the authorities, the administrative and support staff; teachers; parents of pupils; students; persons from socio-professional cycles; [and] regional and local authorities." Johnson-Hanks (2006: 125-31) has lengthily and critically discussed some of these members of the 'educational community', namely, 'The School and Their Teachers'. I cannot therefore see the administration's seriousness in those objectives which are mere smokescreens. It is surely not this same administration that was out to do all the magnificent things that the Education Law purported to represent when, because of its lack of vision, private education establishments have sprouted here and there, including what Boyle (1996: 620 & 622) calls "schools of increasingly dubious quality." Dubious schools with

---

[43] See Chan Jin Kim: "Foreign Investment and National Interests" 2 *Korean Journal of Comparative Law* (1974), 30, & "Legal Aspects of Foreign Investment in Korea" 1 *Korean Journal of Comparative Law* (1973), 2; and Young Moo Kim, "Legal Forms of Doing Business in Korea" 2 *Korean Journal of Comparative Law* (1974), 58.

equally doubtful teachers who the critics say would quickly and sheepishly abdicate "when it comes to the Anglophone Problem or say, decentralization which can spare them the costly trips to Yaoundé" (cited in Fossungu, 2018: 82).

Ambazonia sees part of the remedy of the nonsense in Community Schools.

> When we say community school, it means it is community-based, community-owned. The shareholders are people from the community. That is what we mean. And that is the system we would design. A shareholder approach to ownership of industries, big, medium, or small. We know we have limitations. But we are creating institutions for learning and to acquire knowledge. Not just schools. We are being innovative; we are creating multiple layers of opportunities. That if you miss a couple of days sitting in classroom because there was fighting in that neighbourhood, you go online you are going to catch up. We are transforming, we are disrupting what has existed, we are creating a revolutionary system that totally dismantles what was put in place to turn us from being citizens of a country into becoming slaves to another country. This is going to be a meticulous and tedious job. I appeal to every one of you to bear the burden each time it comes to your door. It would be for you, your family, and to the next generation. Don't forget to pay your Liberation Tax (Ayaba, Lebialem: 29 August 2023).

The authorities cannot be serious about those objectives of education when Boyle's (1996: 621) seasoned research has further clearly shown that "the state lacks the wherewithal and political will to direct [educational] change in Cameroon." A serious administration would not be wanting in this aspect because Mback (2007: 74) thinks only such political will, of course, "would have the potential to transform municipal institutions and, more widely, local governments into the new actors in development they should have been and remained since they were introduced in Cameroon [in 1996]." The much-needed political will is lacking principally because R.B. Sanjo thinks "Cameroon is a nation where, deliberately or otherwise, the political cart is placed before the horse" (cited in Fossungu, 2018: 145).

The debilitating effects of this 'horse before cart' politics on human rights would not require any enormous amount of the stretching of the intellect to grasp. Tell them for me, please, that it is the result of

> A colonial curriculum of education that has made our own efforts worthless. You ask yourself, what has LRC given the people of Lebialem? One of the first places we freed was Bechati. That is the village of Dr Ebenezar Akwanga. That is one of first places General Ivo Mbah freed. We dealt a big blow to the enemy there. And we still control that axis. So, I want to assure the people of Lebialem. Your future in dignity, in wealth, in opportunities, is in Ambazonia. If you see the structures that the Germans left there, they look so beautiful, like the Fon's palace. Who has destroyed it? The enemy has transformed it into its barracks. One of the most prominent schools in Lebialem, was it built by LRC? What has LRC offered the people of Lebialem? It has instead forced you people to abandon your own land. A land that was protected by the blood of your forebears. A place where your own Chief was taken into exile in Garoua. He did not decide to stay there. He came back (Ayaba, Lebialem: 29 August 2023).

Because of that gaping political will void, in the early 1990s the then unique and overcrowded UNIYAO students' *Parlement* surprisingly forced the birth of six universities created by the very controversial legislation on higher education reform. While Mbassi glorifies it as "Fruits et leurres de la réforme", Azebaze describes it as "*six universités créés par le très controversée réforme de l'Enseignement supérieure.*"[44] Steven Langdon has written an interesting essay that elaborately discusses the factors accounting for, trends, consequences and nature of, this 'new form' of power (student-power) in Canada – with some very similar characteristics in the Cameroonian *Parlement* situation. [ee Steven Langdon, "The Politics of Participation: A Student Case," in James A.

---

[44] See Yvette Mbassi, "Fruits et leurres de la réforme" *Cameroon Tribune* (2 novembre 1998), 8; & Alex Gustave Azebaze, "Crise des Universités : Obounou limogé ! Et la session d'Été alors?" *Le Messager* N° 513 (6 juin 1996), 8.

Draper (ed.), *Citizen Participation: Canada* (Toronto: New Press, 1971), 45-56.] The AWOL Leader cannot but laugh at this visionless regime that wants to cajole people now with reconstruction talk when the bone has gotten stuck in its arrogant throat.

> Listen! Look at LRC's budget of 2022. Those people who want to reconstruct Ambazonia! To reconstruct, it means you constructed before, right? Ambazonia has suffered. Ambazonia has really suffered. LRC wants to reconstruct Ambazonia, eh? You did not construct, but you want to reconstruct! What folly! Their budget of 2022 was 6 billion CFA francs, with a population of 20 million. Listen. LRC has a population of 20 million. The amount of money that Singapore makes from palm oil was 11.5 billion US dollars. Singapore has a population of 5 million, I think. Yes, it is about that. Only from palm oil it made 11.5 billion dollars. LRC's budget of 20 million people was 6 million FCFA. What does he (Biya) want to use to reconstruct Ambazonia? (Ayaba, Lebialem: 29 August 2023).

What does Biya also want to use to manage the created universities which included the long-suppressed Ambazonian one in Buea? Because of the student *Parlement*, Cameroon hurriedly dotted itself with four more universities through decreeing previous *Centres Universitaires* (university centers) into full-fledged universities. These are the UNIBU (until then a professional school for the translators and interpreters) in Debundschazone, University of Douala (Wourizone), University of Dschang (Bamboutouszone), and University of Ngaoundéré (Adamawazone). The unique UNIYAO was split into two universities (for Sanagazone), namely, UNIYAO I (being the former University's two Faculties of Arts and Social Sciences and of Sciences) which stayed-put on the original campus of Ngoa-Ékéllé from where *Ngoalingualism* is derived, and UNIYAO II with campus at the city's suburb of Soa (being the mother university's Faculty of Laws and Economics). Five of the ten regions (one English-speaking, four French-speaking) were then without a state university: Benouezone, Guinean-Savannazone, Logonezone, Nyongzone, and Savannazone. But on 13 January 2022 President Paul Biya signed an order to create three new universities in Bertoua (GSZ), Garoua (BNZ) and Ebolowa

(NYZ). "Some experts have equated creating universities without campuses and other enabling infrastructure to putting the cart before the horse."[45]

Decree N° 92/74 of 13 April 1992 established the UNIBU, the then lone state university in West Cameroon. Presidential decree of 14 December 2010 later created the University of Bamenda (UNIBA for SVZ), unlike the UNIBU that came along eight years earlier. Decree N° 93/034 of 19 January 1993 organizing the UNIBU states in Article 1(a) that the University is "conceived in the Anglo-Saxon tradition." But was the talk of Anglo-Saxon tradition and educational dualism in this country then genuine? The answer is NO because this 'Anglo-Saxon' UNIBU which the student *Parlement* "forced" its creation must then have to be destroyed with much subtlety; subtleness that is particularly embedded in Part II of the Education Law itself (as already examined above).

The Anglo-War-Cry Theory of the Inverted Minority

A discussion of the activities of *Parlement* further facilitates the comprehension of the confusion styled higher education (or university) reforms and the reaffirmation of the country's biculturalism. Parlement's splendid success resulted from its obliterating the majority/minority distinction. Talking of minority, it is necessary I also throw light on the confusing phrases 'minority/majority' themselves. I am employing majority/minority in this book simply for analytical convenience because it is not like in Cameroon all Francophones (the majority) are free from the repression and are oppressing all Anglophones (the minority). I am thus in accord with Konings and Nyamnjoh's (1997: 218-19) salient critiques of "this demagogic approach" of "The Buea Declaration" "which is commonplace in ethnic discourse, serv[ing] to emphasise the 'insurmountable' dichotomy that justifies the AAC call for autonomy.... and creat[ing] serious obstacles to any francophone sympathy for the Anglophone

---

[45] Elias Ngalame and Nestor Njodzefe, "Cameroon's New Universities will Get their Buildings Later" 03 March 2022 @ https://www.universityworldnews.com/post.php?story=20220302205022819.

cause." It is such approach ("tend[ing] to blame the wicked francophones as a whole for the plight of the poor anglophones" – Konings and Nyamnjoh, 1997: 218) that makes a common front for change near the impossible in Cameroon, whereas everyone else is being oppressed by the Biya gang, including the gang members themselves. The theory here is heavily relying on Appiagyei-Atua's 'A Prologue on Oppression' (1999: xi-xiv). Specifically, my Ghanaian colleague states at page xii that sycophants like Joseph Dion Ngute (aka Celine Dion), Augustin Kontchou (aka Zero-Mort), Paul Atanga Nji (aka 'Boyses in the Bushes') and others that Biya surrounds himself with "are also oppressed because, by trying to avoid oppression by the oppressor, they betray the rest of the community and so live in constant fear of reprisal. Their conscience haunts them and this oppresses them." Is defeated President Biya not ready to slaughter Camerounese (in like manner as he has been doing to Ambazonians for the past nine years) who are backing Tchiroma's victory to oust him from Etoudi, as per the explosive October 2025 report of Jeune Afrique that exposes Biya's secret call on the military to fight on his side?

It is just that then Southern Cameroonsians, now Ambazonians, felt the oppressive pinch much more deeply because of their different (but not different) cultural and political perspectives, worsened further by the fact that the Etoudi Palace gangsters know and understand well how to easily play what I prefer to describe as the human rights 'Anglos War-Cry' (see Fossungu, 2018: 137-38). They do it with the 'majority' who (on hearing that 'Anglos' are this and that) would not take a minute to think but simply join in the oppressive chorus. Thus, we hear the experts variously postulating in support that, "Since the Biya regime is ill at ease with Anglophones, every opportunity is now used by the regime to prove to the wider public that it is Anglophones causing trouble - not the regime", with another version charging Mr. Biya as saying "*Malgré nos efforts... ce sont les Anglophones qui gâtent le pays*" (cited in Fossungu, 2018: 137 n.17). This thesis provides an explanation of various aspects in Cameroon. It also clarifies, for example, why most English-speaking have come to make 'Francophone' and 'majority' synonyms. I well remember occasions (especially in my student and lecturer days at the UNIYAO). Imagine being in a gathering of, say, fifteen – thirteen Ambazonians and two Camerounese – and finding all thirteen almost talking exclusively in 'bad' French. You then ask them why they cannot talk in the English language they are more comfortable in or with, and here is the response: "We want the majority to understand what is being said."

You can see then that they are not here, as elsewhere, looking at 13/15 as the majority but themselves as Anglophones, the minority in Cameroon that can never count in any circumstance in the country; not even with a half Francophone amid 800,000 of them. And do not make the mistake of thinking this attitude only exhibits while being inside Cameroon because I have had to deal with this same Cameroon-Anglophone frame of mind even while studying/living in Montreal, Canada. Tell me! Who is ever going to give you your language rights if you cannot stand tall and defend or impose them in glaring situations like these? Let their liberator tell them what they must do.

So, as I was saying, I brought up the idea that we should seize that embassy. And we started planning. The COS! When I asked who was going to change the flag, because we had to bring down LRC's flag and then raise the Amba flag. I asked who was ready to change the flag and the COS said he would do it. So, I was going for the military attaché. The COS was going for the flag. You see the great combination of warriors. We planned for about a month. COS, if I am wrong, correct me in the comment section. So, on the morning of 1st of October 2002, I think we were 26 or 30 of us. It should be 26. We had our stickers, Ambazonian stickers that you could just peel and stick on the embassy walls. We stomped the embassy. As I was going in, I saw the COS moving toward the pole of the flag. I was not looking back, I was going straight for the military attaché, to rein him down so that we can take over the embassy. And my people, we did. We took over the embassy. We wanted to hold it for 41 minutes, which was the 41-years of occupation of our Land. We did. The enemy surrounded the embassy within 39 minutes; that is, they called for the German military that surrounded the embassy. LRC staff inside the embassy were crying. You are in one room; you are only hearing slaps in another room. An Amba left scars on the bald head of a LRC official. It was beautiful to occupy that embassy and take it over from the hands of the butchers for a while. We felt powerful, we felt emboldened, we felt free. I think it was just preparation for what began seven years ago (Ayaba, Lebialem: 29 August 2023)

The unprecedented activities of the student revolutionary body did not only come as a giant surprise to the authorities. The vicious Yaoundé regime was also even more gigantically amazed to find out that Ambazonians could have picked up arms to defend themselves after their proud and haughty declaration of genocide on the Two-Cubes-of Sugar in their Drums-of-Water. All thanks to the 'Sense-Pass-King' AWOL Leader and his Team, 'Two Cubes of Sugar' have amazingly almost swallowed up all the drums of water without speedily dissolving as they expected. Dadi in Manyuzone, I hear you well, don't I? But for this IG nonsense, as we all know by now, the swallowing up would long have been over before General Ivo Mbah's passing on to Glory, but his dying wish must happen. We Must Reach Buea Soon, with or without the distracting and enabling IGs. It is a one-way journey! *Parlement* also shook the entire country to the root, with wild rumours that the student body had plans to take over the running of the country. And what is wrong with that? Like those following Ambazonia's brave armed resistance, the whole enterprise of reform that followed the rise of *Parlement* is brutally confusing and controversial. I find all this normal because that is what always happens when an administration has no sharp vision or any at all and events that it never foresaw coming have overtaken it, like the Embassy Takeover which began as a play for the theatre.

Yes, today we are talking about Lebialem. Lebialem! The COS is from Lebialem. Twenty-two years ago, I was in Frankfurt. I was with Fon Gorji Dinka. We were sitting on the podium in a conference that was organized by the Southern Cameroons National Council (SCNC) and Southern Cameroons Youth League (SCYL). And there was a gentleman who was filming the event, especially when I started talking. Then, I was bigger than I look now, before this stage of the struggle. So, this gentleman was filming. I didn't quite know him. Afterwards, I left, boarded the train and was heading back to my hideout. Somebody walked up to me and greeted me and said he was at the conference. That he was the gentleman who was filming. I said, wow! Take a seat. We sat all through, he was living in Mulheim or Dulce Borg. And I was living in Bochum. So, there began a great friendship and brotherhood between myself and my now COS, Mr. Njinkeng Fuabeh. I can attest the relationship I have had with him emboldened me, has nourished me, and has made me a better fighter. One year after we met, I conceived an idea you could only watch it in Bollywood, or in Nollywood. I said to the COS and others that we should seize the Cameroun Embassy in Bonn. Then the capital of Germany was Bonn. At first, everybody was like, really? So, I said yes! I said, you know, we voted to establish a federal union. And in that situation all properties of the federation are jointly owned between Ambazonia and Cameroun. So, Cameroun has been holding it alone illegally (Ayaba, Lebialem: 29 August 2023).

They are particularly good at illegality, including those against the student body. As I said, the whole enterprise of educational reform is inhumanely muddling and contentious. I would nevertheless attempt highlighting few pertinent points. The first is that *Parlement*'s only demands (contrary to the wild rumours spread around to 'justify' the barbaric measures used in trying to disband it) were inevitable wide-ranging reforms in the then 'one and only' and excessively overcrowded UNIYAO. Second, *Parlement* was able to stand as firm as it did – in the face of the heavy deployment of the military – because of its cohesion or solidarity in purpose. There was the marked absence of the usual Anglophone-Francophone division always noticed in the ill-fated fights against human rights violations, notably those regarding the G.C.E. system or those touching uniquely Ambazonian interests. As Canute Tangwa has identified, the divisiveness involved in defending human rights in Cameroon can be attributed to certain factors; one of them being, political parties and interest groups [which] could not rally behind Mbawa [an Ambazonian] as was the case during the Monga-Njawe [Camerounese] trial. Political parties and interest groups, whose manifestoes were espoused by Mbawa, shied away. Either these parties or groups did not react because they have already entrenched themselves in the political mainstream and, as such, did not see Mbawa's case as one of political show of force (as the Monga-Njawe trial was) or they were embroiled in crises. [Canute C.N. Tangwa, "Our Patrick Akoh Mbawa: Casualty of Dare-devilling" *Cameroon Post* N° 0021 (20-26 August 1996), 8.]

Cameroon's empty shells called political parties are everywhere causing discrimination. As I said, those kinds of cultural and genderized divisions were absent in *Parlement,* a body that seems to have understood that to begin by discriminating whose rights should be defended would eventually mean that nobody's rights are safe from the dictatorship. The leaders of the paper political parties never understood this vital lesson and where they are today (begging for the crumbs or remains from Biya's meal table) tells the whole story. It is the same explanation you can attach to the inconsequential IG-Care in December 2022 begging Biya for Amnesty for Ambazonians in the Diaspora (rather than joining at least in the 'Operation 200 AKs' that was ongoing then to fortify Ground Zero for the Take Over)! Who even told them that we even need that amnesty? Tchiroma is now also talking about granting amnesty/pardon to Ambazonians in their jails who humbly request 'pardon' from *la Nation Cam*erounaise as some sort of favour to these unjustly imprisoned freedom fighters!

See, let me tell you people something. When you people see me laughing every time about this struggle, it is not because we have 2,000 rifles. I am looking at the enemy. I am looking at the enemy. See, even if we decide today that we were just going to rest for two weeks, this enemy cannot defeat us. They lack the cause; they lack the money. I was talking to an Ambazonian soldier, a BIR. He is in location XX. He had left the shithole country. He spoke words of wisdom into my head. He spoke from an intellectual mindset, and I was asking myself, how the

174

hell did you find yourself among these rascals? The basin of water has failed to dissolve two cubes of sugar. Rifles that they said they were going to destroy us with in two weeks have failed to do it. Now, they are doing propaganda. Return to normalcy. Had they even accepted that there was no normalcy? Did they even accept that there was a war? Ambazonians, sometimes when you are walking on the road, be laughing alone. And if somebody asks you why you are laughing, tell him or her you just heard good news from Dr Cho Ayaba (Ayaba, Lebialem: 29 August 2023).

Third, *Parlement* 'gave' Cameroon five (rather than one) more hurriedly decreed universities not so much as a response to the students' demands (do see a parallel here with the regime's DDR centres). Public opinion, according to Anyangwe (1996: 826) does not count for anything to the Biya "government [that] is generally insensitive to public opinion and the demands of fairness." Is the Tchiroma-Atanga Nji-Biya tussle over the October 2025 presidential election results not a very clear demonstration? In addition, M.L. Lokanga thinks "there is a growing disenchantment about commissions of inquiry [and new universities and/or constitutional organs] in the Biya regime. For one thing, they have always symbolised official deception at its most treacherous stage.... [G]overnment sponsored commissions of inquiry [and universities and/or constitutional bodies] ... have always tended to cloak rather than shed light on issues.... Since he [Biya] came to power... [43] years ago, he has contrived to create commissions [and universities and/or constitutional organs] only when he intends to shelve an issue" (cited in Fossungu, 2018: 146). Lokanga is heavily corroborated through the comportment of Biya's enablers of genocide in Ambazonia. "One of the most ferocious enablers in Ambazonia comes from Manyu. One of the greatest opportunists in our struggle they come also from Manyu. Flip flop. Why? Because the enemy has abandoned the place to the beast. And the only way you can have an opportunity is through the enablers who call themselves elites.

They are awash all over, serving the devil" (Ayaba, Manyu: 14 September 2024).

The decreeing of those universities, therefore, in the estimation of the authorities, had a double-edged purpose. First, it was a genuinely nice means of diffusing the unprecedented student power; and second, a way of not looking like succumbing to the demands of Ambazonians (the 'two cubes of sugar'), as I further expose. The principal idea behind the creation of these many universities was that of dispersing the exceptional student power that had 'dangerously' developed right there in the very heart of Yaoundé – Cameroon's alpha and omega which, according to President Biya, breathes and the rest of the country lives. *"Lorsque Yaoundé respire, tout le Cameroun vit!"* It is coming from this unauthored piece: "Cameroon: Crisis or Compromise?" 32 *Africa Confidential* (25 October 1991), 2 at page 3. That can also explain why any talk of genuine decentralization becomes heresy or subversion to this administration. Both democracy and federalism preach and further self-governments of local communities. There can be no self-government of a region (or state or province or canton or zone or *Land*) of a federation in the absence of an independent and influential judiciary as well as multiplicity of power centres (such as effective multipartism). I think that the mere absence of the democratic spirit and form at Foumban must render the FRC not a federation. It also makes the acclaimed power-sharing, marked by judicial review in Cameroon, mind-boggling.

Penalizing Students for the Creation of Universities

To Biya then, he had to swiftly eliminate that dangerous student power in the jealously guarded respiratory organ of 'his' Cameroon. That is precisely why the 'nerve centre' of the overcrowded UNIYAO's *Parlement* – the Faculty of Law and Economics – must be moved to the suburb of Soa, done even without adequate (if not actually no) infrastructure there. This theory becomes clear through a look at the consequences, for the students, of bringing about the unplanned and unwilling creation of those universities. As I have already indicated, decreeing the existence of five more universities (rather than just one that should normally have to be in then West Cameroon) provided a convenient way of not looking like "capitulating" to the long suppressed Ambazonian demands for university institutions across the Mungo River. But as *Parlement* had untimely brought that about, the university students must pay dearly for it. How the regime penalized them is interestingly telling relating to the thesis of one-culture biculturalism that I am developing. The punishment given to them, quite apart from the brutal response to the unexpected rise of *Parlement*, came in two ways. The first was the abolition of *epsi* (or *bourse*) and the second was in the form of the imposition of university fees. The authorities purely and speedily scrapped *Epsi* off the books now that there was on the table the same problem it has failed to indefinitely 'solve' or postpone. But its scrapping was not enough chastisement for the students.

The second penalty came in the form of the POR's *Décret Nº 93/032 du 9 janvier 1993* that imposed university fees. This Decree instituted and regulated the payment of fees of 50,000 francs CFA an academic year. Thus, a student who was receiving CFA 40,000 francs a month without paying university fees, for example, is then to pay CFA 50,000 francs a year as fees without *epsi*. Why? It is simply because the 'Anglos' now have a university, thanks to them. It must be emphasized that this introduction of university fees also came at the same time as their parents' salaries had been slashed to unbearable bits: not to mention the full effects of the French devaluation, leading to Jude Waindim's desperate cry on discovering that,

Change in Cameroon has always been in the form of old wine in new wine skins. Yet, that our docility and blind tolerance as future generations are being mortgaged point to the impression that we may after all deserve the leaders we have. Was it otherwise, who, therefore are we? What have we done when leaders force themselves on us? What have we done when our forests are raped; when pseudo law enforcement bandits contemptuously rape our daughters and wives without remorse; when bullets and grenades are hauled at children and women who deserve our protection; when salaries are non-existent and devaluation has made life unbearable; what have we done? ... [Who is ever going] to inject some doses of courage into the inmates of the prison called Cameroon? [Jude Waindim, "Gwangwa'a's Cry of the Destitute" *Cameroon Post* (11-18 December 1995), 4. Also see Jude Waindim, "Did Pope Address Southern Cameroons Issue at UN?" *Cameroon Post* N° 0274 (11-18 December 1995), 1]

Until the devaluation of the French franc (FF) in the early nineties, according to Clément *et al*, CFA 50 francs were equal to 1 FF. Since then, the rate is 100 FCFA = 1 FF. [Jean A.P. Clément, with Johannes Mueller, Stéphane Cossé, and Jean Le Dem, *Aftermath of the CFA Franc Devaluation* (Washington, D.C.: IMF, 1996) at 'Introduction'] Furthermore, at the same moment of imposing fees on the students there was the introduction of too many taxes which, according to Boyle (1996: 618-622), also strangely coupled with the drying up of "public resources" and the stifling of "private initiative" of parents who were opting for better schooling of their children. To the Amba nationalists, "We would be sending out an executive order in the coming days about our education also. We are aware that schools are charging exorbitant prices in terms of school fees. That is unacceptable. We are reviewing the situation carefully. Schools are exempted from paying taxes. And if you are charging students from homes that are facing economic hardship, we would be considering taxing these schools. We would be asking schools to reduce tuition fees because we are also providing an alternative system of learning that can take teachers out of classrooms and put them in other areas where they can produce well" (Ayaba, Manyu: 14 September 2024).

All the above hardship would seem to be the punishment the entire student body in Cameroon must endure for causing the untimely creation of the 'Anglo-Saxon UNIBU' in particular, which the regime must then destroy, one way or the other. This thesis can explain why the 1998 Education Law, which in the opening Section 1(2) declares itself to apply only to pre-university education, would wind up, in a very questionable manner, regulating "all levels of education" in Section 14 of its part II. The UNIBU (and newly created UNIBA) could be clear targets, and keen observers had sternly warned that "The word 'Anglo-Saxon' in the decree creating the University of Buea, to us, was not gratuitous. In fact, on that word hinges a people's lifestyle, indeed, legacy." [The Post Comment, "Five Years After: How Anglo-Saxon is UB?" *The Post* N° 0044 (23 January 1998), 4.]

One cannot therefore validly speak of universities when one has not created appropriate infrastructures and other conditions necessary for the existence and smooth functioning of those universities. It is thus highly doubtful that the 1998 Education Law came to put a stop to (rather than fortify) the sad dog-breeding situation in education in Cameroon. That is why the absence of self-control in politics persists to date, as evidenced especially by both that Education Law itself and the 1996 Constitution. Both laws employ the terms biculturalism, bilingualism, and cultural dualism, when in fact their whole essence is the destruction of any semblance of the existence of those concepts. That is why the creation of a so-called Anglo-Saxon university in this country had to be an involuntary act, with these two pieces of legislation (among others) then being in place to ensure that the said institutions remain 'Anglo-Saxon' only in name and on paper. In short, that they be Anglo-Saxon only in the *Ngoalingual* sense, as even the war between the two educational systems has also largely portrayed.

Once more, how does the Section 18(3) provision also tally in with Section 15(2) that is talking of each sub-system preserving its specific characteristics? Furthermore, how does Section 14 that organizes and controls education at all levels also tie in with a law that conspicuously opens by being limited to only nursery, primary and secondary education in Section 1(2)? All this is surely what critics have chastised as "half a step forward and one hundred steps backward". And in this instance, some critics have asked, how far has one moved? Of course, in Cameroon one would still have 'advanced' a lot because in this country's advanced democracy regression (or 'upside-down rolling-back'[46]) is happily and positively measured since the democracy gets its essence from the absence of self-control and of positive development, as can also be seen in the perfect nation's self-determination and 'pluralistic democracy', capped by useless talk of 'normalcy'.

So, for us, this lockdown was also to remind the occupier
that your notion of normalcy on the dead bodies of our people,

---

[46] See Oben Timothy Mbuagbo and R.M. Akoko, "Roll-Back: Democratization and Social Fragmentation in Cameroon" 13(1) *Nordic Journal of African Studies* (2004), 1-12.

179

on unmarked graves of those you kidnapped and dispose of, is not normalcy for the Ambazonian people. And that we run activities on the Land. It is also to remind all those who enable colonialism, for all of those providing self-interested justifications for colluding with criminals that burn our homes, murder our people, that you aren't ever going to defeat Ambazonia. That we may stumble, we may have our days of rain. But we are poised, we are determined to end the nightmare which is of your creation. To all the enablers who take pride in the death of our people, who allow themselves to be used by the Ngalas, to be put on social media to bastardize and attack our existence as if sixty-two years of butchering is not enough. They laugh when we die, they make jokes about our pain, they make jokes when our men fall. They laugh at us when we stumble. But let me remind them, as a student of history, that all those who sail ashore experience turbulent waters. I would take that as our lesson to remind all of you, the occupier and those who enable the brutality that this is a generation that would not blink. This is a generation that has nothing left to compromise on. This is a generation that would arm itself to the teeth to ensure that the alien system installed in our Land by brute force is dismantled and shipped to wherever it came from. We are not a people with anger. We are not a people who harbour wickedness. We are a people who are struggling simply to exist, to survive under the circumstances that we have lived under (Ayaba, Manyu: 14 September 2024).

Conclusion

Ambazonian nationalism is positive. I have kicked against the nationalist form of government for its tendency to be discriminatory and totalitarian. But nationalism, as Couloumbis and Wolfe (1986: 81) explain, is not always a negative force and can be greatly helpful if it aids people to unite with others in the pursuit of the common good. That is nationalism in its genuine and modern sense. I am sure I hear the Ambazonia Governing Council here very well? In this sense nationalism becomes a behaviour pattern that reduces individualism and alienation and thus provides the individual with a sense of identity and belonging. Such a sense of belonging cannot be realized by merely forcefully effacing the heritage of a portion of the country's population. Therefore, Africans, it is firmly suggested, must simply separate once and for all the concepts of state and of perfect nations and make their states truly pluralistic societies. Doing so necessarily requires the federal devolution or, failing that, a properly decentralized form of governance. Both concepts are nonsensical in the absence of separation of powers, especially judicial independence.

The necessity for governing with due regard for human rights can hardly escape the attention of genuine intellectuals in political science particularly and other intellectuals. Good governance, I suppose, presupposes (for example) that the decision as to what system of government and/or form of state, and as to whether Pauline continues governing or Paul steps in to replace her, must remain with the people and with the people alone for any talk of democracy to be meaningful. It is not democracy if once "elected" or appointed, a government cannot be dethroned by the people except through bloodshed. It is no democracy simply by saying it is democracy in the One-Party. Not even by merely affixing 'Advanced' to it will it become one. Democracy, I believe, is more in the being and doing than in saying and talking. Precolonial African governance never had 'democracy' affixed to it. But, as Gobata indicates, "many of the traditional African kingships (fonships), circumscribed as they were by sundry taboos, ritual restrictions and sanctions, were arguably more democratic than some contemporary western democracies. I could write a whole book defending this thesis but that is not necessary for our purpose here and now." [Gobata, "Western Democrats and African Dictatorships" *Cameroon Post* N° 0021 (20-26 August 1996), 7.] If anything, Davidson also writes, "the comparison between Africa and Europe is likely to be in Africa's favour. Throughout the medieval period most African forms of government were undoubtedly more representative than their European contemporaries. Most African wars were less costly in life and property. And most African ruling groups were less predatory." [Basil Davidson, *Africa in History: Themes and Outlines* revised & expanded edition (New York: Macmillan, 1991) at 145] That is the highly developed and human rights-respecting African political system.

That is also precisely why lawyers and media practitioners who can talk the talk but very easily shrink or only mimic when tested, have been seriously censored and told by the experts to reconsider if they had chosen the right profession. I agree with political pundits who have pointed out that one of the indispensable prerogatives of good leadership is the simple ability of identifying a crisis from a distance and seeing how best to avert it in the general interest. Therefore, they have concluded, to pretend "not to perceive the approach of an ill-wind is itself a negative dispensation of judgement in the fine art of collective bargaining." [A.M. Dipoko, "Was Biya's Speech Necessary?" *Le Messager* N° 029 (18 July 1991), 7.] Politics certainly involves this kind of bargaining and any "politician" who does not recognize this plain fact, I believe, must evoke the same thought as lawyers who do not know that their job is to fearlessly defend human rights without discrimination. Good governance can clearly not exist without the realization of these basic rules. Two distinguished Harvard University professors of government posited as far back as 1963 that a government normally should perform two principal functions – the service and political functions. The first (administrative) involves the provision of goods and services, such as police protection, which are not usually supplied under private auspices. The second (governing) involves the management of conflicts in matters of public importance (Banfield and Wilson, 1963: 18-19). These two functions are often concretely indistinguishable although the tendency in undemocratic states will be to prefer the entire absence of politics since no conflict and struggle for power are tolerated – with all important and unimportant matters being decided by one person or idea; all this solely predicated on purely technical and efficiency grounds. Meanwhile media professionals and university students, for example, who disagree would be systematically singled out and cowed into silence or killed. Simply because these people do not see why and how the regime must reduce them to simple automatons. It is my belief that all this must no longer happen while the bulk of us are looking on helplessly because it is really time Africa stop asking for permission to be itself and grow up constitutionally and stop mumbling feebly that nothing can be done without begging from others. That is President Captain Traoré's message. Research *about* Africa's law (like this book) is obviously an appropriate step in the growing-up direction. Ambazonians are inspiring as well in the domain.

It is doubtful how anyone can expect to sell their goods unless potential buyers are able to trust and believe in the goods' merchantability and fitness (risk-free) for the purpose. Aware of the distrustful and designing nature of the unknown "missions" of most of the appointed officials in the Hinge of Africa, a powerful *Jeune Afrique Economie* editorial (incidentally from a Camerounese) has indicated (like Dr Ayaba has enormously also done above) that if we Africans fail to respect ourselves, we cannot be respected by others, let alone be given the places that are supposed to be ours: "*Si nous ne savons pas nous 'vendre', au sens le plus noble du terme, les autres n'accepteront pas de nous donner la place que nous méritons réellement sur cette planète. Cela est valable dans tous les domains.*" [Blaise-Pascal Talla, "Le poids de nos États" 173 *Jeune Afrique Economie* (novembre 1993), 3.] Traoré's BKF recently proved the point when Europeans who unilaterally cut ties, demanding his returning power to their civilian puppets, are now finding ways to re-establish ties with the same military government. It is about time therefore that we stop allowing people claiming to be our leaders to go about idiotickerizing this beautiful continent and intelligent us. Meaning that personification of public affairs must be erased from this continent because Africa rightly deserves and must get back civilized and patriotic governments and lots of apparatchicks. *Apparatchiks* might so far have been wanting particularly in the Hinge of Africa because of the unnecessary darkness created by the myriads of "intellectuals in politics." Now that Interim-President Captain Ibrahim Traoré of BKF has lit the piecing light and it is shining on the darkness (Bravo also to Ambazonia! Independence means independence!) the *apparatchiks* must surely begin to see the issues differently and, hopefully, come out openly. The concerned Africans thus have the choice: they must have

183

to analyze their situation from top to bottom and either keep on doing what they have been doing or discard even widely held premises whose time has passed. They must avoid bloodshed by solving problems as and when necessary. African lives must matter indeed.

It is my thought that decentralization, if proper and effective, might also ameliorate things in Africa. But federalism and/or decentralization cannot be effective in the absence of liberalism. Liberalism, Corbett has stated, presupposes the presence of disagreement on important questions and recognizes that while religious and ethnic differences require political solutions, no particular ethnic or religious tradition can be the single source of those solutions. Like classical politics, and unlike the ethos of consumer capitalism, liberalism is a political theory grounded in the idea of self-control. [S.M. Corbett, "Book Review of George Grant: A Bibliography (Toronto: University of Toronto Press, 1993) by William Christian" 20:2 *Queen's Law Journal* (1995), 611 at 625-26.] Cameroon's 1996 Constitution (or its offspring: 1998 Education Law) is however not the beginning of this lack of self-control in Cameroon. Everything that has been happening in the country would find roots in the 1961 Federal Constitution; a constitution which grossly betrayed the aspirations of Ambazonians because its architects exhibited a gross lack of self-control and of a sense of duty to the public they were purportedly representing. It is this self-control that makes the struggle for power civilized; with this politically civilizing process being what Riemer (1983: 122) says, at the highest level, "makes fuller individual realization possible." Making this fuller individual realization possible in Africa would necessitate the provision of honestly decent answers to the questions on authentic education and multiculturalism.

There is indeed no reason for useless excuses in Africa; and none for advancing pointless biculturalism, whose real name is assimilation. Assimilation promotes only regression in human rights and that is surely not what Africa deserves from its supposed leader. Africa is not especially interested in having a leader who, moreover, does not genuinely seek to know what holds a society together, where the society is going, nor how it is getting there. Until all these vital issues are properly addressed in Africa, there is just no point in employing terms like democracy and biculturalism in this continent, a continent that would then, according to Frye (1986: 33), simply continue to remain "a blank area of natural resources to be exploited by countries that are more advanced and better organized than we [Africans] are because they've spent more on their education."

Bibliography

Abanda, Abeng (1996) "At Book Launch: Archbishop Verdzekov Decries Assimilation of Anglophones" *The Herald* N° 327 (8-9 July), 1 & 2.

Achanyi, Abia (2010) "Cameroon's Population Hits 19.4 Million" posted by "achanyi abila" achristus2002@ yahoo.com in 2010.

Adams, Melinda. (2006) "Colonial Policies and Women's Participation in Public Life: The Case of British Southern Cameroons" 8(3) *African Studies Quarterly*, 1-22.

Ahidjo, Germaine: (1996) "Confidences: Germaine Ahidjo à cœur ouvert à Honoré De Sumo" *La Nouvelle Expression* N° 319 (28 juin), 1 & 12.

Amang, Protais Ayangma (1997) President of Association of Cameroon Insurance Companies (ASAC) in interview with Michel Eclador Pokoua in *Le Messager* N° 590 (3 mars), 6.

Appiagyei-Atua, Kwadwo (1999) *An Akan Perspective on Human Rights in the Context of African Development* (Doctor of Civil Law Dissertation, McGill University).

Anyangwe, Carlson (1996) "Administrative Litigation in Francophone Africa: The Rule of Prior Exhaustion of Internal Remedies" 8 *Revue Africaine de Droit International et Comparé*, 808-826.

_____ (1989) *The Magistracy and the Bar in Cameroon* (Yaoundé: PANAG-CEPER).

_____ (1987) *The Cameroonian Judicial System* (Yaoundé: CEPER).

Archer, Peter and Lord Reay (1966) *Freedom at Stake* (London: The Bodley Head).

Arthurs Report (1983) *Law and Learning: Report to the Social Sciences and Humanities Research Council of Canada.*

Ayaba, Lucas Cho (2024, Manyu) "The State of Manyu – My State-to-State Address of the Potentials of Each Ambazonia State" (14 September) @ youtube.com.

_____ (2024, Ngoketunjia) "The State of Ngoketunjia – My State-to-State Address of the Potentials of Each Ambazonia State" (September) @ youtube.com.

_____ (2023, Lebialem) Dr Cho Ayaba's Address to the Citizens of Lebialem" (29 August) @ youtube.com.

_____ (2023, Ndian) "The State of Ndian – My State-to-State Address of the Potentials of Each Ambazonia State" (27 August) @ youtube.com.

Banfield, Edward C. and James Q. Wilson (1963) *City Politics* (Cambridge, Mass.: Harvard University Press and The M.I.T. Press).

Bayefsky, Anne F. (1989) *Canada's Constitution Act 1982 and Amendments* Vol. 1 (Toronto: McGraw-Hill Ryerson).

Benjamin, Jacques (1972) *Les Camerounais occidentaux : la minorité dans un état bicommunautaire* (Montréal : Université de Montréal).

Bissonnette, Bernard (1963) *Essai sur la constitution du Canada* (Montréal: Les Éditions du Jour).

Biya, Paul (1986) *Communal Liberalism* (London: Macmillan).

Bjornson, Richard (1991) *The African Quest for Freedom and Identity: Cameroonian Writing and the National Experience* (Indianapolis: Indiana University Press).

Boyle, Patrick M. (1996) "Parents, Private Schools, and the Politics of an Emerging Civil Society in Cameroon" 34(4) *Journal of Modern African Studies*, 609-622.

Bringer, Peter (1981) "The Abiding Influence of English and French Criminal Law in One African Country: Some Remarks Regarding the Machinery of Criminal Justice in Cameroon" 25(1) *Journal of African Law*, 1.

Britannica (2002) *The New Encyclopaedia Britannica* Volume 4, 15th edition (Chicago: Encyclopaedia Britannica Inc.).

Brunnell, Matthew A. (2005) "What *Lawrence* brought for 'Show and Tell': The Non-Fundamental Liberty Interest in Minimally Adequate Education" 25(2) *Boston College Third World Law Journal*, 342-82.

Chinje B. (1997) "Promises… Promises…" *The Herald* N° 521 (10-12 October), 7.

Couloumbis, Theodore A. and James H. Wolfe (1986) *Introduction to International Relations: Power and Justice* 3rd edition (Englewood Cliffs, N.J.: Prentice-Hall Inc.).

Dawson, R. MacGregor (1970) *The Government of Canada* [5th edition revised by Norman Ward] (Toronto: University of Toronto Press).

Day, Frank D. (1964) *Criminal Law and Society* (Springfield, Illinois: C.C. Thomas).

de Jorge, Hans (1993) "Democracy and Economic Development in the Asia-Pacific Regions: The Role of Parliamentary Institutions" 14:9-10 *Human Rights Law Journal*, 301.

de Smith, Stanley A. (1964) "Federalism, Human Rights, and the Protection of Minorities", in David P. Currie (ed.), *Federalism and the New Nations of Africa* (Chicago: University of Chicago Press), 279-341.

Delancey, Mark W. (1989) *Cameroon: Dependence and Independence* (Boulder: Westview Press).

Dumont, Hugues, Nicolas Lagasse, Marc van der Hulst, and Sébastien van Drooghenbroeck (2008) "Kingdom of Belgium", in Ahktar Majeed, Ronald L. Watts and Douglas M. Brown (eds.), *Distribution of Powers and Responsibilities in Federal Countries* (Montreal & Kingston: McGill-Queen's University Press), 35-65.

Dunlop, C.R.B. (1991) "Literature Studies in Law Schools" 3 *Cardozo Studies in Law and Literature*, 63.

Driedger, Leo (1989) *The Ethnic Factor: Identity in Diversity* (Toronto: McGraw-Hill).

Eleazu, Uma O. (1977) *Federalism and Nation-Building: The Nigerian Experience, 1954-1964* (Elms Court: Stockwell).

Enonchong, H.N.A. (1967) *Cameroon Constitutional Law – Federalism in a Mixed Common-Law and Civil-Law System* (Yaoundé: Centre d'Édition et de Production de Manuel et d'Auxiliares de l'Enseignement).

Etinge, C.N. (1991) "Proposition for the Agenda of a National Conference" *Le Messager* **Special Political Issue** (6 June), 6-7.

Eyinga, Abel (1996) "Le régime néocolonial actuel a atteint un autre niveau dans la lutte contre la conscience nationale" *La Nouvelle Expression* N° 338 (30 août), 6-7.

Eyoum'a Ntoh, Patrick-Thomas (1996) "13 millions de voyous !" *Le Messager* (12 septembre), 2.

Flanz, Gisbert H. (1968) "West Indian Federation", in T.M. Franck (ed.), *Why Federations Fail: An Inquiry into the Requisites for Successful Federalism* (New York: New York University Press), 91-123.

Fombad, Charles Manga (2014) "Strengthening Constitutional Order and upholding the Rule of Law in Central Africa: Reversing the Descent towards Symbolic Constitutionalism: 14 *African Human Rights Law Journal*, 412-48.

_____ (2005) "The Separation of Powers and Constitutionalism in Africa: The Case of Botswana" 25(2) *Boston College Third World Law Journal*, 301-42.

_____ (2003) "Protecting Constitutional Values in Africa: A Comparison of Botswana and Cameroon" 36(1) *Comparative and International Law of Southern Africa*, 83-105.

Fohtung, Barry B. (1996) "Yaoundé or the ACME of Anglophone Masturbation-I" *Cameroon Post* N° 0028 (8-14 October), 8.

_____ (1995) "The Gambler" *Cameroon Post* (11-18 December) 11.

Fonkeng, E.F. (1990) *The Captive* (Ottawa: Bhakti Press).

Forbin, Boniface (1997) "North West Terrorism: Gov't Provokes Anti-Anglophone Violence" *The Herald* (18-20 April), 4.

Fossungu, Peter Ateh-Afac (2025) *History in History of Ambazonian Resistance: The Metaphysics of Assimilation and Independence* (Chitungwiza, Zimbabwe: Mwanaka Media and Publishing).

_____ (2024) *Ayabacholization Classroom in my Life: The Longest Shortcut to University Education* (Chitungwiza, Zimbabwe: Mwanaka Media and Publishing).

_____ (2023) *Royal Burial and Enthronement in Ambazonia: Interrogating the Relevance of Postcolonial Education in Africa* (Chitungwiza, Zimbabwe: Mwanaka Media and Publishing).

_____ (2021) *Battling Language Rights Governance in Africa: Swisselgianism, Ubackism, and the Ambazonia-Cameroun War* (Chitungwiza, Zimbabwe: Mwanaka Media and Publishing).

_____ (2019) *Getting Africa Out of the Dungeon: Human Rights, Federalism, and Judicial Politics in Cameroon* (Masvingo, Zimbabwe: Africa Talent Publishers).

_____ (2018) "Political Naivety, Corruption, and Poverty Promotion in Africa: Riding the 'Poorest-ugliest French' Bijuralism Horse from Cameroon to Canada via Britain", in Munyaradzi Mawere (ed.), *The Political Economy of Poverty, Vulnerability and Disaster Risk Management: Building Bridges of Resilience, Entrepreneurship and Development in Africa's 21st Century* (Bamenda: Langaa RPCIG), 123-73.

_____ (2013a) *Understanding Confusion in Africa: The Politics of Multiculturalism and Nation-building in Cameroon* (Bamenda: Langaa RPCIG).

189

_____ (2013b) *Democracy and Human Rights in Africa: The Politics of Collective Participation and Governance in Cameroon* (Bamenda: Langaa RPCIG).

Franck, Thomas M. (1968a) "East African Federation", in T.M. Franck (ed.), *Why Federations Fail: An Inquiry into the Requisites for Successful Federalism* (New York: New York University Press), 3-36.

_____ (1968b) "Why Federations Fail", in T.M. Franck (ed.), *Why Federations Fail: An Inquiry into the Requisites for Successful Federalism* (New York: New York University Press), 167-99.

Frye, Northop (1986) "Language as the Home of Human Life", in Michael Owen (ed.), *Salute to Scholarship: Essays Presented at the Official Opening of Athabasca University* (Athabasca, Alberta: Athabasca University), 20-33.

Gold, Marc (1985a) "The Mask of Objectivity: Politics and Rhetoric in the Supreme Court of Canada" 7 *Supreme Court Review*, 455.

_____ (1985b) "Constitutional Scholarship in Canada" 23 *Osgoode Hall Law Journal*, 495.

Gorji-Dinka, Fongum (1991) "The Gorji-Dinka Concept of a New Social Order" *Le Messager* **Special Political Issue** (Thursday 6 June), 5.

Green, William (1999) "Schools, Signs, and Separation: Quebec Anglophones, Canadian Constitutional Politics, and International Language Rights" 27 *Denver Journal of International Law and Policy*, 449.

Hodgins, Bruce W., John J. Eddy, Shelagh D. Grant and James Struthers (1989) *Federalism in Canada and Australia: Historical Perspectives, 1920-1988* (Peterborough, Ontario: Frost Centre for Canadian Heritage and Development Studies).

Hogg, Peter W. (1996) *Constitutional Law of Canada* 4th Student edition (Toronto: Thomson Canada Limited).

Ikeda, Daisaku (1987) *A Lasting Peace* Vol. II (New York & Tokyo: Weatherhill).

Johnson, Willard R. (1970) *The Cameroon Federation: Political Integration in a Fragmentary Society* (Princeton, N.J.: Princeton University Press).

Johnson-Hanks, Jennifer (2006) *Uncertain Honor: Modern Motherhood in An African Crisis* (Chicago: The University of Chicago Press).

Kah, Henry Kam (2011) "Women's Resistance in Cameroon's Western Grassfields: The Power of Symbols, Organization, and Leadership, 1957–1961" 12(3) *African Studies Quarterly*, 67-91.

Kanyongo, Gibbs Y. (2005) "Zimbabwe's Public Education System Reform: Successes and Challenges" 6(1) *International Education Journal*, 65-74.

Konings, Piet (1999) "The Anglophone Struggle for Federalism in Cameroon", in L.R. Basita and J. Ibrahim (eds.), *Federalism and Decentralization in Africa: The Multiethnic Challenge* (Fribourg: Fribourg Institut du Fédéralisme), 289-325.

Konings, Piet and Francis B. Nyamnjoh (1997) "The Anglophone Problem in Cameroon" 35(2) *The Journal of Modern African Studies*, 207-29.

Lantum, Dan N. (1991) "Dr. Bernard Nsokika Fonlon: An Intellectual in Politics" *Le Messager* **Special Political Issue** (Thursday 6 June), 20-22, continued in *Le Messager* N° 028 (20 June 1991), 11-13.

Le Vine, Victor T. (1971) *The Cameroon Federal Republic* (Ithaca: Cornell University Press).

Loewenstein, K. (1967) *British Cabinet Government* (London: Oxford University Press).

Magstadt, Thomas M. (1991) *Nations and Governments: Comparative Politics in Regional Perspective* (New York: St Martin's Press, Inc.).

Majeed, Ahktar (2008) "Introduction: Distribution of Powers and Responsibilities", in Ahktar Majeed, Ronald L. Watts and Douglas M. Brown (eds.), *Distribution of Powers and Responsibilities in Federal Countries* (Montreal & Kingston: McGill-Queen's University Press), 3-7.

Maneli, Mieczyslaw (1994) *Perelman's New Rhetoric as Philosophy and Methodology for the Next Century* (Dordrecht: Kluwer Academic Publishers).

Mback, Charles Nach (2007) "One Century of Municipalization in Cameroon: The Miseries of Urban Democracy", in Dickson Eyoh and Richard Stren (eds.), *Decentralization and the Politics of Urban Development in West Africa* (Washington D.C.: Woodrow Wilson International Centre for Scholars), 53-76.

Muabe, Fidèle (1997) "Women Bemoun Their Decline in Politics. Say Representation Has Dropped From 23 to 10 in Parliament" *The Herald* N° 485 (16-17 July), 3.

Ndamukong, Gilbert (1996) "Financial Subvention to the G.C.E. Board" *Cameroon Post* N° 0028 (8-14 October), 2.

Ndi Chia, Charly (1995) "We May Not Be the World, but We Are the People" *Cameroon Post* N° 0274 (11-18 December), 4.

191

_____ (1995b) "Why Gov't Is Bent on Destroying North West Traditional Authority – Dr. Nantang Jua" *Cameroon Post* N° 0274 (December 11-18), 6.

Newman, Peter C. (1975) *The Canadian Establishment* Volume 1 (Toronto: McClelland and Stewart Limited).

_____ (1968) *The Distemper of our Times – Canadian Politics in Transition: 1963-1968* (Toronto: McClelland and Stewart Limited).

Nfi, Joseph L. (2014) "The Anglophone Cultural Identity in Cameroon 50 Years After Re-Unification" 2(2) *International Journal of Advanced Research*, 121-29.

Ngwana, A.S. (2009) "Cameroon: Genesis and Reality of the Anglophone Problem", available at http//topics192.com/2009/02/cameroongenesis-and-reality-of-html.

Ntenga, George Chebe (1997) "Cameroon Calling: Who is Destroying National Unity?" *The Herald* (10-11 March), 4.

Ofege, Ntemfac (1995a) "Constitutional Revision: Vistas of Anglophone Exclusion and Presidential Hypocrisy" *Cameroon Post* N° 0274 (11-18 December), 8.

_____ (1995b) "Autopsy of a Most Outrageous Document" *Cameroon Post* N° 0274 (11-18 December), 8.

Ojwang, J.B. and D.R. Salter (1988-89) "Legal Education in Kenya" 33(1) *Journal of African Law*, 78-90.

Okondo, Peter J.H. (1964) "Prospects of Federation in East Africa", in David P. Currie (ed.), *Federalism and the New Nations of Africa* (Chicago: University of Chicago Press), 29-74.

Ondoa, Magloire (1996) "Commentaire" 25 *Juridis Périodique* (*Revue de Droit et de Science Politique*), 11-14.

Pearson, F.S. and J.M. Rochester (1984) *International Relations: The Global Condition in the Late Twentieth Century* 2nd edition (New York: Random House).

Peaslee, Amos J. (1974) *Constitutions of Nations* Vol. I – Africa (The Hague, Netherlands: Martinus Nijhoff).

Pirie, Andrew J. (1987) "Objectives in Legal Education: The Case for Systematic Instructional Design" 37 *Journal of Legal Education*, 576-97.

Riemer, Neal (1983) *Political Science: An Introduction to Politics* (New York: Harcourt Brace Jovanovich, Inc.).

Rubin, Neville (1971) *Cameroon: An African Federation* (New York: Praeger Publishers).

Schneider, Hans-Peter (2008) "The Federal Republic of Germany", in Ahktar Majeed, Ronald L. Watts and Douglas M. Brown (eds.), *Distribution of Powers and Responsibilities in Federal Countries* (Montreal & Kingston: McGill-Queen's University Press), 124-154.

SDF (1996) 'SDF Launches National Economic Salvation Programme (NESPROG)" *Cameroon Post* Special Edition (December), 1.

Shapiro, Evan Joel (1995) *The Supranational Challenge: Federal and Decentralized Unitary States Within the European Union* (LL.M. Thesis, McGill University).

Simon, Richard and Martin Papillion (2008) "Canada", in Ahktar Majeed, Ronald L. Watts and Douglas M. Brown (eds.), *Distribution of Powers and Responsibilities in Federal Countries* (Montreal & Kingston: McGill-Queen's University Press), 92-122.

Southall, Roger (1974) *Federalism and Higher Education in East Africa* (Nairobi: East African Publishing House).

SCFAQ: "Southern Cameroons Frequently Asked Questions", available @ http://www.southerncameroons.org/index3.htm (last visited in March 2021).

Stark, Frank M. (1976) "Federalism in Cameroon: The Shadow and the Reality" 10(3) *Canadian Journal of African Studies*, 423-42.

Stevenson, Garth (1989) *Unfulfilled Union: Canadian Federalism and National Unity* 3rd edition (St. Catherines, Ontario: Gage Educational Publishing Company).

Students' Letter of 20th August 1985: "Letter from the English-speaking Students of the North West and South West Provinces to their Parents", available at "Southern Cameroons Landmark Documents": http://www.southerncameroons.org/index3.htm (last accessed in August 2020).

Suifon, Takwa (1997) "University of Buea: The Place to Be..." *The Herald* N° 523 (20-21 October), 6.

Taku, Charles Achaleke (1995) "Lawyer Alerts British Gov't: C'wealth Systems Are Being Destroyed in Cameroon" *Cameroon Post* N° 0274 (11-18 December), 1.

Tixier, Gilbert (1974) *A Comparative Study of the Economic Policies of the Cameroons and Ivory Coast* (Paris: International Institute for Economic Research & LGDJ).

Trager, Frank N. (1968) "Introduction: On Federalism", in Thomas M. Franck (ed.), *Why Federations Fail: An Inquiry into the Requisites for Successful Federalism* (New York: New York University Press), ix-xv.

Tremblay, André (1993) *Droit Constitutionnel: Principes* (Montréal : Les Éditions Thémis).

_____ (1967) *Les compétences législatives au Canada et les pouvoirs provinciaux en matière de propriété et de droits civils* (Ottawa: Éditions de l'Université d'Ottawa).

Wheare, K.C. (1963) *Federal Government* (London: Oxford University Press).

Williams, Patricia J. (1987) "Alchemical Notes: Reconstructing Ideals from Deconstructed Rights" 22 Harvard Civil Rights-Civil Liberty Review, 401-33.

Zang-Atangana, Joseph-Marie (1989a) *Les forces politiques au Cameroun réunifié: Tome 1 – Les partis politiques avant la réunification* (Paris : L'Harmattan).

_____ (1989b) *Les forces politiques au Cameroun réunifié: Tome 2 – L'expérience de l'UC et du KNDP* (Paris: L'Harmattan).

_____ (1989c) *Les forces politiques au Cameroun réunifié: Tome 3 – Les groupes de pression* (Paris: L'Harmattan).

Mmap Nonfiction and Academic books

If you have enjoyed *Education and Federalism in History of Ambazonian Resistance: The Gymnastics and Folly of Assimilation,* consider these other fine **Mmap Nonfiction and Academic books** from *Mwanaka Media and Publishing:*

Cultural Hybridity and Fixity by Andrew Nyongesa
Tintinnabulation of Literary Theory by Andrew Nyongesa
South Africa and United Nations Peacekeeping Offensive Operations by Antonio Garcia
A Case of Love and Hate by Chenjerai Mhondera
A Cat and Mouse Affair by Bruno Shora
The Scholarship Girl by Abigail George
The Gods Sleep Through It All by Wonder Guchu
PHENOMENOLOGY OF DECOLONIZING THE UNIVERSITY: *Essays in the Contemporary Thoughts of Afrikology* by Zvikomborero Kapuya
Africanization and Americanization Anthology Volume 1, Searching for Interracial, Interstitial, Intersectional and Interstates Meeting Spaces, Africa Vs North America by Tendai R Mwanaka
Africa, UK and Ireland: Writing Politics and Knowledge Production Vol 1 by Tendai R Mwanaka
Writing Language, Culture and Development, Africa Vs Asia Vol 1 by Tendai R Mwanaka, Wanjohi wa Makokha and Upal Deb
Zimbolicious: An Anthology of Zimbabwean Literature and Arts, Vol 3 by Tendai Mwanaka
Drawing Without Licence by Tendai R Mwanaka
Writing Grandmothers/ Escribiendo sobre nuestras raíces: Africa Vs Latin America Vol 2 by Tendai R Mwanaka and Felix Rodriguez
Nationalism: (Mis)Understanding   Donald Trump's Capitalism, Racism, Global Politics, International Trade and Media Wars, Africa Vs North America Vol 2 by Tendai R Mwanaka
It Is Not About Me: Diaries 2010-2011 by Tendai Rinos Mwanaka

Chitungwiza Mushamukuru: An Anthology from Zimbabwe's Biggest Ghetto Town by Tendai Rinos Mwanaka

The Day and the Dweller: A Study of the Emerald Tablets by Jonatha Thompson

Zimbolicious Anthology Vol 4: An Anthology of Zimbabwean Literature and Arts by Tendai Rinos Mwanaka and Jabulani Mzinyathi

Parks and Recreation by Abigail George

FAMILY LAW AND POLITICS WITH BIOLOGY AND ROYALTY II AFRICA AND NORTH AMERICA by Peter Ateh-Afec Fossungu

Writing Robotics, Africa Vs Asia, Vol 2 by Tendai Rinos Mwanaka

Zimbolicious Anthology Vol 5: An Anthology of Zimbabwean Literature and Arts by Tendai R. Mwanaka

Love Notes: Everything is Love, An Anthology of Indigenous Languages of Africa an East Europe by Tendai R Mwanaka

Zimbolicious Anthology Vol 6: An Anthology of Zimbabwean Literature and Arts by Tendai R. Mwanaka and Chenjerai Mhondera

BATTLING LANGUAGE RIGHTS GOVERNANCE IN AFRICA SWISSELGIANISM, UBACKISM, AND THE AMBAZONIA CAMEROUN WAR by Peter Ateh-Afec Fossungu

Otherness and Pathology: The Fragmented Self and Madness in Contemporary Africa Fiction by Andrew Nyongesa

Zimbabwe: The Urgency of Now by Tendai Rinos Mwanaka

Zimbabwe: The Blame Game, Recollected essays and Non-fictions by Tendai Rino Mwanaka

The Trick is to Keep Breathing: Covid 19 Stories From African and North America Writers, Vol 3 by Tendai Rinos Mwanaka

Recentring Mother Earth by Andrew Nyongesa

Zimbabwe: Beyond Robert Mugabe by Tendai Rinos Mwanaka

Language, Thought, Art and Existence: New and Recollected Essays and Non Fiction by Tendai Rinos Mwanaka

Experimental Writing, Africa Vs Latin America Vol 1 by Tendai Rino Mwanaka and Ricardo Felix Rodriguez

Fixing Earth Anthology: An anthology of Africa, UK and Ireland Writers, Vol 2 by Tendai Rinos Mwanaka

Africa Must Deal with Blats for Its True Decolonisation: Unclothed Truth abou Internalised Internal Colonialism by Nkwazi N. Mhango

ROYAL BURIAL AND ENTHRONEMENT IN AMBAZONIA INTERROGATING THE RELEVANCE OF POSTCOLONIAL EDUCATION IN AFRICA by Peter Ateh-Afec Fossungu

196

SCHOOL BASED HIV EDUCATION AFFECTING GIRLS IN SELECTED COUNTRIES IN SUB SAHARAN AFRICA by Ivainesu Charmaine Musa

HIV AND AIDS IN ZIMBABWE: A REVIEW ON THE RELATIONSHIP BETWEEN PERCEPTION OF MASCULINITY AMONGST UNMARRIED YOUNG MEN AND THEIR SEXUAL BEHAVIORS by Lucas Kudakwashe Muvhiringi

AFRICA'S CONTEMPORARY FOOD INSECURITY: SELF-INFLICTED WOUNDS THROUGH MODERN VENI VIDI VICI AND LAND GRABBING by Nkwazi Mhango

I Can't Breathe and other Essays by Zvikomborero Kapuya

Ayabacholization Classroom In My Life: The Longest Shortcut To University Education by Peter Ateh-Afec Fossungu

Gathering Evidence by Tendai Rinos Mwanaka

Best New African poets 10th anniversary: Interviews and Reviews by Tendai Rinos Mwanaka

In the footsteps of a Bipolar Life by Ambrose Cato George and Abigail George

No Business Like Love Business by Peter Atec-Afec Fossungu

RE-ENGINEERING UNDER-EXPLORED RENEWABLE ENERGY by Blessing Barnet Chiniko

Manifestations of trauma in the post-2000 Zimbabwean Literature by Nyarai Maria Kanyemba

Donald Trump's Second Coming: Is Democracy, Dead, Dying or Alive by Tendai Rinos Mwanaka

HISTORY IN HISTORY OF AMBAZONIA RESISTENCE by Peter Afec-Ateh Fossungu

Zimbolicious 10th Anniversary Anthology: New and Collected Non-fictions by Tendai Rinos Mwanaka

Letters to Dariah by Rumbi Chen

THE KALEIDOSCOPE OF LIFE: Essays on Identity and Indigenous Knowledge Systems by Sithembe Isaac Xhegwana

Pulse of the Sub-Saharan Dunes by Moussa Traore

Conundrum and other essays by M-Soga Mlandu

Upcoming books

https://facebook.com/MwanakaMediaAndPublishing

www.ingramcontent.com/pod-product-compliance
Lightning Source LLC
Chambersburg PA
CBHW070333270326
41926CB00017B/3854